Circular Economy Strategy for SDG Business Management

Young Won Park · Kin'ya Tamaki

Circular Economy Strategy for SDG Business Management

New Theories and System Techniques

Springer

Young Won Park
Graduate School of Humanities and Social Science
Saitama University
Shinjuku-ku, Tokyo, Japan

Kin'ya Tamaki
Department of Business Administration
Aoyama Gakuin University
Shibuya-ku, Tokyo, Japan

ISBN 978-981-96-4193-2   ISBN 978-981-96-4194-9 (eBook)
https://doi.org/10.1007/978-981-96-4194-9

This Springer imprint is published by the registered company Springer Nature Singapore Pte Ltd.
The registered company address is: 152 Beach Road, #21-01/04 Gateway East, Singapore 189721, Singapore

Preface

This book offers a strategic framework for advancing Circular Economy (CE) strategies to align with Sustainable Development Goals (SDGs) amid the shifts of Digital Transformation (DX), Sustainability Transformation (SX), and Green Transformation (GX). By examining global policies, industry practices, and innovative systems, the book presents actionable insights for fostering CE adoption. Highlighting the role of technological integration, policy frameworks, and cross-sector collaboration, it underscores CE's potential to balance economic growth with sustainability. This work was supported by JSPS KAKENHI (Grant-in-Aid for Scientific Research (B) Grant Number 22H01717 and Scientific Research (C) Grant Number 23K01578).

Chapter 1: Circular Economy Trends in the DX, SX, and GX Era
This chapter traces the evolution from linear to circular economic models, emphasizing the integration of DX, SX, and GX to advance CE. It links CE to SDGs by focusing on waste reduction, resource optimization, and lifecycle management. Technologies like IoT, AI, and blockchain enable innovations such as reverse logistics and product-as-a-service models. However, barriers like regulatory gaps and cultural resistance require solutions such as extended producer responsibility (EPR) and eco-innovation. The 9R framework—Recycle, Remanufacture, Reuse, Refuse, Rethink, Reduce, Repair, Refurbish, and Repurpose—guides resource value retention throughout lifecycles. By synergizing digital advancements, social equity, and environmental imperatives, CE emerges as a transformative paradigm for achieving systemic sustainability. Through policy innovation and consumer engagement, the chapter establishes a foundation for the book, exploring CE's potential to redefine global economic practices.

Chapter 2: International Trend Researches on CE Policy and International Standard: Impact of New CE Policies and Regulations on Sustainable Business Model Transform
This chapter highlights the influence of global CE policies and standards on sustainable business models. Initiatives like the EU's New Circular Economy Action Plan and Japan's Advanced Resource Recycling Act focus on lifecycle management,

waste reduction, and resource efficiency. Standards such as ISO 59000 and certifications like "Cradle to Cradle Certified®" offer structured pathways for CE adoption, emphasizing product sustainability and material health. Technological innovations, including the Digital Product Passport, enhance traceability and recycling processes. These initiatives align CE with broader sustainability goals, addressing challenges such as regulatory complexities and market adaptation. The chapter underscores the role of policy frameworks and international collaboration in scaling CE strategies globally, contributing to both environmental conservation and economic transformation.

Chapter 3: CE Strategy in the Automotive Industry
In the automotive industry, CE addresses environmental challenges by shifting from "take-make-dispose" to resource-efficient systems. Honda's "Triple Action to ZERO" strategy exemplifies this approach, targeting carbon neutrality, clean energy adoption, and resource circulation. CE practices like recycling, remanufacturing, and shared mobility reduce environmental impact and create economic opportunities. Despite obstacles such as complex supply chains and regulatory disparities, CE adoption is supported by policies like Japan's recycling laws and global standards such as ISO 59000. This chapter highlights Honda's leadership in integrating CE principles, demonstrating how innovative practices can transform the automotive sector while aligning with sustainability goals.

Chapter 4: CE Strategy in the Cosmetics Industry
The cosmetics industry is adapting to CE through strategies like Shiseido's "5Rs" framework: Reduce, Reuse, Recycle, Replace, and Respect. This approach integrates environmental, social, and ethical dimensions, supported by technological innovation and cross-industry collaboration. Despite challenges such as high initial investments and the need for consumer engagement, Shiseido's initiatives exemplify CE's competitive advantages. By addressing lifecycle management and fostering sustainable consumer habits, Shiseido positions itself as a leader in CE. This chapter emphasizes the importance of corporate responsibility and sustainability as drivers of long-term success in the cosmetics industry.

Chapter 5: CE Strategy in the Multifunction Printer Industry
Fujifilm Business Innovation Corp. demonstrates how CE principles—Reduce, Reuse, Recycle—can enhance operational efficiency and profitability. Its robust recycling systems and visionary leadership illustrate the importance of integrating resource management and innovation into manufacturing practices. However, challenges like substantial upfront costs and supply chain coordination remain significant. This chapter provides insights into overcoming these barriers, emphasizing the role of capability building and collaboration in achieving sustainable business models.

Chapter 6: CE Strategy in the Food Industry
The food industry leverages CE to tackle food loss and promote sustainability through initiatives like Mizkan Group and TABETE's surplus food-sharing platform. Using the 9R framework, these practices optimize resource use while addressing cultural and regulatory challenges. The chapter emphasizes Japan's "mottainai" ethos in

fostering consumer awareness and sustainable practices. By scaling these efforts through technology and policy, CE presents a pathway to a more sustainable and equitable food system.

Chapter 7: CE Strategy in the Electric Vehicle Batteries Industry
This chapter examines CE's role in managing electric vehicle batteries (EVBs) to achieve SDGs. Companies in Europe, China, and Japan adopt varied approaches such as recycling, remanufacturing, and repair, leveraging advanced technologies and regulatory support. Despite challenges like cost and regulatory complexity, these practices highlight the potential for CE to revolutionize the automotive sector. Collaborative efforts and innovations are essential for scaling CE globally, fostering a sustainable, resource-efficient future.

Chapter 8: CE Strategy in the Chemical Industry
The chemical industry plays a critical role in CE by driving resource efficiency and sustainability. Case studies of Mitsui Chemicals, Mitsubishi Chemical, and Kaneka illustrate innovative practices like chemical recycling and biodegradable materials. These companies address challenges such as technological barriers and supply chain complexities, showcasing CE's potential to transform global value chains. The chapter advocates for collaboration and innovation as essential drivers for achieving CE goals in the industry.

Chapter 9: Advancing CE Strategies for a Sustainable Future
The final chapter underscores the transformative potential of the Circular Economy (CE) as a framework to address global challenges like resource scarcity, environmental degradation, and climate change. By integrating Digital Transformation (DX), Sustainability Transformation (SX), and Green Transformation (GX), CE can decouple economic growth from resource consumption, fostering innovation and resilience. Technological advancements such as AI, IoT, and blockchain enable traceability, optimize resource flows, and create closed-loop systems, as demonstrated by initiatives such as Mitsubishi Chemical's AI-driven production and Hitachi's IoT-enabled monitoring of elevators. Globally, the EU leads in regulatory frameworks, the USA in market-driven innovation, China in industrial symbiosis, and South Korea in technological approaches. Key challenges include high costs, regulatory complexity, and consumer skepticism. Addressing these requires robust policies, public-private partnerships, and consumer engagement. CE's alignment with carbon neutrality goals highlights its role in fostering resilience, sustainability, and long-term prosperity through innovation, collaboration, and systemic change.

Young Won Park, Ph.D.
Saitama University and University of Tokyo
Tokyo, Japan

Kin'ya Tamaki, Ph.D.
Aoyama Gakuin University
Tokyo, Japan

Contents

About the Authors

Young Won Park is a Professor of the Faculty of Economics, Graduate School of Humanities and Social Sciences at Saitama University and an Endowed Chair Professor of the Management Education and Research Center at the University of Tokyo, Japan. He holds a Ph.D. degree in the Department of Advanced Social and International Studies from the University of Tokyo, Japan. His articles have been published in journals including *Management Decision, International Journal of Production Economics, International Journal of Technology Management, International Journal of Information Management, Business Horizons, Journal of Business Research, Journal of Purchasing and Supply Management, Benchmarking: An International Journal, International Journal of Services and Operations Management, International Journal of Logistics Systems and Management, International Journal of Business Excellence, International Journal of Procurement Management, Akamon Management Review, Japan Academy of International Business Studies, Japanese Society for Science and Technology Studies, and the Japan Society of Information and Communication Research.* He has received research awards including a Certificate for Highly Cited Research in Business Horizons, Dissertation Paper Awards from the Japan Association for Social Informatics (JASI), Best Paper Awards from the Japan Society of Information and Communication Research (JSICR), Research Awards of the Social Science Field from the Telecommunications Advancement Foundation (TAF), and Research Students Awards of the Social Science Field from the Telecommunications Advancement Foundation (TAF). His research interests are in technology management, global strategy and IT strategy, and global supply chain management.

Kin'ya Tamaki is Professor of the Faculty of School of Business, Aoyama Gakuin University, and a Director, SDGs and Circular Economy Partnership Institute, Aoyama Gakuin University. He received a Ph.D. degree from Waseda University, School of Science and Engineering, 1989. His research interests are in business model innovation, future business strategy and product design and production management, circular economy, operational technology cybersecurity, and SDGs regional vitalization. He is engaged with the International Association of Project & Program

Management as the president of the academic Japanese society, and Asia Pacific Industrial Engineering and Management Systems as a board member of the international academic society. His books have been published in "Automation in Education, Training, and Learning Systems" (Springer Handbook of Automation), "Educational Programs of Business Producers and System Creators for Future Strategy Design Based on Action Project Group Activities through Industry and University Cooperation" (Higher Education - Reflections From the Field), "Automation in Education/ Learning Systems" (Springer Handbook of Automation), "Robotics in Construction and Shipbuilding" (Handbook of Industrial Robotics, Jhon Wiley & Sons, Inc.), and "Assembly" (Handbook of Industrial Engineering, Jhon Wiley & Sons, Inc.). His articles have been published in journals including *Journal of Community Medicine and Health Research, Journal of Strategic Management Studies, Journal of International Association of Project & Program Management, Journal of Mechanics Engineering and Automation, Journal of Global Tourism Research, International Journal of Business Information Systems, and AOYAMA BUSINESS REVIEW*. He has received research awards including Aoyama Gakuin Academic Commendation, the Japan Industrial Management Association Paper Encouragement Award, and the Robotics Society of Japan Research Encouragement.

Chapter 1
Circular Economy Trends in the DX, SX, and GX Era

Young Won Park

1.1 Introduction

Over the past decade, the concept of the circular economy (CE) has garnered significant attention from scholars, practitioners, and policymakers. At its heart, CE represents a fundamental shift from the traditional "take-make-dispose" linear economic model to one that prioritizes restorative and regenerative practices. These principles aim to minimize waste, pollution, and other negative externalities while fostering economic resilience and generating social and environmental benefits. Across various research initiatives and policy directives, CE's strategic importance has been increasingly recognized—evidenced by its integration into international, European, and national policies. This growing consensus underscores CE's potential to address sustainability challenges comprehensively and holistically.

Despite this progress, the transition to a circular economy on a broad scale remains complex. Organizations must navigate substantial barriers, adopt enabling technologies, and incorporate strategic frameworks often described using the acronyms DX (Digital Transformation), SX (Sustainability Transformation), and GX (Green Transformation). These three interconnected transformation processes create new opportunities for advancing CE initiatives. Digital Transformation (DX) leverages cutting-edge technologies such as the Internet of Things (IoT), Artificial Intelligence (AI), and blockchain to optimize processes like reverse logistics, resource tracking, and product lifecycle management. Sustainability Transformation (SX) embeds sustainability and social equity principles more deeply into organizational practices and policymaking. Meanwhile, Green Transformation (GX) focuses on mitigating environmental impacts by reducing carbon emissions, addressing resource overuse, and promoting low-carbon economic futures.

This chapter explores current CE trends within the context of DX, SX, and GX. It highlights advancements in lean production, Industry 4.0, supply chain management, eco-innovation, policy frameworks, and other domains identified in recent scholarly literature. Beyond summarizing existing research, this chapter seeks to illustrate

Y. W. Park and K. Tamaki, *Circular Economy Strategy for SDG Business Management*,
https://doi.org/10.1007/978-981-96-4194-9_1

the intersections of digital, sustainability, and green transformations, showcasing dynamic pathways for expanding CE practices and driving systemic change.

1.2 Circular Economy Recent Trends

1.2.1 Shifting from Linear to Circular: The Foundational Landscape

From the onset of industrialization, mainstream economic systems have hewed to a linear model, wherein natural resources are extracted, processed, used, and ultimately discarded. Researchers have long noted that this model exacerbates resource depletion, environmental damage, and social inequality. As Kirchherr et al. (2017) explain, CE aims to reverse these negative outcomes by focusing on reducing, reusing, and recycling (the "3Rs") and by catalyzing broader systemic changes. These encompass product redesign for durability and reparability, remanufacturing to extend product life, and material repurposing to increase overall resource efficiency. Nonetheless, Kirchherr et al. (2017) underscore that CE's conceptual contours differ among stakeholders, sometimes complicating matters of measurement and definition.

Murray et al. (2017) trace CE's origins to earlier developments in economics, ecology, and systems thinking, including industrial ecology, cradle-to-cradle design, and biomimicry. Despite the theoretical richness of these traditions, Korhonen et al. (2018) caution that more detailed, practice-oriented guidance is needed to operationalize CE in real-world business or policymaking contexts. This challenge is especially germane today, given the mounting urgency of environmental issues and shifting public expectations around sustainability. Hence, bridging the "knowing-doing gap" emerges as a pressing objective: the literature is robust on CE concepts, but far less explicit about implementation pathways.

Simultaneously, the digital revolution offers a suite of tools—Internet of Things (IoT) networks, big data, AI, and blockchain among them—that hold potential to enhance CE's practicability. Chauhan et al. (2022) show how firms can employ these technologies to innovate business models, reconfigure operational processes, and implement reverse logistics systems that close resource loops. At the same time, expansions in sustainability transformation (SX) and green transformation (GX) complement digital efforts by reducing carbon emissions and redefining consumption patterns.

1.2.2 Barriers and Critical Factors in Transitioning to Circular Models

Despite CE's growing visibility, substantial hurdles continue to impede widespread uptake. De Jesus and Mendonça (2018) note that these barriers range from insufficient infrastructure and technologies, to lack of awareness, entrenched cultural attitudes, and unsupportive market and policy conditions. One recurrent example is the shortage of robust reverse logistics capabilities. Ciliberto et al. (2021) emphasize that without integrated, transparent systems to recirculate resources efficiently, organizations often struggle to capture the value inherent in reuse, remanufacturing, and recycling.

Financial and market constraints likewise loom large. As Centobelli et al. (2020) observe, small and medium-sized enterprises (SMEs) can find it difficult to raise capital for circular economy investments and may lack green incentives from local or national governments. Chauhan et al. (2022) further identify psychological barriers (e.g., lack of trust in digital monitoring systems, reluctance to adopt AI or blockchain solutions) and ambiguous policy frameworks. These challenges are frequently exacerbated by incomplete articulation of how circular transitions address social as well as environmental justice—an oversight that Kirchherr et al. (2017) suggest can lead to inequities or unintended social harms. As a result, questions persist about how best to integrate the social dimension of sustainability—embodied in SX—within CE initiatives.

1.2.3 Intersections of Digital, Sustainable, and Green Transformations

In parallel, organizations are grappling with three overlapping forms of transformation, commonly referred to as DX, SX, and GX. DX (Digital Transformation) denotes the uptake of data-intensive technologies—IoT, AI, big data, and more—that enhance real-time monitoring, connect operations, and automate processes. As Kristoffersen et al. (2020) illustrate, digital transformation initiatives reveal inefficiencies in resource use, thereby facilitating more effective circular production and waste diversion. SX (Sustainability Transformation) widens the focus to systemic changes in how resources are allocated, economic activities are structured, and social equity is upheld. The United Nations' Sustainable Development Goals (SDGs) capture these broad themes, and CE is often cited as a direct pathway for fulfilling SDG 12 ("responsible consumption and production") and related goals. GX (Green Transformation) centers on decarbonization, environmental stewardship, and preservation of ecological assets. Zhou et al. (2020) discuss how green transitions in countries like China support the adoption of Industry 4.0 technologies and facilitate the implementation of circular models that help reduce emissions and pollution.

When DX, SX, and GX align within organizational or policy contexts, they can generate a synergistic effect, overcoming the challenges to implementing CE at scale. However, synergy is hardly automatic. Coordinated governance, stakeholder buy-in, incentive structures, and a collective vision of future outcomes are needed if CE is to progress beyond small pilot projects and become a new social and economic paradigm.

1.2.4 Production Systems and the Role of Industry 4.0

One vital nexus where DX, SX, and GX converge is Industry 4.0—the increasingly networked, automated, data-driven model of manufacturing. Ciliberto et al. (2021) detail how merging lean production and Industry 4.0 can reduce waste, optimize processes in real time, and thus advance CE objectives. Industry 4.0 solutions include smart machines, advanced analytics, robotics, and cloud computing, which dramatically extend traditional lean practices.

Manavalan and Jayakrishna (2019) show the impact of integrating 6R (Recover, Reuse, Remanufacture, Recycle, Redesign, Reduce) strategies into supply chains, reorienting them from linear end-of-pipe processes to continuously looping resource flows. Doing so entails capital investment, changes in workforce skills, and top-down leadership dedicated to sustainable outcomes. Yet for firms capable of implementing these Industry 4.0 solutions, benefits range from improved brand reputation and reduced material and energy costs, to supply chain resilience and compliance with evolving environmental regulations.

1.2.5 Emerging Digital Technologies and the Future of Circularity

Digital technologies can bridge the gap between conceptual frameworks and operational practice. Kristoffersen et al. (2020) put forward the Smart CE framework, mapping out how digital solutions, from blockchain to advanced analytics, can enable manufacturers to adopt circular strategies. By automating product tracking and verifying chain-of-custody, these technologies buttress extended producer responsibility schemes and help manage complex reverse logistics networks.

Blockchain, for instance, introduces immutable ledgers that document a product's composition, origin, and movement through supply chains. Murthy and Ramakrishna (2022) underline its significance for e-waste management, where tracking devices from cradle to grave are notoriously problematic. The transparency engendered by blockchain can incentivize producers to reclaim discarded devices, properly recycle components, and meet extended producer responsibility obligations. Similarly, AI can refine sorting processes in recycling facilities, improve product design (e.g., through generative design methods that minimize raw inputs), and facilitate predictive maintenance, extending the lifespan of capital equipment.

Chauhan et al. (2022) note that adopting IoT sensors, AI, and cloud computing also sets the stage for "product-as-a-service" business models. Here, manufacturers or third parties retain ownership of an asset while offering a service to customers; the incentive, therefore, shifts toward maintaining product longevity rather than selling high volumes of new products. However, such radical shifts hinge on consumer openness, regulatory support, and organizational capacity—reminding us that technology alone is insufficient to realize CE's potential.

1.2.6 Policy, Regulation, and Governance: Key Elements for CE Enablement

Underpinning all these advancements is robust governance and supportive policies. Zhou et al. (2020) suggest that national innovation policies can accelerate pollution-abatement technologies, ecological industrial restructuring, and the adoption of Industry 4.0 tools that enable CE. Nonetheless, policy success varies by region due to diverging economic, infrastructural, and cultural contexts.

In supply chain contexts, regulations—such as extended producer responsibility (EPR), eco-design directives, and deposit-refund schemes—can align market incentives with CE practices. Centobelli et al. (2020) highlight how stakeholder pressures on SMEs can help these smaller organizations adopt circular strategies, especially when incentives for green commitments are provided and when supply chain management embraces sustainability. Meanwhile, De Jesus and Mendonça (2018) advocate a broader "innovation systems" perspective, suggesting that public–private partnerships, capacity-building initiatives, and supportive institutional arrangements are required if CE is to fulfill its transformative potential.

1.2.7 Eco-Innovation: Linking Circularity with Broader Sustainability Agendas

Eco-innovation integrates environmental objectives into product design, production processes, and service offerings in ways that create both economic value and reduced ecological footprints. Prieto-Sandoval et al. (2018) assert that eco-innovation acts as a conduit for putting CE principles into practice, encouraging research partnerships, and scaling new business models like product-service systems or sharing platforms.

Additionally, green and low-carbon policies necessitate synergy with CE. Xie et al. (2023) highlight the interplay between carbon emission reductions and green economic strategies in a Chinese province, illustrating how improving energy efficiency or substituting coal with renewables aligns with CE's resource optimization goals. Meanwhile, Mhatre et al. (2021) stress the need for macro-level government engagement to build supportive infrastructure. Investments in digitalization, infrastructure for collecting and sorting materials, and targeted incentives for material loops can help multiple industries adopt eco-innovations. When aligned with social equity aims—consistent with the broader SX agenda—eco-innovation can produce local jobs in repair, remanufacturing, or recycling, thus reinforcing the social pillar of sustainability.

1.2.8 Extended Producer Responsibility and the Role of Consumers

An essential aspect of CE is shared responsibility across product lifecycles. Extended Producer Responsibility (EPR) mandates that manufacturers assume some, if not full, accountability for post-consumer stages of their products. Murthy and Ramakrishna (2022) highlight how EPR can be especially impactful for e-waste, compelling producers to design devices for easier refurbishment, recycling, or take-back. However, they also point out that global frameworks and improved enforcement are often needed to bridge the gap between policy ambitions and real-world practice.

Consumer attitudes remain equally crucial. Whether it is the acceptance of refurbished electronics or willingness to participate in product-as-a-service schemes, user behavior can make or break a circular business model. Kirchherr et al. (2017) note that consumer awareness is often underemphasized in CE definitions. Nonetheless, building trust among consumers—by, for example, labeling or providing guarantees for reused and remanufactured goods—will be pivotal for scaling up circular activities. Successful adoption thus requires a cultural shift that values longevity, resource conservation, and services over individual ownership.

1.2.9 Circular Strategies, Indicators, and Monitoring Frameworks

Effective measurement is a linchpin in implementing circular principles. Moraga et al. (2019) identify the proliferation of CE indicators, including recycling rates, resource productivity, and monitoring frameworks. However, limiting assessment to recycling alone may overlook more nuanced or higher-level strategies like reuse, remanufacturing, or rethinking product-service systems. Reike et al. (2018) propose a 10R typology (Refuse, Rethink, Reduce, Reuse, Repair, Refurbish, Remanufacture, Repurpose, Recycle, Recover), ranking circular strategies by the level of resource retention they offer.

While the policy emphasis frequently leans toward recycling, it is noteworthy that "inner loops"—such as repair or reuse—may yield greater environmental benefits if effectively pursued. Mhatre et al. (2021) discuss how, under the 2015 EU CE Action Plan, multiple nations advanced waste management and recycling. Still, fewer have systematically integrated product design for disassembly, extended warranties, or advanced remanufacturing. As a result, the net effect on resource consumption and waste generation has been partial. More comprehensive frameworks, built on robust data, are required to align "macro" interventions—like national recycling targets—with "micro" actions—like corporate eco-innovation or consumer-based repair programs.

Advancing from theoretical acceptance to real operational change requires pragmatic metrics and indicators. Moraga et al. (2019) examine how governments and corporations increasingly adopt monitoring frameworks—targeting recycling rates, resource productivity, or material footprints—to assess their circular progress. Still, merely tracking recycling can obscure broader lifecycle considerations. For instance, some policy approaches emphasize recycling over product longevity or reuse, which can undermine higher-order CE strategies.

As shown before, Reike et al. (2018) propose a 10R typology (Refuse, Rethink, Reduce, Reuse, Repair, Refurbish, Remanufacture, Repurpose, Recycle, Recover), ranking circular strategies by the level of resource retention they offer. By mapping specific initiatives to different "R" categories, policymakers and businesses may better align with sustainability goals. Furthermore, Mhatre et al. (2021) explore how these frameworks have informed CE action plans in the European Union, generating momentum in sectors such as e-waste, construction, and electronics. Nonetheless, the picture remains partial: the literature and policy practice often privilege the more traditional "downstream" aspects of CE (e.g., recycling), rather than innovative "upstream" interventions (e.g., product-service systems, design for disassembly).

1.2.10 The Future of CE Amid DX, SX, and GX

The intersection of DX, SX, and GX foretells a dynamic future for CE. On one level, digital transformations can yield real-time intelligence, reduce resource inputs, and facilitate circular design. On another level, sustainability transformations stress that these technical fixes must come packaged with social equity and stakeholder engagement. Green transformations, in turn, push industries to cut carbon emissions and implement closed-loop resource practices.

Despite the promise, key questions persist: Will the computational resources required for large-scale AI or IoT solutions undermine environmental gains by raising energy consumption? Are there rebound effects—like greater e-waste from faster obsolescence of electronics used to run these systems? How do cultural attitudes toward ownership and convenience influence the adoption of rental or sharing models? CE is thus inseparable from broader deliberations about justice, ethics, and planetary boundaries. Proponents of a "just circular economy" call for inclusive processes that ensure benefits—jobs, lower costs, local resilience—are equitably distributed rather than captured by a select few.

1.2.11 Organization of This Book and Chapter Contributions

This chapter introduces the key themes around circular economy strategies, metrics, and applications, underscoring their intersection with DX, SX, and GX. Through a careful exploration of CE enablers, barriers, and technological drivers, the chapter frames CE not as a stand-alone initiative, but as part of a broader societal reconfiguration. The synergy between circular models, digital tools, green principles, and sustainability considerations increasingly permeates industries and supply chains, reshaping how resources flow through the economy.

By foregrounding these emergent technologies and policy trends—ranging from e-waste management to Industry 4.0 innovations—this chapter suggests the 9R framework and reveals both the opportunities and obstacles that define today's CE landscape. As subsequent chapters in this book will illustrate, engineers, policymakers, economists, supply chain professionals, and social scientists each have vital roles to play in developing comprehensive, ethically grounded circular systems. The future of CE will rely on bridging these disciplinary and practical domains, ensuring that the transition is both effective and equitable.

1.3 Circular Economy Framework for SDGs: 9R Framework

The concept of the circular economy (CE) is increasingly recognized as an effective framework for addressing interconnected economic, environmental, and social challenges. By emphasizing the principles of resource efficiency, waste reduction, and sustainable consumption, CE offers a pathway to meet multiple Sustainable Development Goals (SDGs). As global urgency accelerates to achieve the SDGs, scholars and practitioners have positioned CE as a transformative tool capable of decoupling economic growth from resource depletion and environmental degradation (Park et al. 2024).

At its essence, the circular economy shifts away from the conventional "take-make-dispose" approach, focusing instead on maintaining material value within the economic system for as long as possible. This shift promotes not only environmental sustainability but also economic resilience and social equity. The Ellen MacArthur Foundation has been instrumental in popularizing CE principles, and subsequent studies have refined these ideas across various industries, including automotive, construction, and consumer goods (Shakhnoza and Park 2023; Park et al. 2024). Research underscores CE's ability to lower emissions, ensure resource security, and safeguard biodiversity, aligning closely with SDGs related to clean energy, responsible production, and climate action (Bonsu 2020; Husgafvel and Sakaguchi 2023).

Despite its potential, implementing CE on a large scale remains challenging. Barriers include operational inefficiencies, cultural resistance, and fragmented policy frameworks. Consequently, a range of methodologies and indicators have been developed to assist stakeholders in designing, implementing, and assessing circular strategies aligned with the Sustainable Development Goals (SDGs). For instance, frameworks such as the 9R typology have been developed to categorize and clarify CE strategies, offering a systematic approach to maximizing material efficiency and minimizing waste.

1.3.1 The 10R Typology

The 10R typology serves as a comprehensive framework for understanding and implementing circular strategies. Each "R" represents a distinct action that preserves or regenerates material value at different points in a product's lifecycle. This typology includes R0 Refuse, R1 Rethink, R2 Reduce, R3 Reuse, R4 Repair, R5 Refurbish, R6 Remanufacture, R7 Repurpose, R8 Recycle, and R9 Recover (Potting et al. 2017; Reike et al. 2018).

Refuse emphasizes avoiding unnecessary production or consumption. By abandoning resource-intensive or polluting products and processes, organizations and individuals can reduce material demand at the source.

Rethink focuses on making products more efficient through innovative design and multi-functionality. For example, shared mobility services rethink transportation by maximizing the utility of vehicles.

Reduce involves minimizing resource use during production and consumption. Lightweight design, efficient manufacturing processes, and energy-saving technologies exemplify this strategy.

Reuse promotes extending the life of products by transferring them to new users without significant alterations, as seen in second-hand markets.

Repair ensures products remain functional through maintenance or minor fixes, delaying the need for replacement.

Refurbish restores older products to modern standards, enhancing their usability and extending their lifespan. This strategy is prevalent in industries such as electronics and furniture.

Remanufacture involves disassembling products, restoring components, and reassembling them into like-new products. For instance, remanufacturing engines in the automotive industry preserves significant material value.

Repurpose adapts discarded products or components for new functions. Creative applications, such as using old tires in construction, illustrate this principle.

Recycle focuses on processing materials to recover raw resources for new products. While recycling is widely practiced, it often results in material degradation, making it a less preferred option compared to strategies like reuse or remanufacture.

Finally, Recover emphasizes energy recovery from waste through methods such as incineration. However, this strategy is considered the least desirable within the CE hierarchy as it typically destroys material integrity.

Table 1.1 The 10R typology

R Strategy	Description
R0 Refuse	Avoid making a product redundant by abandoning its function or offering the same function differently
R1 Rethink	Make product use more intensive, for example, through sharing or multi-functionality
R2 Reduce	Increase efficiency in production or use by consuming fewer resources and materials
R3 Reuse	Use discarded products by another consumer in good condition for the same purpose
R4 Repair	Repair and maintain defective products to be used for their original function
R5 Refurbish	Restore an old product and bring it up to date with improved functionality or appearance
R6 Remanufacture	Use parts of discarded products to make new products with the same functionality
R7 Repurpose	Use discarded products or parts in new products with a different function
R8 Recycle	Process materials to obtain the same (high-grade) or lower (low-grade) quality recycled materials
R9 Recover	Recover energy from materials that cannot be recycled through incineration or other means

The 10R typology provides a structured approach to CE, enabling organizations to evaluate and implement strategies that align with their sustainability goals. Each R represents a specific strategy for retaining value within the system, ranging from avoiding resource use altogether (Refuse) to recovering energy from materials that cannot be reused or recycled (Recover). This framework not only clarifies the range of CE strategies but also highlights their interconnectedness, emphasizing the importance of adopting a holistic approach to sustainability (Table 1.1).

1.3.2 The 9R Approach in This Book

This book adopts a 9R framework, consolidating "Recover" under "Recycle" to emphasize the importance of preserving material value over energy recovery. The rationale for this modification stems from the growing recognition that energy recovery through incineration often contradicts the principles of circularity by permanently removing materials from the economic system (Park et al. 2024).

Engineering and supply chain management are pivotal in operationalizing the 9R framework. Engineering innovations, such as design-for-disassembly and material optimization, enable circular strategies like reuse, remanufacturing, and recycling. Advanced technologies, including 3D printing and digital twins, enhance production efficiency and reduce material waste, aligning with CE principles.

Supply chain management ensures the seamless flow of materials and products within circular systems. Circular supply chains integrate reverse logistics to collect, sort, and process used products for refurbishment, remanufacturing, or recycling. Technologies such as blockchain and IoT enhance transparency and accountability, enabling companies to track material flows and measure progress toward sustainability goals.

The synergy between engineering and supply chain management is essential for achieving circularity. For instance, designing products for modularity simplifies disassembly and repair, while efficient supply chain processes ensure that materials are returned to production cycles. However, implementing these practices requires addressing challenges such as high upfront costs, technological gaps, and global supply chain fragmentation. Collaborative efforts among stakeholders, including policymakers, industry leaders, and researchers, are crucial for overcoming these barriers and advancing CE implementation.

Figure 1.1 offers a concrete visualization of these concepts in terms of engineering and supply chain phases. The 9R framework comprises Refuse, Rethink, Reduce, Reuse, Repair, Refurbish, Remanufacture, Repurpose, and Recycle. Each of these strategies is designed to minimize resource extraction, reduce waste, and maximize the lifespan and utility of products and materials. By addressing various stages of a product's lifecycle—from design and production to use and end-of-life management—the 9R framework offers a holistic approach to achieving circularity.

Refuse focuses on eliminating unnecessary products and materials at the design stage. For example, refusing single-use plastics or hazardous chemicals can significantly reduce environmental impact. Rethink encourages reimagining business

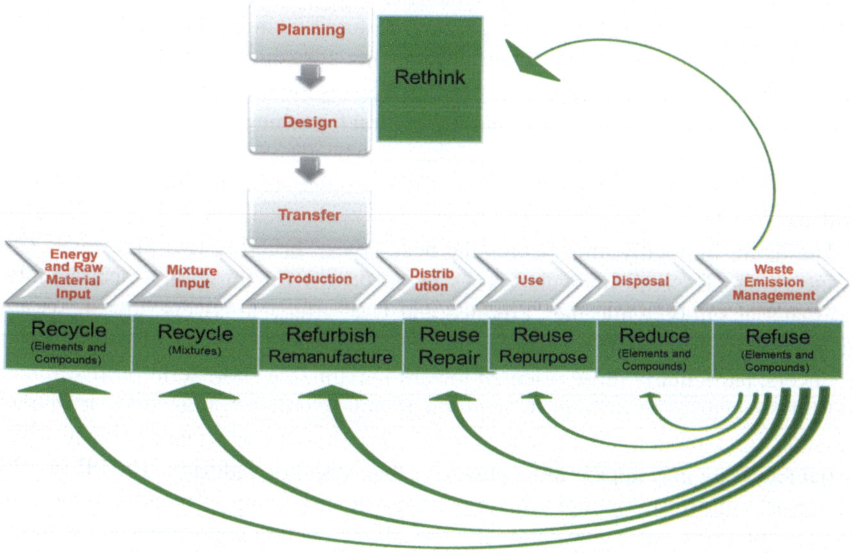

Fig. 1.1 Framework for 9R strategies

models and consumption patterns. Sharing economies, product-as-a-service models, and modular product designs are all examples of rethinking traditional approaches to production and consumption. Reduce targets resource efficiency by minimizing material inputs and energy use. Lightweight packaging, energy-efficient appliances, and digital solutions that replace physical products exemplify this strategy. Reuse promotes extending the life of products with minimal processing, fostering second-hand markets and donation platforms. Repair addresses product longevity by fixing broken or malfunctioning items, reducing the need for new products. Refurbish and Remanufacture represent strategies that restore or rebuild products to extend their lifecycle. Refurbishing often involves cosmetic or functional updates, while remanufacturing typically requires disassembling and rebuilding products to near-original standards. These strategies are particularly relevant in industries with high-value products, such as automotive and electronics. Repurpose adapts products or components for entirely new uses. This strategy fosters creativity and innovation, as seen in the use of industrial waste for art or construction materials. Recycle remains a critical component of the framework, focusing on recovering materials to produce new products. However, the framework prioritizes recycling as a last resort, emphasizing its role only when higher-value strategies are not feasible.

Curving arrows in Fig. 1.1 demonstrate that Rethink spans the planning and design stages, capturing the need to reconsider core assumptions about product function, structure, and expected lifespan. Meanwhile, different green arrows trace out strategies such as recycle or refurbish that feedback from later stages in the supply chain to earlier phases, thereby preserving materials at higher value. The figure incorporates a rationale that consolidates "recover" within "recycle," echoing recent scholarly trends that view energy-from-waste as a last resort, less aligned with high-value circular loops. The note on the figure clarifies that the original references to 10R have been modified into 9R in order to focus on more function-preserving strategies. This schematic integrates both engineering chains, focusing on product conception and design elements, and supply chains, addressing production, distribution, and disposal. The synergy of these two chains is central for achieving meaningful circular transformations, since well-designed products can be disassembled more readily and reused, thereby lowering dependency on virgin resources and curbing environmental burdens.

The figure implicitly underscores the necessity of bridging two lifecycles. The "Concept and Design" lifecycle zeroes in on design for durability, disassembly, and material safety, while the "Produce and Use" lifecycle covers how items are manufactured, distributed, consumed, and eventually managed at end of life. Many producers, particularly those oriented toward maximizing short-term profits, might find little incentive to revamp their products unless policy frameworks or market pressures force them to do so. Indeed, production-based compliance measures like partial recycling may appear more attractive than systemic redesign. The 9R or 10R frameworks thus also highlight the importance of supporting or mandating design-oriented solutions, since conventional disposal or recycling approaches alone rarely deliver the full potential of the circular economy.

Although the figure was developed to illustrate the logic behind the 9R framework, it also aligns with the aim of clarifying the "engineering chain" (where product structures are decided and prototypes tested) and the "supply chain" (where raw materials, manufacturing, and distribution meet consumer demand and, eventually, waste management). In bridging these elements, the figure and its green arrows capture feedback loops that route materials back into different stages. That said, implementing this approach depends on coherent policies, well-planned reverse logistics, consumer acceptance of secondhand or remanufactured goods, and corporate willingness to adopt new business models such as product-service systems. The evolution of such models is influenced by digital transformations that enable real-time tracking of products, advanced sensor technology for predictive maintenance, and big data analytics that can optimize resource distribution. However, none of these technological enablers automatically guarantee that businesses or consumers will choose more circular options.

Cultural norms, habitual behaviors, and entrenched linear assumptions about product ownership remain significant obstacles. While design changes can make repair simpler, a cultural shift that values maintaining goods for the long haul is likewise crucial, especially in sectors where fast fashion or rapid product turnover is deeply embedded. Overcoming these ingrained consumption patterns often requires educational campaigns, labeling that indicates the environmental credentials of products, and economic disincentives for single-use or disposable items. The tension around how "R" words are defined only heightens when stakeholders do not share a consistent perspective on what a more circular approach truly entails. Some might see incineration with energy recovery as "good enough," whereas others interpret that approach as a last-resort measure that contradicts higher-level loops.

Policymakers seeking to implement the 9R or 10R schemes might pursue distinct targets for each R, encouraging companies to demonstrate how they are meeting benchmarks for reuse, repair, or remanufacturing. They might also adopt more wide-ranging policies, from extended warranties that make companies responsible for product performance over longer cycles to restrictive bans on disposable packaging or single-use plastics. Meanwhile, from a business standpoint, adopting certain R strategies can become profitable if it aligns with consumer expectations or if raw materials become more expensive. However, the complexities of measuring success remain, especially when it comes to capturing intangible benefits like extended product life and avoided resource extraction. Despite ongoing complexity, the 9R framework introduced in Fig. 1.1 helps clarify the relationships between each R strategy and the overall product lifecycle, showing how different loops channel materials and components back into earlier phases.

In conclusion, the 10R typology articulates a broad range of strategies for sustaining and maximizing resource value across supply chains, while the 9R approach specifically merges "recover" into "recycle" to emphasize the priority of maintaining product integrity above energy-based solutions. The reference image, dubbed "9R Framework," depicts how planning, design, production, distribution, use, disposal, and waste management can be reoriented around circular ideals, with "Rethink" bridging the early conceptual phases and "Refuse" representing the removal of problematic materials or processes. By embedding that logic into both engineering and supply chain considerations, organizations can move beyond incremental recycling to more transformative changes. Nonetheless, the operationalization of these frameworks depends on thoughtful policy, supportive consumer culture, and cross-sectoral collaboration. Empirical research on target-setting, systematic data collection, and robust governance structures all enhance the likelihood of meaningful outcomes. If done properly, the circular economy can address immediate ecological threats, reduce material throughput, and build more resilient and equitable societies, yet it demands a concerted effort to unify definitions, align incentives, and cultivate a holistic mindset that values long-lasting solutions over quick disposals.

1.4 Conclusion

Over the last decade, the circular economy (CE) has transitioned from a niche concept to a foundational element of global, regional, and local strategies for sustainability. Its principles align closely with the need for systemic change in how societies produce, consume, and manage resources. The integration of CE with Digital Transformation (DX), Sustainability Transformation (SX), and Green Transformation (GX) significantly amplifies its potential impact. However, this integration also introduces new complexities. While digital technologies like IoT, AI, and blockchain enhance resource optimization and enable innovative circular business models, they also bring challenges, such as the generation of e-waste and potential rebound effects. Similarly, sustainability frameworks emphasize equity and resilience, ensuring CE transitions are inclusive and socially just, while green imperatives align CE strategies with climate goals, such as reducing emissions and curbing resource exploitation.

The implementation of CE concepts across industries demonstrates how they are being operationalized through efforts such as lean manufacturing, reverse logistics, and digital solutions for supply chain realignment. These approaches highlight both the tangible benefits and persistent barriers of CE adoption. Challenges like e-waste management and innovations in bioplastics provide valuable insights into the specific obstacles and opportunities in advancing circular practices. Despite the availability of technical solutions and supportive policies, scaling up these practices requires overcoming institutional inertia, market fragmentation, and cultural resistance.

Insights from foundational work emphasize that CE is not just about recycling. It encompasses designing out waste, extending product lifespans, and shifting from ownership-based to service-based models where feasible. This transition challenges conventional economic metrics like GDP, which often prioritize resource throughput over long-term sustainability. Overcoming such systemic obstacles necessitates new frameworks that value resource durability and ecosystem health.

Moving forward, the following chapters explore the theoretical foundations, methodological tools, and practical applications of the circular economy (CE) through a diverse range of case studies. These include policy recommendations, advanced digital solutions, and cross-sector collaborations essential for scaling CE practices. By harmonizing DX's technological innovations, SX's focus on resilience and equity, and GX's environmental imperatives, CE can move from pilot projects to a transformative economic paradigm.

Chapter 1 has established that CE is no longer a theoretical construct but an evolving framework intersecting with digital, sustainability, and green transformations. From early concepts like closed loops to contemporary frameworks such as the 9R approach, CE has expanded in scope. While recycling remains critical, the focus has shifted toward higher-value strategies like design for disassembly, long-term product use, and collaborative consumption models. These approaches challenge GDP-driven metrics, calling for new systems that prioritize stock (durable resources and sustainable infrastructure) over flow (short-term resource throughput).

The governance challenges of CE are as diverse as its potential solutions. Regional disparities in infrastructure, cultural attitudes, and economic priorities necessitate tailored approaches. Effective strategies include well-designed Extended Producer Responsibility (EPR) schemes, macro-level targets incentivizing upstream interventions, and digital tools for resource tracking and circular logistics. Lean production, bolstered by Industry 4.0 technologies, offers significant opportunities for efficiency gains, provided human factors such as workforce training and stakeholder collaboration are equally prioritized.

The chapters ahead will explore these themes in depth, offering analytical frameworks, case studies, and actionable insights. Together, they affirm that while transitioning to a circular economy is ambitious, the alignment of DX, SX, and GX—coupled with the collective efforts of innovators, policymakers, and consumers—brings this vision closer to reality. By addressing ecological challenges, reducing material dependence, and fostering economic resilience, CE can evolve into a transformative model for sustainable development in the twenty-first century.

References

Bonsu, N. O. (2020). Towards a circular and low-carbon economy: Insights from the transitioning to electric vehicles and net zero economy. Journal of Cleaner Production, 256, 120659.

Centobelli, P., Cerchione, R., Chiaroni, D., Del Vecchio, P., & Urbinati, A. (2020). Designing business models in circular economy: A systematic literature review and research agenda. Business Strategy and the Environment, 29(4), 1734–1749.

Chauhan, C., Parida, V., & Dhir, A. (2022). Linking circular economy and digitalisation technologies: A systematic literature review of past achievements and future promises. Technological Forecasting and Social Change, 177, 121508.

Ciliberto, C., Szopik-Depczyńska, K., Tarczyńska-Łuniewska, M., Ruggieri, A., & Ioppolo, G. (2021). Enabling the Circular Economy transition: A sustainable lean manufacturing recipe for Industry 4.0. Business Strategy and the Environment, 30(7), 3255–3272.

De Jesus, A., & Mendonça, S. (2018). Lost in transition? Drivers and barriers in the eco-innovation road to the circular economy. Ecological Economics, 145, 75–89.

Husgafvel, R., & Sakaguchi, D. (2023). Circular economy development in the wood construction sector in Finland. Sustainability, 15(10), 7871.

Kirchherr, J., Reike, D., & Hekkert, M. (2017). Conceptualizing the circular economy: An analysis of 114 definitions. Resources, Conservation and Recycling, 127, 221–232.
Korhonen, J., Honkasalo, A., & Seppälä, J. (2018). Circular economy: The concept and its limitations. Ecological Economics, 143, 37–46.
Kristoffersen, E., Blomsma, F., Mikalef, P., & Li, J. (2020). The smart circular economy: A digital-enabled circular strategies framework for manufacturing companies. Journal of Business Research, 120, 241–261.
Manavalan, E., & Jayakrishna, K. (2019). An analysis on sustainable supply chain for circular economy. Procedia Manufacturing, 33, 477–484.
Mhatre, P., Panchal, R., Singh, A., & Bibyan, S. (2021). A systematic literature review on the circular economy initiatives in the European Union. Sustainable Production and Consumption, 26, 187–202.
Moraga, G., Huysveld, S., Mathieux, F., Blengini, G. A., Alaerts, L., Van Acker, K., de Meester, S., & Dewulf, J. (2019). Circular economy indicators: What do they measure? Resources, Conservation and Recycling, 146, 452–461.
Murray, A., Skene, K., & Haynes, K. (2017). The circular economy: An interdisciplinary exploration of the concept and application in a global context. Journal of Business Ethics, 140, 369–380.
Murthy, K., & Ramakrishna, S. (2022). A review on global E-waste management: urban mining towards a sustainable future and circular economy. Sustainability, 14(2), 647.
Park, Y. W., Sugie, R., & Mizuguchi, K. (2024). Circular Economy Strategy of Japanese Firms: A Comparative Study of Manufacturing and Other Industries. Communication of JIMA, 34(1), 15–22.
Potting, J., Hekkert, M. P., Worrell, E., & Hanemaaijer, A. (2017). Circular economy: measuring innovation in the product chain. Planbureau voor de Leefomgeving, (2544).
Prieto-Sandoval, V., Jaca, C., & Ormazabal, M. (2018). Towards a consensus on the circular economy. Journal of Cleaner Production, 179, 605–615.
Reike, D., Vermeulen, W. J., & Witjes, S. (2018). The circular economy: New or refurbished as CE 3.0?—Exploring controversies in the conceptualization of the circular economy through a focus on value retention options. Resources, Conservation and Recycling, 135, 246–264.
Shakhnoza, N. K., & Park, Y. W. (2023). Circular Economy in Automobile Industry: Literature Analysis. Management Review: An International Journal, 18(1), 83–113.
Xie, S., Li, T., & Cao, K. (2023). Analysis of the Impact of Carbon Emission Control on Urban Economic Indicators based on the Concept of Green Economy under Sustainable Development. Sustainability, 15(13), 10145.
Zhou, X., Song, M., & Cui, L. (2020). Driving force for China's economic development under Industry 4.0 and circular economy: Technological innovation or structural change?. Journal of Cleaner Production, 271, 122680.

Chapter 2
International Trend Researches on CE Policy and International Standard: Impact of New CE Policies and Regulations on Sustainable Business Model Transform

Kin'ya Tamaki

2.1 Introduction

In the past, the Japanese manufacturing industry was primarily based on the business model of selling products introduced into the market, and the 3R tactics (reuse, reduce, and recycle) for following up on waste disposal. "SDGs Target 12.5: Waste reduction" included in "SDGs Goal 12: Producer and consumer responsibility" are related to the circular economy (CE). The European Union's (EU) CE Commission has defined CE as follows: "CE is an economic policy that will enhance new competitiveness by creating new business opportunities and innovative and efficient production methods and consumption styles, protecting companies from resource depletion and price volatility".

First, the CE principles, circular cycle models, and circular product certificated conditions will be described. Next, we will explore the international trend researches on CE policies, master plans, regulations, and laws in the EU and Japan. Then the international standards (ISO 59000 series) of CE documents still under development by ISO/TC (Technical Committee) 323 Secretariat will be presented. Finally, we will discuss the influence of new CE policies and regulations regarding ecodesign on the future business models, and product and service design.

The main issues addressed in each chapter are as follows:

Section 2.2 describes the CE principles, and biological or technical cycle models by Ellen Mac Arthur Foundation.

Section 2.3 introduces the "CRADLE TO CRADLE CERTIFIED®" by Cradle to Cradle Products Innovation Institute.

Section 2.4 explores the trend researches on CE policies, master plans, regulations in the EU: Ecodesign Working Plan, the EU Action Plan for Circular Economy (CE Package), and New Circular Economy Action Plan.

Y. W. Park and K. Tamaki, *Circular Economy Strategy for SDG Business Management*,
https://doi.org/10.1007/978-981-96-4194-9_2

Section 2.5 shows the trend surveys regarding CE Policies and Industry Case Studies in Japan: Circular Economy Vision 2020 Compiled by the Ministry of Economy, Trade and Industry (METI), Growth—Oriented, Resource-Autonomous Circular Economy Strategy by the METI, and industry case studies such as Japan Partnership for Circular Economy (J4CE) by Japan Business Federation (Keidanren).

Section 2.6 investigates evolution of CE legislations in Japan: Basic Law on Resources, the 6th Basic Environmental Plan, the Advanced Resource Recycling Act, and the Fifth Fundamental Plan for Establishing a Robust Material-Cycle Society.

Section 2.7 summarizes how the international standards (ISO)/TC (Technical Committee) 323 Secretariat began designing the ISO 59000 series of CE documents to harmonize the understanding of the CE and to support its implementation and measurement.

Section 2.8 explores the impact of new CE Regulations for ecodesign Requirements for sustainable products, and Digital Product Passport for CE for verification of product information in the EU.

Section 2.9 discusses influence of above-mentioned new CE regulations such as ecodesign requirements on business model transformation for recycling resources and sustainable product design.

2.2 CE Principles and "Butterfly Model" by Ellen Mac Arthur Foundation

2.2.1 CE Definition and CE Principles

The Ellen Mac Arthur Foundation (EMF) founded in 2010 is promoting the concepts of the CE and the sustainable transition. The EMF defines CE as: "a system solution framework that tackles global challenges like climate change, biodiversity loss, waste, and pollution. It is based on three principles, driven by design: eliminate waste and pollution, circulate products and materials (at their highest value), and regenerate nature" (Ellen Mac Arthur Foundation, 2023). In addition, the EMF presents the "Three Principles of the Circular Economy":

- Product design in a manner that does not generate waste and pollution
- Continue to use products and raw materials
- Regenerate natural systems

2.2.2 *The "Biological Cycle" and "Technical Cycle" in the "Butterfly Model"*

With the aim of realizing the aforementioned CE principles, the EMF theorized the "butterfly model" (Ellen Mac Arthur Foundation, 2015) which explained how the flows of both "biological cycle" and "technological cycle" can be maintaining products and resources at their highest value, through regeneration, repair, reuse, refurbish, and only lastly recycle (Fig. 2.1).

The central part of the figure expresses the conventional "linear model (procurement, production and disposal of resources)." This linear model is used by consumers through a series of corporate activities that procure and invest resources, process and manufacture, and provide services. After consumer use, the disposal of resources is incinerated or landfilled.

Renewable resources in the "biological cycle" cannot move through the cycle indefinitely. It gradually deteriorates as it undergoes cycles using resources. This process of recycling renewable resources as their original quality deteriorates are called "cascade recycling." It is nearly impossible for a single company to achieve such cascading recycling.

The cycle should then be repeated several times. When the resource finally becomes unusable, it will eventually return to nature. It can be returned to the soil through biodegradation or composting, and organic waste can be converted into

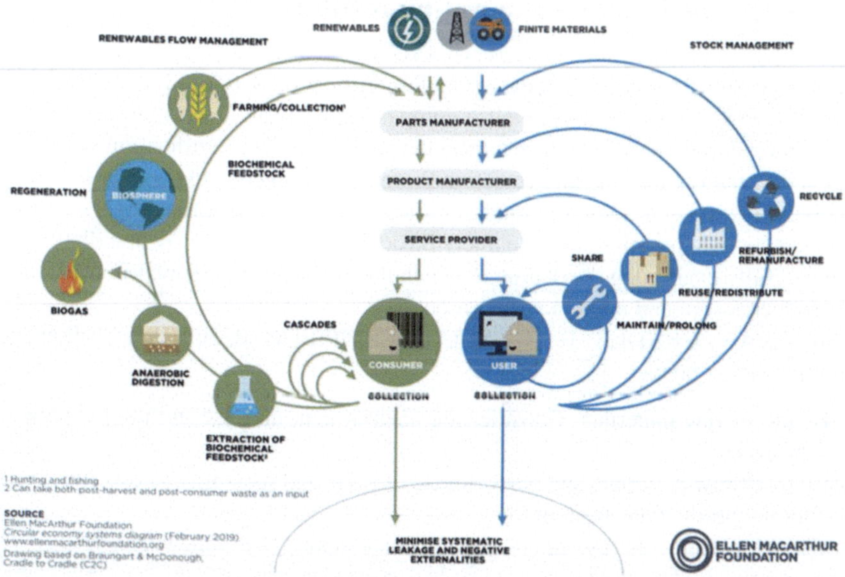

Fig. 2.1 The "butterfly model" by Ellen Mac Arthur Foundation (Ellen Mac Arthur Foundation, 2015)

biogas and can be used as energy. When it returns to the soil, it creates circulation by generating new plants and organisms. However, if the product itself contains harmful chemical substances, the above will be extremely difficult.

In the “technological cycle,” it is fundamental to use depleted resources in economic activities without waste and to continue to circulate them. Since it requires less energy, resources, and labor to newly input resources, they should be circulated from the inside as much as possible (referred to as the “inner loop”).

When the original owner no longer uses it, it will be reused and redistributed, which generates CO_2 and requires new energy in the form of fuel consumption. Specifically, one must first eliminate waste by maintaining and repairing and using it for a long time or by sharing it. Next, when reuse and redistribution are no longer possible, the product that has been used once is disassembled, cleaned or otherwise maintained, and then reassembled into a product (remanufacturing, refurbishment).

When it becomes impossible to remanufacture, it will be recycled as the outermost loop. In other words, recycling involves the return to raw materials to remake parts and products.

Therefore, at the product design stage, it is important to apply about “system technique for product life cycle design” that allows the inner loop to flow as much as possible.

2.3 “CRADLE TO CRADLE CERTIFIED®” by Cradle to Cradle Products Innovation Institute

It is now possible to acquire “Cradle to Cradle certification (CRADLE TO CRADLE CERTIFIED®)” based on how well a company can create a recycling cycle and whether it incorporates products that meet the conditions. The certification system is operated by the Environmental Protection Promotion Agency (EPEA) established in Hamburg, Germany (Cradle to Cradle Products Innovation Institute, 2021). EPEA evaluates applicants in five stages, namely Basic, Bronze, Silver, Gold, and Platinum, after carefully examining the degree to which the cyclical cycle is incorporated into the product design and manufacturing process.

To receive “CRADLE TO CRADLE CERTIFIED® (C2C)”, the following conditions must be met:

1. Health of raw materials: Consider the environment and use minimal chemical substances.
2. Reuse of raw materials and parts: Reuse of parts and recycling as raw materials after the product has been used.
3. Use of natural energy and carbon management: Use renewable energy in production and work to reduce greenhouse gas emissions.
4. Water Stewardship: Do not pollute water during production.
5. Social fairness: Respect people and the environment, from raw material procurement to production.

2.4 CE Policy Trend Surveys in the EU

2.4.1 Ecodesign Working Plan

The "Ecodesign working plan (2016–2019)" was issued in November 2016, with the purpose of identifying working commissions' priorities under ecodesign and energy labelling (European Commission, 2016). In Europe, the ecodesign and energy labelling directive are framework directives; therefore, they should be transposed by Member States, which establish binding requirements that are specific to each product group. Working plans are designed to help identify categories of products to be investigated in depth in the upcoming three years and for which new measures can be prepared.

Ecodesign directive and energy labelling measures have been then modified, including new material efficiency requirements, such as ease of repair and the facilitation of end-of-life treatment. Beyond these mandatory aspects, voluntary tools have been developed such as the EU Ecolabel and the Green Public Procurement criteria. In October 2019, 10 ecodesign implementing regulations were adopted specially concerning household appliances such as refrigerators, washing machines, dishwashers and televisions.

2.4.2 The EU Action Plan for Circular Economy (CE Package)

Starting in 2015, the first "circular economy action plan" was adopted in previous initiatives promoted by the European Commission. This initial plan included measures stimulating the Europe's transition towards a CE while fostering sustainable economic growth and the generation of new jobs (European Commission, 2015). Fifty-four actions were included in the plan, and after three years of implementation, all of them had been achieved, even if the work continues beyond 2019 for some actions. Actions were related to the entire life cycle and included details of different phases of the production and consumption process. The actions were divided according to the topic they mainly refer to and thus included the following: production, consumption, waste management, market for secondary raw materials, and sectorial actions concerning some on strategic sectors (e.g., plastic, food waste, critical raw materials, construction and demolition, biomass and bio-based materials, innovation and investments, monitoring).

2.4.3 New Circular Economy Action Plan

As one of the main pillars of the European Green Deal, in March 2020, the European Commission adopted the "New Circular Economy Action Plan" (European Commission, 2020). The new action plan is composed of thirty-five actions to be implemented in the timeframe 2020–2023; it focuses on different areas from the previous action plan. The key actions are listed under seven macro-areas that correspond to as many overall goals and targets: a sustainable product policy framework; key product value chains; "less waste more value;" making the CE work for people, regions, and cities; crosscutting actions; leading efforts at a global level; and monitoring progress.

The design of sustainable products is intended to help broaden the ecodesign directive beyond energy-related products, thereby improving product durability, reusability, upgradability and reparability and increasing the amount of recycled content. Prioritized areas of intervention include electronics, textiles and ICT (Information and Communication Technology).

In the three years since the adoption of the CE action plan, many results have been achieved. The Commission adopted a proposal for a new regulation regarding sustainable batteries (2020); a Global Alliance on CE and Resource Efficiency (GACERE) was launched in 2021; and new proposals about organic pollutants in waste and waste shipments were adopted.

2.5 Trend Surveys Regarding CE Policies and Industry Case Studies in Japan

2.5.1 Circular Economy Vision 2020

Background

With the aim to present basic future directions of policies for a CE, the Ministry of Economy, Trade and Industry (METI) in Japan conducted surveys on the current state of challenges related to resource circulation at home and abroad and analyzed the results. As part of this effort, the "Study Group on Circular Economy Vision" held repeated discussions since July 2018 and compiled the discussion results into a report titled "Circular Economy Vision 2020" (METI, 2020).

Outline of the Circular Economy Vision

In addition to the need to transform to a CE, Japan should consider development of digital technologies and growing demand for environmental considerations from markets and society as new drivers. In line with this, all industries in Japan should regard this transformation as a new business opportunity that can guide their businesses to a virtuous cycle of the environment and growth: this should be considered as a marked shift from the existing 3Rs initiative as a measure for addressing waste and the environment, to new business models with higher circularity as management and business strategies.

With the aim to encourage Japanese companies to exercise their strengths related to mid to long-term industrial competitiveness by advancing their efforts in the 3Rs program, the METI compiled the "Circular Economy Vision 2020" with three different viewpoints in mind (METI, 2020):

1. **shift to new business models with higher circularity,**
2. acquire appropriate evaluation from the market and society, and
3. establish a resilient resource circulation system early to present Japan's basic policy directions for a circular economy.

In the following, the "(1) shift to new business models with higher circularity" is discussed in particular.

1. **Shift to new business models with higher circularity**

To create a highly cyclical business, it is necessary to make various efforts beyond the traditional 3Rs. It is essential for companies to select appropriate recycling-oriented initiatives according to each industry at every stage of design, production, use, and disposal, and to design circularity throughout the entire product life cycle.

[**Artery industry**]: Toward a recycling industry that ensures circularity and leads recycling, and towards the shift to a CE within all arterial industries, including the manufacturing industry, the distribution industry, and even service platforms that utilize digital technology.

In addition to the role of the generator of industrial waste (responsibility of the generator), it is necessary to design highly cyclical products and business models and build a circulation system that includes recycling.

As described above, it is important to place each used product on the most appropriate collection route and reuse or recycle it in the most appropriate manner, according to the product's value chain, properties, and emission sources.

- Distribution and collection while maintaining product ownership through leasing, sharing, subscription.
- Efforts should be made to circulate resources throughout the product lifecycle via voluntary collection of used products and the establishment of recycling routes in cooperation with venous industries.

[**Venous industry**]: Shift from recycling industry to resourcing industry.

For daily necessity products that are widely distributed among end consumers, it is difficult to predict collection times and discharge locations. For this reason, the venous industry should collect these various used products over a wide area, and stably supply high-quality recycled materials by actively utilizing automatic sorting technology.

It is important to expand the use of recycled materials by facilitating communication between the arteries and veins regarding the quality, origin, and product characteristics that are necessary when deciding whether to buy or sell materials based on these quality and usage standards. Through these efforts, it is expected that the cost of recycled materials will decrease.

2.5.2 Growth—Oriented, Resource-Autonomous Circular Economy Strategy

The METI formulated a document titled "Growth-Oriented, Resource-Autonomous Circular Economy Strategy" in March 2023 (METI, 2023). It is essential to carefully assess and enhance the adequacy of current policy measures from the following three perspectives:

1. Enhancement of new policy instruments,
2. Expansion of coverage for existing policies,
3. Creating a Robust Market Environment.

1. **Enhancement of New Policy Instruments** (Challenge of Discontinuities: Fostering Competition in Competitive Domains)

In line with the objectives of the circular economy, appropriate goal-setting is essential. To avoid dissipation of policy resources, resources should be strategically allocated according to the established goals and their respective intensities.

- Understanding circulation realities (Macro/Micro) and setting targets (clarification of KPIs)
- Establishing obligations to make efforts toward KPIs (qualitative/quantitative)
- Support based on commitments to quantitative targets benefiting circulation

Through initiatives like GX upfront investment support, which includes about a two-trillion-yen investment over the next decade in the resource circulation sector, providing assistance via "Pledge & Support". These measures aim to streamline efforts and effectively allocate resources to achieve circular economy goals.

2. **Expanding Coverage of Existing Policies** (Raising the Baseline: Shifting from the 3Rs to Circular Economy Concepts)

To achieve a transformative, non-linear transition toward a CE, it is essential to shift the foundational approach from the 3Rs (Reduce, Reuse, Recycle) to a broader and more integrated CE framework. This requires elevating the baseline of the existing policy system.

- Deepening the 4Rs (Reduce, Reuse, Recycle, Renewable) Policies
  - Consideration of adding new items to the scope of the Act on the Promotion of Effective Utilization of Resources (3Rs Act), including solar panels, clothing, batteries, etc.
  - Expansion and enforcement of circularity-conscious design
  - Strengthening efficient collection of circular resources

  - Measures to enhance the value of circular resources, such as standardizing labeling
  - Development of the recommerce market, etc.

- Cross-cutting measures for efficient recovery of metal resources and others
- Establishment of cooperative relationships to promote international resource circulation with willing countries, especially in the Indo-Pacific region
- Enhancement of wide-area regional circulation

3. **Creating a Robust Market Environment** (Establishing a Nonlinear Foundation: Expansion of Cooperative Domains)

To achieve a nonlinear transition toward a CE, it is essential to expand cooperative domains through collaboration among relevant stakeholders, as individual corporate efforts alone cannot ensure economic viability. Therefore, industry, government, and academia should work together toward shared goals to develop the necessary market environment.

- Strengthening partnerships among industry, government, and academia
- Creating an environment for data sharing
- Attracting risk capital

Three Gears: transmission for growth-oriented resource-autonomous Economy

To accelerate the commercialization of the circular economy in Japan and gain international competitiveness through the establishment of a growth-oriented, resource-autonomous economy, the CE policy framework outlined in "Deepening of 4R Policies" is organized into the following three "gear" packages.

Gear I: Establishing a Competitive Environment (Regulations & Rules)

- Deepening of 4R Policies
  - Expanding and implementing circularity-conscious design
  - Increasing the supply of circular resources: strengthening efficient collection
  - Expanding demand for circular resources: implementing standardization and life cycle assessment (LCA)
  - Ensuring proper labeling: visualizing circular value
  - Developing the recommerce market: strengthening product safety, etc.
- **Improving Collaboration with Overseas Partners**
  - Securing critical minerals
  - Aligning regulations and rules (e.g., plastic pollution measures [UNEP], international standardization of circular economy [ISO], development of information-sharing platforms)

Gear II: Circular Economy Toolkit (Policy Support)

- Investment Support for the Circular Economy

  - Support for research and development, and proof of concept (PoC)
  - Support for capital investment, including investment in recommerce
- Support for Digital Transformation (DX)
  - Assistance in building architecture to ensure information traceability
  - Support for the development and implementation of digital systems
- Standardization Support
  - Assistance in establishing quality indicators
- Support for Startups and Ventures
  - Attracting risk capital (circular economy-focused investment)

Gear III: Circular Economy Partnership (industry-government-academia collaboration)

- Industry: Setting ambitious voluntary targets, committing to them, and managing progress
- Government: Establishing a competitive environment and allocating the Circular Economy Toolkit based on the ambition level of targets
- Developing a Vision and Roadmap
- Solving Issues in Cooperative Domains
  - Developing projects and creating use cases such as establishing a circular economy information platform, standardization, and promoting regional circularity on a wide scale
- Branding the Circular Economy
  - Promoting and embedding circular economy values, education, and corporate management policies

2.5.3 Japan Partnership for Circular Economy (J4CE)

The Japan Partnership for Circular Economy (J4CE) was founded on March 2021 by the Japanese Ministry of the Environment (MOE), the METI, and Japan Business Federation (Keidanren). J4CE works to strengthen public–private partnerships to foster the understanding of the CE among a wide range of stakeholders, including companies in Japan, and to promote initiatives in response to the accelerating global trend toward a CE.

The launch of J4CE attracted widespread attention and more than 150 companies and industrial organizations have joined J4CE as of September 2022. Approximately 160 cases and initiatives have been submitted by participating companies and organizations, and all these cases are introduced on the J4CE website. In September 2021, J4CE selected 28 noteworthy cases and initiatives and published a brochure entitled

"Noteworthy Cases 2021 Edition." They were also actively involved in international outreach by distributing the brochure at a side event of COP26.

When J4CE were preparing for their 2022 edition of the "Noteworthy Cases", they selected related to resource and recycling in diverse industries. According to the UNEP International Resource Panel (IRP), the extraction and processing of natural resources into materials, fuels and food accounts for about half of all global GHG emissions (excluding climate impacts related to land use). J4CE recognizes that promoting the circular economy is important for advancing decarbonization (Keidanren, 2022) and hopes that the Noteworthy Cases will become widely known inside and outside Japan, and that Japanese companies will continue to promote the circular economy through their excellent technologies, ideas and collaborations. J4CE also aims to help promote the circular economy in Japan and around the world by further disseminating their efforts. Below is a table of contents for CE Noteworthy Cases by industry:

- Noteworthy Area 1: Steel
- Noteworthy Area 2: Non-Ferrous Metals
- Noteworthy Area 3: Cement
- Noteworthy Area 4: Paper and Woody Resources
- Noteworthy Area 5: Bioplastics
- Noteworthy Area 6: Collection and Recycling of Plastic
- Noteworthy Area 7: Recycling Technologies (Home Appliances, Plastic, Textile)
- Noteworthy Area 8: Formulating a Recycling Loop (Plastic, Food Waste)

2.6 Evolution of CE Legislation in Japan

2.6.1 Basic Law on Resources

"**Basic Law on Resources**" (officially titled "Law for the Promotion of the Effective Utilization of Resources") was established by the Ministry of Economy, Trade and Industry (then called the Ministry of International Trade and Industry) in 1991 and plays a significant role as a policy foundation related to the CE. The core principles of this law are the sustainable use of resources and the decreasing of environmental burdens through waste reduction. Specifically, it aims to enhance overall resource efficiency in society by providing guidelines that promote 3Rs (reduce, recycling, and reuse), and it aims to improve resource efficiency for businesses and consumers.

Building on the Basic Law on Resources, Japan has enacted industry-specific recycling laws facilitating the efficient reuse of resources and the appropriate management of waste. Representative examples of these industry-specific recycling laws include:

- **Home Appliance Recycling Law** (enforced in 1998): Mandates the recycling of home appliances such as televisions, refrigerators, washing machines, and air conditioners, establishing a system where manufacturers and consumers share the costs of recycling.

- **Food Recycling Law** (enforced in 2001): Promotes the reuse of food waste with the aim of utilizing it for the production of animal feed and fertilizers.
- **Automobile Recycling Law** (enforced in 2005): Systematizes the dismantling and reuse of automobiles by mandating the proper disposal of airbags and fluorocarbons.
- **Small Appliance Recycling Law** (enforced in 2013): Promotes the reuse of precious metals and rare metals contained in small electronic devices, such as mobile phones and digital cameras.

However, there are several disadvantages and limitations associated with these industry-specific recycling laws:

- **Lack of consistency among industries**: Differences in standards across industries can lead to inefficiencies in resource circulation.
- **Increased expenses**: The rising costs of recycling may decrease economic rationality.
- **Vertical Structure**: Cooperation among different industries is difficult, making the recycling of composite products challenging.
- **Delayed response to new technologies**: Laws may not be able to keep up with the advancements in new materials and technologies.
- **Insufficient consumer participation**: The lack of awareness among consumers regarding recycling necessitates efforts to promote their participation.
- **Incompatibility with international standards**: Japan's unique regulations may act as a barrier in the international market.

2.6.2 The 6th Basic Environmental Plan

The "**6th Basic Environmental Plan**", established on May 21, 2024, introduces new measures aimed at realizing a sustainable society (Japanese Government, 2024). This plan strengthens responses to environmental challenges and promotes the CE advancement. In particular, it emphasizes the importance of promoting recycling and efficient resource utilization with an expectation that these efforts will contribute to reducing environmental impact while ensuring consistency with existing regulations

The 6th Basic Environmental Plan also sets forth policies to address a broad spectrum of environmental issues, including climate change countermeasures and biodiversity conservation. Furthermore, it emphasizes collaboration with industry and proposes specific targets and measures to provide guidance for local governments and businesses to engage actively. In this way, the revisions to regulations aim to deepen environmental policies and enhance sustainability efforts.

To advance environmental policies concretely, six priority measures have been outlined for key environmental fields, focusing on environmental, economic, and societal perspectives:

1. Climate change countermeasures
2. **Formation of a circular society**

3. Securing biodiversity and harmonizing with nature
4. Management of environmental risks, etc.
5. Foundational measures for various policies
6. Reconstruction and revitalization following the Great East Japan Earthquake, and preparedness and response to future major disasters

Focusing on "**(2) Formation of a Circular Society**", the following details outline the expansion of the CE activities.

Developing sustainable communities and societies through the CE transition for circular society formation

To enforce effective CE approaches for resource efficiency and for circularity improvements across the entire value chain, and to connect the CE with net-zero (aiming for zero waste) or with nature-positive initiatives, or by implementing integrated measures related all three.

Inter-enterprise collaboration for comprehensive resource circulation throughout the entire lifecycle

To accelerate resource circulation, a coordinated approach between "arterial industries" (e.g., manufacturing and retail) and "venous industries" (e.g., waste management and recycling) will be fostered. This collaboration will support the creation of a resilient resource circulation market over the medium-to-long term.

Establishing diverse regional circulation systems and implementing regional revitalization

To form sustainable regions and a circular society with high resource productivity, this plan will promote initiatives that will take into account the local natural capital and implement the appropriate circulation scale for each region and resource. Efforts will include the continuous use of renewable resources within regions, effective maintenance of regional stock to use as extensively and wisely as possible, and reduction of input resources and generated waste amounts, ultimately fostering sustainable and vibrant communities.

Strengthening resource circulation and waste management infrastructure, and implementing robust, appropriate disposal and environmental restoration

This plan aims to reinforce waste management infrastructure through utilizing digital technology, robotics, and traceability systems that will strengthen resource circulation and facilitate decarbonization in the sector by advancing recycling processes such as, dismantling, shredding, and sorting used products, promoting biomass and recycled material use, establishing 3R principles for the rapidly spreading new products and materials, and making environmental burdens visible. Additionally, data platforms will be developed to enhance resource circulation information and promote arterial-venous collaboration.

Establishing an appropriate international resource circulation framework and promoting overseas expansion of the circular industry

Through platforms such as the G7, G20, OECD, and ASEAN, as well as bilateral and multilateral collaborations, Japan will address the international agreements related to 3Rs including the CE, resource efficiency policies, and resource circulation. Japan will also lead the discussions on the responsible trade of recyclable waste, plastic pollution measures, and international resource circulation.

2.6.3 The Advanced Resource Recycling Act

The **Advanced Resource Recycling Act** (Act on the Advancement of Resource Recycling Businesses to Promote Resource Circulation) was enacted by the Ministry of the Environment on April 9, 2024 (Ministry of the Environment, April, 2024). The purpose of the Act is to contribute to environmental protection by promoting efficient resource recycling practices and reducing greenhouse gas emissions through improved productivity in recycling processes. This act introduces measures to advance the technologies and facilities involved in waste collection, transportation, disposal, and recycling to achieve highly effective resource circulation. Through these actions, the Act seeks to enhance the efficiency and effectiveness of resource recycling systems, thereby supporting sustainable environmental management and economic growth.

The term "**advancement of resource recycling businesses**" in this act refers to measures that enhance greenhouse gas reduction in recycling processes through one of the following approaches:

Efficient Recycling for Demand-Driven Production: Conducting recycling operations (including collection, transportation, and disposal) to meet the needs of manufacturers, processors, or retailers, while focusing on efficient recycling practices.

Productivity Improvement: Advancing technologies for separating valuable materials from waste to increase the productivity of recycling.

Introduction of Equipment for Efficiency in Recycling: Measures to introduce equipment for streamlining the recycling process and other measures aimed at reducing the volume of greenhouse gas emissions generated from that process.

In addition to the measures listed above, other measures contributing to the reduction of **greenhouse gas emissions** associated with the implementation of recycling are

Businesses can create and submit an advanced resource recycling plan that corresponds to one of the four aforementioned measures. If the plan meets the specified criteria, the submitted company can receive "certification" from the Minister of the Ministry of the Environment as an Advanced Resource Recycling Operator. This certification acknowledges the company's commitment to high-efficiency recycling practices and contributes to overall environmental sustainability efforts.

2.6.4 *The Fifth Fundamental Plan for Establishing a Robust Material Cycle Society*

The **Basic Act for Establishing a Robust Material Cycle Society** was enacted in year 2000 under the jurisdiction of the Ministry of the Environment. Based on this law, the Fundamental Plan for Establishing a Robust Material Cycle Society has been formulated. This plan is reviewed approximately every five years. In 2023, the Minister of the Ministry of the Environment submitted an inquiry to the Central Environment Council regarding the plan's revision. Following deliberations, **the fifth fundamental plan** was approved by the Cabinet on August 2, 2024 (Ministry of the Environment, August, 2024).

Overview of the Fifth Fundamental Plan for Establishing a Robust Material Cycle Society

The transition to a CE is a critical national policy issue that should be addressed as a state strategy. It not only addresses environmental challenges such as climate change, biodiversity conservation, and pollution prevention, but also contributes to solving social issues like "strengthening industrial competitiveness," ensuring economic security, revitalizing local communities, and achieving a "high quality of life."

The key issues, policy responses, and envisioned future scenarios that are particularly closely related to CE within the context of "strengthening industrial competitiveness" and achieving a "high quality of life" are summarized in Table 2.1.

Resource Circulation Throughout the Entire Lifecycle Through Inter-Enterprise Collaboration

In this fundamental plan, the CE transition is positioned as a national strategy, with **five key priority areas** established as important directions, aiming for the target year of 2030. For the realization of these priority areas, specific initiatives, along with evaluation indicators and numerical targets corresponding to these initiatives, have been set. The following are the five key priority areas:

- Developing sustainable communities and societies through the CE transition for circular society formation.
- Inter-enterprise collaboration for comprehensive resource circulation throughout the entire lifecycle.
- Establishing diverse regional circulation systems and implementing regional revitalization.
- Strengthening resource circulation and waste management infrastructure, and implementing robust, appropriate disposal and environmental restoration.
- Establishing an appropriate international resource circulation framework and promoting overseas expansion of the circular industry.

Among those five key priority areas, particularly relevant to "**CE business strategy and CE value chain management**" is "Inter-enterprise collaboration

Table 2.1 Points of **CE Relevance** in "Strengthening Industrial Competitiveness" and Achieving a "High Quality of Life"

Key Issues / Background	Main Policy Responses	Future Achieving Goals
- Movement to strengthen the **use of recycled materials** in batteries, automobiles, packaging, etc.	- Expansion of the use and supply of **recycled materials** through **environmentally considerate designs** and **advanced resource recycling** - Leading the formation of **international rules for value chain circularity**	- Realization of thorough **resource circulation throughout the entire lifecycle** - Establishment of **domestic and international resource circulation systems** - Improvement of **product and service competitiveness** - Enhancement of **Japan's international presence**
- Increased global demand for resources leading to **competition for resource acquisition** - Rising prices and supply concerns for **minerals and other resources**	- Maximization of the recycling and utilization of **imported minerals, food, and other resources** - Strengthening **domestic and international resource circulation for minerals** and other materials	
- **Need to shift away** from a society characterized by **mass production, mass consumption, and mass disposal**	- **Transitioning lifestyles** through the use of recycled materials in products, reuse and repair, and reduction of food and fashion waste	- Achieving a high quality of life by **transforming behaviors and lifestyles from diverse choices**

for comprehensive resource circulation throughout the entire lifecycle." This area emphasizes the importance of collaboration among companies and businesses to effectively implement resource circulation strategies.

[Background]

- Through inter-enterprise collaboration between the [**artery industries**], such as manufacturing and retail, and the [**vein industries**], such as waste management and recycling (known as [**artery-vein collaboration**]), advanced examples of circular economy (CE) are beginning to emerge, creating new value in the market.

[Medium-to-Long Term Direction]

- Through inter-enterprise collaboration, support the creation of a resilient resource circulation market in the medium-to-long term by expanding the use and ensuring the stable supply of recycled materials.
- Promote thorough resource circulation across the entire lifecycle for resources that are important from the perspectives of environmental impact, waste generation, and contributions to decarbonization:
  - Waste plastics and waste oils
  - Utilization of biomass technologies (including waste-derived biomass, under-utilized resources, food waste, sewage sludge, wood, paper, and sustainable aviation fuel [SAF])

- Improvement of recovery rates and recycling of used products containing base metals and rare metals
- Promotion of construction recycling with an emphasis on "quality" for used earth, rocks, and construction materials

- Promote business models that maximize service offerings and added value while effectively utilizing stocks:
  - Containers and packaging
  - Buildings
  - Automobiles
  - Small home appliances and electronics
  - Textile products (fashion)
  - For products and materials that have become widespread due to global warming countermeasures, clarify the policy direction for each product.

In Table 2.2 descriptions of the [**Future Vision for Resource Circulation and CE Business Models**] regarding "Resource Circulation Throughout the Entire Lifecycle through Inter-Enterprise Collaboration" have been extracted from the basic plan report.

2.7 CE International Standards /TC 323

International Standardization in the field of "**Circular Economy**" to develop frameworks, guidance, supporting tools and requirements for the implementation of activities of all involved organizations, to maximize the contribution to Sustainable Development. International standards related to "**circular economy**" are still under development by **ISO/TC (Technical Committee) 323 Secretariat**. The **ISO 59000 series** of documents are designed to deepen the understanding of the circular economy and to support its implementation and measurement.

2.7.1 ISO/CD 59004—Circular Economy—Terminology, Principles and Guidance for Implementation

This document defines key terminology, establishes a CE vision and principles for organizations, and provides guidance, including possible actions, for implementation (ISO/CD 59004). It is applicable to organizations seeking to understand and commit or contribute to a CE while contributing to sustainable development. These organizations can be either private or public, acting individually or collectively, regardless of type or size, and located in any jurisdiction, or position within a specific value chain or value network.

Table 2.2 [**Future Vision for Resource Circulation and CE Business Models**] Achieved Through Inter-Enterprise Collaboration Across the Entire Lifecycle

Lifecycle Stage	**Future Vision** for Resource Circulation Across Entire Lifecycle (Summary)
Resource Acquisition Stage	• Maximize the proportion of safe circular resources and renewable resources while minimizing the use of depleting resources and harmful substances • Ensure that the utilization of renewable resources does not exceed the natural regeneration rate
Production Stage	• As the proportion of renewable resources increases, the utilization of recycled materials is promoted • Produce only what is necessary, at the necessary time, and in the necessary quantity (Just-in-Time production) • Products that align with expanded producer responsibility through environmentally conscious design are becoming more widespread, enhancing the brand value of such business models
Distribution Stage	• The spread of new business models utilizing technologies and systems such as optimizing distribution routes and building sharing platforms for the sharing of goods and services
Usage Stage	• The spread of business models that focus on supporting individual consumers by providing only the minimum necessary goods for services, while ensuring the long-term functionality of those goods through inspection, repair, replacement, and reuse
Disposal Stage	• [Reuse] Reuse items within the limits of technical and economic feasibility • [Recycle] For items that cannot be reused, recycle those that can be reprocessed into resources • For items that cannot be recycled but can recover energy, carry out energy recovery • Only items that cannot be recycled or have energy recovery options are subjected to intermediate processing, such as reduction, before final disposal • Establish waste collection systems that offer high convenience for residents
Overall Lifecycle	• The certification of sustainable resources and materials, along with green procurement based on such certifications • The encouragement of voluntary efforts by consumers and provision of economic incentives to promote these efforts • The optimization of the overall lifecycle through a combination of various means, such as developing circularity indicators for the value chain to visualize the progress of initiatives • An appropriate sharing of information regarding resource circulation among related businesses

This document gives guidance for any kind of organization. It describes the main terms and definitions, a circular economy vision, the circular economy principles, provides practical guidance on actions that contribute to a circular economy, and guidance to implement a circular economy in any kind of organization.

2.7.2 *ISO/CD 59010—Circular Economy Guidance on the Transition of Business Models and Value Networks*

Circular value creation models continuously improve their resource management practices and contributions to a CE and more sustainable business pathways (ISO/CD 59010). Circular value creation models establish measurable indicators (see ISO 59020) which can track resource use and losses over time, and monitor their impacts on and benefits to society and the natural environment.

In addition to its potential environmental benefits, studies show that a circular economy offers opportunities worth trillions of United States dollars, including job creation, which builds resiliency in national and international economies. These findings have propelled momentum towards a global CE, and as a result, organizations have begun the transition to take advantage of these many opportunities.

However, transitioning from a linear to a circular value creation model can be challenging because it typically demands that an organization's value creation models and value networks be restructured. Accordingly, this document gives guidance for organizations wishing to transition their linear value creation models and value networks to circular ones. This document is divided into eight clauses, of which Clauses 4 to 8, including their subclauses and interrelationships, are shown in Fig. 2.2.

2.7.3 *ISO/CD 59,020—Circular Economy—Measuring and Assessing Circularity Performance*

This document specifies requirements and gives guidance to organizations for measuring and assessing a defined economic system to determine their circularity performance at a specific time (ISO/CD 59020). Measurement and assessment are performed by the collection and calculation of data with the help of mandatory and optional circularity indicators.

This document provides a framework to guide users within organizations of all types and sizes through the measurement and assessment process, including system boundary setting and choice of indicators, as well as processing and interpreting data in a consistent and reproducible manner to generate meaningful and verifiable results. The framework is applicable to multiple levels of an economic system, ranging from regional, interorganizational and organizational to the product level.

To measure and assess social, environmental and economic impacts that are caused by the actions of the organization to achieve circular goals and objectives, the document provides a list of complementary methods that can be used in addition to this document.

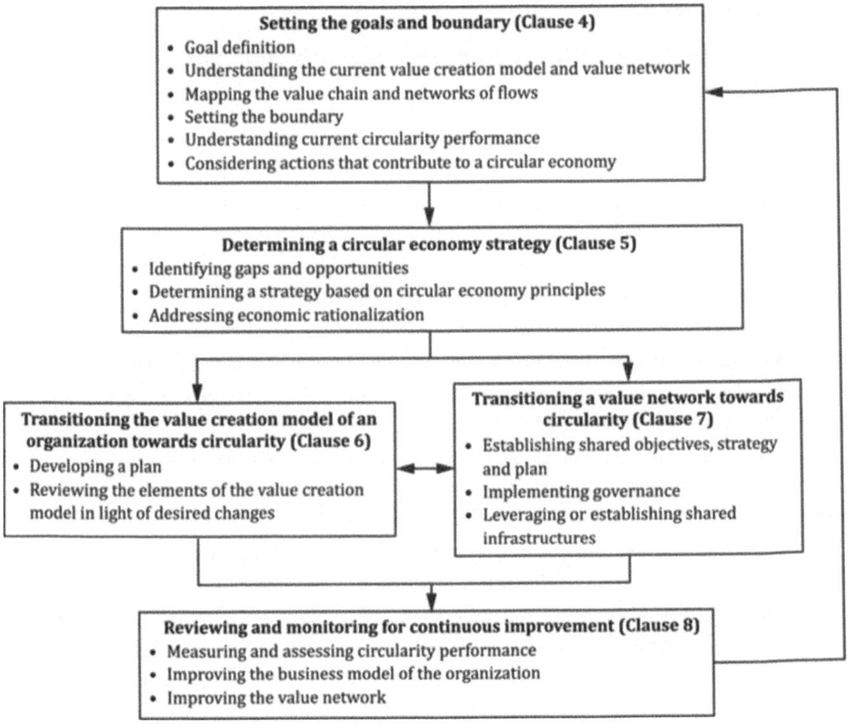

Fig. 2.2 The structure of this document: "ISO/CD 59010: Guidance on the transition of business models and value networks" (ISO/CD 59010)

2.7.4 ISO/CD TR 59031—Circular Economy—Performance-Based Approach—Analysis of Cases Studies

*Status: Under development.

2.7.5 ISO/CD TR 59032—Circular Economy – Review of Existing Value Networks

ISO 59010 provides guidance on supporting an organization's business model and processes from linear to circular by transforming an organization's business ecosystem into a value network. The contents of this document support the users of ISO 59010 in providing further detail on the development of value networks in a circular economy. In the development of ISO 59010, a survey was conducted to review and analyze the examples of globally existing value networks.

This document provides an analysis of the survey results (ISO/CD 59032). It reviews examples of value networks to illustrate their characteristics and structures and how they can accelerate a CE transition process, and therefore supports ISO 59010. This document investigates suitable examples of value networks to promote CE transition. ISO 59010 gives guidance on a critical aspect in transitioning an organization's business model and processes from linear to circular and transforming an organization's business ecosystem into a value network. This document complements ISO 59010 by providing further information on value networks.

The characteristics and structure of the value networks reflect multiple organization cooperation. The multiple organizations work together to advance their businesses and accelerate their circular economy transition process. A specific organization does not necessarily control the others. This document addresses the methods used to establish and organize a value network to meet the desired requirements. This document collects and analyses existing relevant cases, examples of the creation of value networks, to demonstrate what is a value network in the context of the CE.

2.7.6 ISO/ FDIS 59040 - Circular Economy – Product Circularity Data Sheet

*Status: Under development.

The document provides a general methodology for improving the accuracy and completeness of the CE -related information based on the usage of a "Product Circularity Data Sheet" when acquiring or supplying products (ISO/WD 59040). The Product Circularity Data Sheet provides essential information on product lifecycle and circularity, including data relevant to resource reuse, recycling, and environmental impact reduction.

This general methodology contains then a set of requirements that need to be established by an organization aiming to use the concerned data sheet when acquiring or supplying products, which also includes the trusted reporting and exchanging of circular economy related information. The document also provides guidance for the definition and sharing of a Product Circularity Data Sheet, considering the type, content and format of information to be provided. This guidance and these requirements are intended to be applicable to all organizations, regardless of type, size and nature.

These requirements implement a qualitative approach for business-to-business data exchange to be inclusive with small and medium businesses/enterprises and to protect confidential information.

2.8 Impact of New CE Regulations for Ecodesign and Digital Product Passport in the EU

SECTION I GENERAL PROVISIONS: Article 1 Subject matter and scope

This Regulation (EU) 2024/178 (13 June, 2024) for the setting of "**ecodesign requirements for sustainable products**" establishes a framework for the setting of **ecodesign requirements** that products have to comply with to be placed on the market or put into service, with the aim of improving the environmental sustainability of products in order to make sustainable products the norm and to reduce the overall carbon footprint and environmental footprint of products over their life cycle, and of ensuring the free movement of sustainable products within the internal market (European Parliament and of the Council, 2024).

This Regulation also establishes a **digital product passport (DPP)**, provides for the setting of mandatory green public procurement requirements and creates a framework to prevent unsold consumer products from being destroyed.

2.8.1 Regulations Related to Ecodesign Requirements for Sustainable Products

Ecodesign requirements should include, as appropriate, performance requirements or information requirements, or both. Those requirements should be used to improve product aspects relevant for environmental sustainability, such as durability, reusability, repairability, energy efficiency, recyclability, and carbon and environmental footprints. Ecodesign requirements should be transparent, objective, proportionate and in compliance with international trade rules.

The ecodesign requirements shall be such as to improve the following product aspects ('**product aspects**') where necessary supplemented by others, be used, individually or in combination, as a basis for improving the product aspects:

1. durability;
2. reliability;
3. reusability;
4. upgradability;
5. repairability;
6. the possibility of maintenance and refurbishment;
7. the presence of substances of concern;
8. energy use and energy efficiency;
9. water use and water efficiency;
10. resource use and resource efficiency;
11. recycled content;
12. the possibility of remanufacturing;
13. recyclability;

14. the possibility of the recovery of materials;
15. environmental impacts, including carbon footprint and environmental footprint;
16. expected generation of waste.

2.8.2 *Regulations Related to Digital Product Passport for Verification of Product Information*

Where a "**Digital Product Passport**" is available, the required information shall be provided therein and shall, where necessary, also be provided in one or more of the following forms:

1. on the product itself;
2. on the product's packaging;
3. on a label;
4. in a user manual or other documentation accompanying the product;
5. on a free access website or application.

Information that makes it possible to track substances of concern pursuant to paragraph 5 shall be given either on the product or be accessible through a data carrier included on the product.

The "**Digital Product Passport**" is scheduled to be gradually introduced based on the "2024 EU Sustainable Product Regulation (**ESPR**)" and will initially apply to specific product categories. According to the report, the initial stages will focus on categories such as electronic devices, textiles, and batteries, with potential expansion to other product categories under consideration.

The "Digital Product Passport" requires the inclusion of "**product information**" that covers various aspects throughout the product's entire lifecycle, from its basic characteristics to detailed technical specifications. The purpose of providing this information is to facilitate consumers and recyclers in understanding the environmental impact of products and to promote sustainable usage and proper disposal. The main categories of information required in the "product information" section are as follows.

1. **Basic Product Information**
   - Product Name and Model Number: The name, model, and number of the product.
   - Manufacturer: Name of the manufacturer, location, and contact information (for customer support).
   - Country of Origin: The country and region where the product was manufactured.
2. **Information on Materials and Raw Materials**
   - Types and Proportion of Materials Used: Proportion of recycled materials, types of materials used such as plastic, metal, and fiber, and their respective proportions.

- Presence of Hazardous Substances: Information on hazardous chemicals contained in the product (e.g., compliance with RoHS regulations).
- Sustainability of Raw Materials: Verification of sustainable sourcing, such as forest certification and use of recycled materials.

3. **Product Performance and Function**
   - Energy Efficiency: Energy consumption and efficiency of the product (with applicable certifications such as Energy Star or eco-labels).
   - Functional Specifications: Overview of the primary functions, performance, and durability data of the product.
4. **Information on Use and Maintenance**
   - Product Lifespan: Recommended usage period and estimated lifespan of the product.
   - Repairability and Maintenance: Feasibility of repair, repair methods, and availability of replaceable parts.
   - Safety Guidelines: Instructions for use and safety precautions to prevent accidents.
5. **End-of-Life and Recycling Information**
   - Recycling Methods: Information on parts that require disassembly, recyclable components, and appropriate recycling facilities.
   - Disposal Methods: Environmental impact of improper disposal and guidelines on proper disposal methods.

2.9 Discussion: Influence of New CE Regulations on Sustainable Business Model Transform

Looking back at the business models related to the "**technological cycle**" included in the "**butterfly model**" by Ellen Mac Arthur Foundation in Sect. 2.2, the following "**CE business models**" were proposed:

- Reusing and redistribution business model
- Maintenance and repairing business model for extended product life
- Refurbishment and remanufacturing business model after disassembling products and parts
- Recycling business model involving the return to raw materials to remake parts and products
- Sharing business model with sharing platform services

Accenture consultants above-mentioned similar "**five business models for circular growth**" (Lacy and Rutqvist, 2015).

- **Circular supply chain**: Provide renewable energy and bio-based or fully recyclable materials so the same resources can be used again and again.
- **Recovery and recycling**: Recover useful resources or energy from end-of-life products or production waste, thus running waste disposal costs into revenue.
- **Product life extension**: Prolong the useful life of products and components through resale, repair, remaking and upgrading.
- **Sharing platform**: Increase product utilization by enabling users to use and/or exchange products and services.
- **Product as a service**: Provide access to products and equipment, including contracts for performance, and including incentives that products last longer and can be maintained, repaired and upgraded.

The "**Fifth Fundamental Plan for Establishing a Robust Material-Cycle Society**" was approved by the Cabinet on August, 2024. In Table 2, the descriptions of the [Future Vision for Resource Circulation and **CE Business Models**] regarding "Resource Circulation Throughout the Entire Lifecycle through Inter-Enterprise Collaboration" have been extracted from the basic plan report. The "CE Business Models" related to each lifecycle stage are described as following:

[Resource Acquisition Stage]

- Maximize the proportion of safe circular resources and renewable resources while minimizing the use of depleting resources and harmful substances.
- Ensure that the utilization of renewable resources does not exceed the natural regeneration rate.

[Production Stage]

- As the proportion of renewable resources increases, the utilization of recycled materials is promoted.

[Distribution Stage]

- The spread of new business models utilizing technologies and systems, such as optimizing distribution routes and building sharing platforms for the sharing of goods and services.

[Usage Stage]

- The spread of business models that focus on supporting individual consumers by providing only the minimum necessary goods for services, while ensuring the long-term functionality of those goods through inspection, repair, replacement, and reuse.

[Disposal Stage]

- [Reuse] Reuse items within the limits of technical and economic feasibility.
- [Recycle] For items that cannot be reused, recycle those that can be reprocessed into resources.
- For items that cannot be recycled but can recover energy, carry out energy recovery.

- Establish waste collection systems that offer high convenience for residents.

[Overall Lifecycle]

- Certification of sustainable resources and materials, along with green procurement based on such certifications.
- Encouragement of voluntary efforts by consumers and provision of economic incentives to promote these efforts.
- Optimization of the overall lifecycle through a combination of various means, such as developing circularity indicators for the value chain to visualize the progress of initiatives.
- Appropriate sharing of information regarding resource circulation among related businesses.

The significance of the "Fifth Fundamental Plan" lies in its inclusion of the core elements of the two previously mentioned CE business models. It aligns with each stage of the CE value chain and provides a future-oriented vision as a guideline within Japanese legislation.

The significance of positioning **ISO/CD 59010**—Guidance on the Transition of **Business Models** and Value Networks as a core component within the **ISO 59000 serie**s of documents is considerable. In the future, companies aiming to expand globally, along with their products, will be expected to comply with the ISO 59000 series.

This Regulation (EU) 2024/178 (13 June, 2024) established a framework for the setting of **ecodesign requirements**. The ecodesign requirements shall be such as to improve the following **product aspects** where necessary supplemented by others, be used, individually or in combination, as a basis for improving the product aspects:

1. durability;
2. reliability;
3. reusability;
4. upgradability;
5. repairability;
6. the possibility of maintenance and refurbishment;
7. the presence of substances of concern;
8. energy use and energy efficiency;
9. water use and water efficiency;
10. resource use and resource efficiency;
11. recycled content;
12. the possibility of remanufacturing;
13. recyclability;
14. the possibility of the recovery of materials;
15. environmental impacts, including carbon footprint and environmental footprint;
16. expected generation of waste.

The original ecodesign Directive limited its scope to energy-related products. It is important to note that the 2024 revision, known as the **ecodesign for Sustainable**

Products Regulation (ESPR), has expanded its scope to cover nearly all products distributed within the EU market, including components and intermediate products. However, it does not apply to food, feed, pharmaceuticals, live plants and animals, or vehicles regulated by other legislation.

Notably, products exported to the EU market from outside the region must also comply with this regulation. Additionally, it mandates that information on the required **product aspects**, as mentioned previously, be provided to consumers through the "**Digital Product Passport**."

For the implementation of the ESPR, the European Commission plans to release a work plan that will gradually address compliance with the ESPR, starting with high-priority product groups. The first work plan will target product groups such as iron and steel, aluminum, textiles (particularly clothing and footwear), furniture including mattresses, tires, detergents, paints, lubricants, chemicals, energy-related products, information and communications technology products, and other electronic devices.

Additionally, this proposed regulation introduces new provisions concerning the disposal of unsold consumer goods. It requires businesses, excluding small and medium-sized enterprises (SMEs), to disclose information such as the annual volume of disposed consumer goods, reasons for disposal, and efforts toward recycling or remanufacturing. Furthermore, if disposal poses a significant adverse impact on the environment, the European Commission may prohibit such disposal.

2.10 Conclusion

Section 2.2 described the CE principles from the Ellen Mac Arthur Foundation (EMF). (1) designing in a manner that does not generate waste and pollution; (2) continue to use products and raw materials; and (3) regenerate natural systems. Based on the CE Principles, the EMF presented an "EC butterfly model" consisting of both a "biological cycle" and "technological cycle".

Section 2.3 described the "Cradle to Cradle certification (CRADLE TO CRADLE CERTIFIED®)" operated by the Environmental Protection Promotion Agency (EPEA). To receive the certification, five conditions must be met: (1) health of raw materials; (2) reuse of raw materials and parts; (3) use of natural energy and carbon management; (4) water Stewardship; and (5) social fairness.

Section 2.4 introduced CE policy trends in the EU. The "Ecodesign working plan (2016–2019)" was issued in 2016, with the purpose of identifying working commissions' priorities under ecodesign and energy labelling, The first "circular economy action plan" was adopted in 2015 as part of previous initiatives promoted by the European Commission. The European Commission adopted the "New Circular Economy Action Plan" in March 2020. The key actions were listed under seven macro areas that correspond to seven overall goals and targets: a sustainable product policy framework; key product value chains; less waste more value; making the circular economy work for people, regions and cities; crosscutting actions; leading efforts at global level; and monitoring the progress.

Section 2.5 presented trend surveys regarding circular economy policy and industry case studies in Japan. The Study Group on Circular Economy Vision at the METI compiled a report titled "Circular Economy Vision 2020." The METI also formulated a document titled "Growth—Oriented, Resource-Autonomous Circular Economy Strategy", in March 2023. The Japan Business Federation (Keidanren), in cooperation with the METI and the Ministry of Economy, established the "Japan Partnership for Circular Economy (J4CE)" on 2 March 2021. They selected especially noteworthy cases and initiatives, and published brochures entitled "Noteworthy Cases" as 2021/2022 Edition.

Compared to the EC policy mentioned above, the responses to the circular economy trend in Japan, the Japanese government's circular economy policy and the circular economy management strategy in the industrial world were considerably behind. In the future, when Japanese companies conduct global business transactions, it will be pivotal to be able to implement a circular economy management strategy compatible with the ISO 59000 series.

Section 2.6 investigated evolution of circular economy legislations in Japan. "Basic Law on Resources" was established in 1991 and played a significant role as a policy foundation related to the circular economy. Building on the Basic Law on Resources, Japan had enacted industry-specific recycling laws, facilitating the efficient reuse of resources and the appropriate management of waste. The "6th Basic Environmental Plan", established on May 21, 2024, introduced new measures aimed at realizing a sustainable society. To advance environmental policies concretely, six priority measures had been outlined for key environmental fields, especially including "Establishment of a Circular Society." The "Advanced Resource Recycling Act" was enacted by Ministry of the Environment on April, 2024. Businesses can create and submit an advanced resource recycling plan that corresponds to one of the four aforementioned measures. If the plan meets the specified criteria, the submitted company can receive "certification" from the Minister of the Environment as an Advanced Resource Recycling Operator. The "Fifth Fundamental Plan for Establishing a Robust Material-Cycle Society" was approved by the Cabinet on August, 2024. The descriptions of the "Future Vision for Resource Circulation and Circular Economy Business Models" regarding "Resource Circulation Throughout the Entire Lifecycle through Inter-Enterprise Collaboration" had been extracted from the basic plan report.

In Sect. 2.7, the international standards (ISO)/TC (Technical Committee) 323 started to design the ISO 59000 series of CE documents to harmonize the understanding of the circular economy and to support its implementation and measurement: (1) ISO/CD 59004: Terminology, Principles and Guidance for Implementation and CE international standards; (2) ISO/CD 59010: Guidance on the transition of business models and value networks; (3) ISO/CD 59020: Measuring and assessing circularity performance; (4) ISO/CD TR 59031: Performance-based approach – Analysis of cases studies; (5) ISO/CD TR 59032: Review of existing value network; and (6) ISO/ FDIS 59040: Product circularity data sheet.

Section 2.8 explored the impact of new circular economy Regulations for Ecodesign Requirements for Sustainable Products, and Digital Product Passport for CE for verification of product information in the EU. This Regulation (EU) 2024/178 (13 June, 2024) established a framework for the setting of "ecodesign requirements for sustainable products," including "digital product passport (DPP)."

Acknowledgements This research is conducted as a part of the Grant-in-Aid for Scientific Research Activity, Basic Research (B) in Japan, which aimed to the"Development, Empirical Research and Dissemination of New Theories and System Techniques for Circular Economy (CE) to Meet "SDGs Goal 12; Producer and Consumer Responsibility" (Principal investigator: Kin'ya Tamaki, Academic period: from 2022 to 2025 [4 years], Research project number: 22H01717), (Tamaki, 2022).

References

Cradle to Cradle Products Innovation Institute: "CRADLE TO CRADLE CERTIFIED® User Guidance VERSION 4.0, Product Standard", 2021.

Ellen Mac Arthur Foundation: Towards the circular economy. Journal of Industrial Ecology, 2(1), 23–44, 2015. Available at: https://www.werktrends.nl/app/uploads/2015/06/Rapport_McKinsey-Towards_A_Circular_Economy.pdf.

Ellen Mac Arthur Foundation (EMF) website, accessed on February 2023: https://ellenmacarthurfoundation.org/network/overview.

European Commission, "First Circular Economy Action Plan", 2015, website, accessed on June 2023: https://environment.ec.europa.eu/topics/circular-economy/first-circular-economy-action-plan_en

European Commission, "Ecodesign Working Plan 2016–2019", 2016.

European Commission," New Circular Economy Action Plan", 2020. Available at: https://eur-lex.europa.eu/resource.html?uri=cellar:0638aa1d-0f02-11eb-bc07-01aa75ed71a1.0003.02/DOC_1&format=PDF.

European Parliament and of the Council," Regulation (EU) 2024/178: Ecodesign requirements for sustainable products", 13 June, 2024: http://data.europa.eu/eli/reg/2024/1781/oj.

ISO/TC 323:

ISO/CD 59004—Circular Economy—Terminology, Principles and Guidance for Implementation: https://www.iso.org/standard/80648.html?browse=tc.

ISO/CD 59010—Circular Economy—Guidance on the transition of business models and value networks: https://www.iso.org/obp/ui/#iso:std:iso:59010:ed-1:v1:en.

ISO/CD 59020—Circular Economy—Circular Economy—Measuring and assessing circularity: https://www.iso.org/standard/80650.html?browse=tc.

ISO/CD TR 59031—Circular economy—Performance-based approach—Analysis of cases studies: https://www.iso.org/standard/81183.html?browse=tc.

ISO/CD TR 59032—Circular economy—Review of Existing Value Networks: https://www.iso.org/obp/ui/#iso:std:iso:tr:59032:ed-1:v1:en.

ISO/WD 59040—Circular economy—Product Circularity Data Sheet: https://www.iso.org/standard/82339.html?browse=tc.

Japan Business Federation (Keidanren): "Noteworthy Cases for Initiatives on the Circular Economy by Japanese Companies", Vo.2 2022 Edition. (Japanese)

Japanese Government Cabinet Decision, "6th Basic Environmental Plan", May 21, 2024. (Japanese)

Kin'ya Tamaki, "New Management Strategy that Integrates Circular Economy (CE) and DX: Proposals for CE Domestic and International Surveys and CE New Theories and System Techniques", Journal of Management Systems, Japan Industrial Management Society, Vol.32 No.1, pp.49–49, 2022. (Japanese)

Ministry of Economy, Trade and Industry (METI), Japan, “Circular Economy Vision 2020”, May 22, 2020. https://www.meti.go.jp/english/press/2020/0522_003.html.

Ministry of Economy, Trade and Industry (METI), Japan, “Growth—Oriented, Resource-Autonomous Circular Economy Strategy”, March 2023. (Japanese)

Ministry of the Environment,” Advanced Resource Recycling Act (Act on the Advancement of Resource Recycling Businesses to Promote Resource Circulation)”, April 9, 2024. (Japanese)

Ministry of the Environment,” Fifth Fundamental Plan for Establishing a Robust Material Cycle Society”, August 2, 2024. (Japanese)

Petter Lacy and Jakob Rutqvist, “Waste to Wealth: Creating Advantage in a Circular Economy”, Accenture, London, 2015.

Chapter 3
CE Strategy in the Automotive Industry

Young Won Park and Sugie Ryosuke

3.1 Introduction

Under growing environmental challenges and the urgent need for sustainable practices, the concept of a Circular Economy (CE) has emerged as a transformative framework for reshaping how economies operate. CE redefines traditional "take-make-dispose" economic models, emphasizing waste minimization, resource efficiency, and regenerative practices. Its principles align with global sustainability priorities, such as the United Nations' Sustainable Development Goals (SDGs), particularly focusing on responsible consumption and production to address climate change, resource scarcity, and waste accumulation. This paradigm shift is recognized by policymakers, industries, and scholars as a pathway to achieving significant environmental, economic, and social benefits.

The automotive industry, with its extensive supply chains and notable environmental footprint, is a prime candidate for implementing CE principles. This sector's lifecycle, encompassing raw material extraction, manufacturing, product usage, and disposal, involves significant energy and material consumption and generates substantial waste. Circular strategies like recycling, remanufacturing, and shared mobility models provide viable approaches to mitigate these environmental challenges. Recycling retrieves materials from end-of-life products and reintegrates them into production cycles, reducing dependence on virgin resources. Remanufacturing extends product lifespans by restoring used components to their original quality, decreasing the demand for new materials. Shared mobility enhances resource efficiency by reducing the overall number of vehicles required to meet transportation needs.

Despite the evident advantages, transitioning to CE in the automotive sector presents notable challenges. The complexity of global supply chains introduces logistical and regulatory hurdles, as varying environmental regulations across regions necessitate significant compliance efforts. Small and medium-sized enterprises (SMEs) may find these requirements particularly burdensome. Consumer skepticism about the quality and performance of remanufactured products further complicates

Y. W. Park and K. Tamaki, *Circular Economy Strategy for SDG Business Management*,
https://doi.org/10.1007/978-981-96-4194-9_3

adoption, with some customers preferring new products. Additionally, logistical difficulties in transporting end-of-life products to recycling or remanufacturing centers highlight the need for streamlined processes to support CE practices.

Nonetheless, the potential benefits for the automotive industry from adopting CE are significant. Reducing reliance on raw materials can result in considerable cost savings, while recycling and remanufacturing open new revenue streams. Demonstrating a commitment to sustainability enhances brand reputation and appeals to environmentally conscious consumers. In recent years, leading automakers have started incorporating CE principles into their operations, setting ambitious goals and fostering collaborations with suppliers, policymakers, and other stakeholders to facilitate systemic change.

Honda stands out as a leader in implementing CE principles within the automotive industry. Its "Triple Action to ZERO" framework, aimed at achieving zero environmental impact by 2050, encompasses three core pillars: carbon neutrality, clean energy, and resource circulation. By addressing these interconnected objectives, Honda underscores its dedication to sustainability across its operations and products.

The company has committed to achieving carbon neutrality throughout its product lifecycle and corporate activities by 2050. A significant milestone in this journey is Honda's pledge to transition 100% of its automobile sales to electric vehicles (EVs) and fuel cell vehicles (FCVs) by 2040. This shift reflects Honda's focus on electrification and alternative energy solutions, contributing to global climate goals and positioning the company as a leader in sustainable transportation. Alongside reducing emissions, this transition supports broader efforts to mitigate climate change by integrating innovative technologies into its offerings.

Honda is also advancing clean energy initiatives as part of its CE framework. It is working to establish carbon–neutral production facilities, beginning with its Saitama plant in Japan. This factory incorporates renewable energy sources and advanced CO_2 reduction technologies, serving as a model for other production sites globally. By minimizing dependence on fossil fuels and enhancing energy efficiency, Honda's clean energy strategies align with societal goals for energy security and resilience, further reinforcing its commitment to sustainability.

Central to Honda's CE strategy is resource circulation, which prioritizes reducing, reusing, and recycling materials across the company's operations. Honda aims to achieve 100% sustainable material utilization by 2050, focusing on designing products for durability, disassembly, and recyclability. This approach reduces dependence on finite resources and promotes conservation. The use of Lifecycle Assessment (LCA) enables Honda to evaluate the environmental impact of its products at each stage of their lifecycle, from raw material extraction to disposal. This comprehensive analysis helps identify opportunities to reduce CO_2 emissions and improve resource efficiency during product development.

Electrification is another critical aspect of Honda's sustainability efforts. By targeting carbon-free automobiles by 2040, Honda is advancing electrification while addressing CE goals of recyclability and waste reduction through innovative product design. This dual focus on environmental and resource sustainability demonstrates Honda's leadership in aligning business objectives with global sustainability priorities.

Collaboration is a cornerstone of Honda's CE approach. The company works with industry leaders to advance recycling technologies and establish dismantling and recycling networks, ensuring a stable supply of recycled materials. These partnerships enhance Honda's ability to minimize reliance on virgin resources and promote sustainability across its supply chain. Honda also invests in hydrogen as a clean energy carrier, supporting the development of hydrogen fuel cell technology and related infrastructure. This investment aligns with Honda's broader objectives of clean energy adoption and carbon neutrality, fostering the growth of a hydrogen ecosystem.

Despite these ambitious efforts, Honda and the broader automotive sector face significant challenges in implementing CE principles. The global nature of supply chains, coupled with regional regulatory disparities, creates logistical hurdles. Consumer skepticism regarding remanufactured or recycled products can limit market acceptance, while transporting end-of-life vehicles for recycling adds complexity. Addressing these challenges requires systemic innovation, effective stakeholder collaboration, and robust policy support.

Honda's "Triple Action to ZERO" framework exemplifies how CE principles can drive transformative change within the automotive industry. By integrating carbon neutrality, clean energy, and resource circulation into its strategy, Honda addresses critical environmental issues while fostering innovation and sustainability. Through collaboration, resource efficiency, and clean energy investment, Honda demonstrates that economic growth and environmental stewardship can coexist. This leadership not only positions Honda as a model for the industry but also reinforces the viability and impact of CE as a strategic approach to sustainable development. Honda's comprehensive approach highlights the importance of aligning business practices with sustainability goals, paving the way for a more resilient and circular economy.

3.2 Literature Review

3.2.1 The Emergence of Circular Economy (CE) and Its Global Importance

The concept of the Circular Economy (CE) has garnered significant attention over the last decade, aligning closely with global sustainability goals, particularly the United Nations' Sustainable Development Goals (SDGs). CE provides a transformative framework for minimizing waste, maximizing resource efficiency, and promoting sustainable production and consumption patterns (Park et al. 2024). In contrast to the traditional "take-make-dispose" linear economic model, CE focuses on regenerative systems that reduce environmental impact while creating economic and social value. As climate change, resource scarcity, and waste accumulation intensify, CE has emerged as a critical strategy for fostering sustainable development and ensuring resource security.

The Ellen MacArthur Foundation (2021), a leading advocate of CE, has played a pivotal role in defining and popularizing the concept. Their framework emphasizes the transition from linear economic models toward circular systems that prioritize resource efficiency, waste reduction, and the regeneration of natural systems (Shakhnoza and Park 2023; Park et al. 2024). A fundamental goal of CE is to decouple economic growth from the consumption of finite resources, enabling businesses and societies to achieve long-term sustainability. By redesigning systems to retain the value of materials and products throughout their lifecycle, CE offers a pathway to address pressing environmental challenges and achieve SDG 12, which focuses on responsible consumption and production.

Scholars and policymakers increasingly recognize the multifaceted benefits of CE. Beyond its environmental advantages, CE offers economic opportunities by reducing dependency on virgin materials, lowering production costs, and unlocking new revenue streams. Social benefits, such as job creation in repair, remanufacturing, and recycling industries, further underscore the holistic potential of CE. Moreover, CE fosters innovation by encouraging the development of sustainable business models, such as product-service systems, which shift the focus from ownership to access and utility.

However, the transition to CE is not without challenges. Systemic barriers, including insufficient infrastructure, fragmented policies, and cultural resistance to change, complicate the adoption of circular practices. The complexity of global supply chains and the lack of standardized metrics for measuring circularity further hinder progress. Despite these challenges, the momentum behind CE continues to grow, driven by the increasing recognition of its role in achieving a more sustainable and resilient global economy.

3.2.2 The Importance of CE in the Automotive Industry

The automotive industry, with its extensive supply chains and significant environmental impact, represents a critical sector for implementing CE principles. This industry's lifecycle—encompassing resource extraction, manufacturing, usage, and disposal—is resource-intensive and contributes substantially to waste and greenhouse gas emissions. As such, adopting CE strategies in the automotive sector is vital for mitigating these environmental challenges while creating economic and social value (Shakhnoza and Park 2023).

Recycling, remanufacturing, and the sharing economy are three key strategies identified in CE research for transforming the automotive sector (Guarnieri et al. 2023; Patel and Singh 2023; Park et al. 2024). Recycling involves reclaiming materials from end-of-life vehicles (ELVs) and reintegrating them into production processes. This approach conserves resources and reduces reliance on virgin materials, aligning with sustainability goals. For instance, advances in recycling technologies enable the recovery of high-value materials such as aluminum, steel, and rare earth metals from ELVs, which are then used in manufacturing new vehicles.

Remanufacturing, another critical CE strategy, focuses on restoring used vehicle components to their original quality. This process not only extends the lifespan of products but also reduces the demand for raw materials and energy-intensive production processes. Remanufactured parts, such as engines and transmissions, are increasingly popular among consumers due to their cost-effectiveness and environmental benefits. By integrating remanufacturing into their operations, automotive companies can enhance resource efficiency and reduce waste.

The sharing economy, which promotes shared access to vehicles, also plays a pivotal role in advancing CE in the automotive industry. Car-sharing and ride-hailing services exemplify how shared mobility models can optimize resource utilization and reduce the number of vehicles required to meet transportation needs. This approach aligns with CE principles by shifting the focus from ownership to usage, thereby minimizing waste and maximizing the value derived from existing assets.

Despite its potential, the automotive industry faces significant challenges in adopting CE practices. The complexity of global supply chains, which involve diverse materials and numerous stakeholders, poses logistical and regulatory hurdles. Differing environmental regulations across regions further complicate the implementation of circular strategies, as companies must navigate varying compliance requirements. Additionally, consumer perceptions of remanufactured or recycled products can impact market acceptance. Concerns about quality and performance often deter consumers from embracing these products, highlighting the need for robust quality assurance measures and public awareness campaigns.

Logistical challenges related to the collection, transportation, and processing of ELVs also hinder the widespread adoption of CE in the automotive sector. Establishing efficient reverse logistics systems is essential for enabling the recovery and recycling of materials. Investments in infrastructure and technology, such as automated disassembly and material sorting systems, are critical for overcoming these barriers and streamlining circular practices.

Despite these obstacles, the automotive industry stands to gain significantly from transitioning to a circular economy. Circular strategies can reduce costs associated with raw materials and waste disposal while creating new revenue opportunities through remanufacturing and recycling. Moreover, adopting CE practices can enhance brand reputation by demonstrating a commitment to sustainability, which is increasingly valued by consumers and stakeholders. Leading automotive companies are already incorporating CE principles into their operations, setting ambitious targets to reduce their environmental footprint and collaborating with policymakers, suppliers, and consumers to drive systemic change.

3.2.3 The Role of Policy and Regulation in Advancing CE

Government policies and regulations are instrumental in promoting the adoption of CE principles. By establishing legal frameworks, setting targets, and providing incentives, governments can encourage businesses and industries to transition to circular practices. In Japan, for instance, policies such as the Basic Law for Establishing a Recycling-Based Society and various recycling laws have laid the groundwork for CE implementation. These regulations aim to reduce waste, promote resource efficiency, and encourage the development of circular business models.

However, regulatory frameworks also present challenges for businesses, particularly small and medium-sized enterprises (SMEs). Compliance with environmental regulations often requires significant investments in infrastructure, technology, and training. SMEs, which typically operate with limited resources, may struggle to meet these requirements. The complexity of navigating regulatory landscapes, especially in industries with intricate supply chains like manufacturing, further complicates the adoption of CE practices.

To address these challenges, governments can implement measures to support businesses in their transition to a circular economy. Financial incentives, such as subsidies, tax breaks, and grants, can offset the costs associated with CE initiatives. Public–private partnerships can also play a crucial role in fostering innovation and building the infrastructure needed for circular practices. For example, collaborative projects between governments, academic institutions, and industry stakeholders can drive advancements in recycling technologies and reverse logistics systems.

In addition to domestic policies, international standards and frameworks are essential for harmonizing CE practices across borders. The development of global standards, such as the ISO 59000 series, provides a common language and set of guidelines for implementing CE principles. These standards facilitate the exchange of best practices and promote consistency in measuring and reporting circularity.

Extended Producer Responsibility (EPR) is another regulatory approach that has proven effective in advancing CE. EPR policies hold manufacturers accountable for the entire lifecycle of their products, from design to disposal. By incentivizing companies to design products for durability, reparability, and recyclability, EPR encourages the adoption of circular practices. For instance, EPR schemes in the electronics and automotive sectors have led to the establishment of take-back programs and the development of recycling networks.

Public awareness and consumer behavior also play a critical role in the success of CE policies. Governments can launch educational campaigns to inform consumers about the benefits of CE and encourage sustainable consumption patterns. Labeling systems that indicate the environmental impact of products can further empower consumers to make informed choices.

While policies and regulations are vital for advancing CE, they must be designed to balance environmental objectives with economic feasibility. Overly stringent regulations can stifle innovation and impose undue burdens on businesses, while lax policies may fail to drive meaningful change. A collaborative approach that involves stakeholders from government, industry, academia, and civil society is essential for developing effective and equitable CE policies.

In conclusion, the role of policy and regulation in promoting CE cannot be overstated. By providing a supportive framework, addressing systemic barriers, and fostering collaboration, governments can accelerate the transition to a circular economy. As the global momentum for CE continues to grow, aligning policy efforts with technological advancements and market trends will be critical for achieving sustainable and inclusive economic growth.

3.3 Case Study of Honda

3.3.1 Honda's Sustainability: Before and After 2000

Before 2000: Pioneering Environmental and Social Responsibility

Honda has long been known as a pioneer in environmental and social responsibility, rooted in a corporate philosophy established with its founding in 1948. From its inception, Honda committed itself to making a positive societal impact, integrating principles of environmental stewardship and corporate responsibility into its core values. Over the decades—especially during the 1960s and 1970s—Honda implemented proactive environmental policies well before they became standard or required by regulations.

First, Honda took early action on pollution control, demonstrating remarkable foresight in tackling environmental issues. In 1966, Honda established its Air Pollution Research Group and created an air pollution control laboratory, marking its commitment to addressing pollution concerns. This occurred before stringent environmental regulations were introduced in the late 1960s, underscoring Honda's proactive approach. In 1971, Honda developed the Compound Vortex Controlled Combustion (CVCC) engine, designed specifically to meet stringent U.S. Clean Air Act standards, which were among the world's most rigorous at the time. The CVCC engine's development was more than a technological breakthrough—it was a testament to Honda's dedication to environmental responsibility at a time when global emission standards were minimal.

Second, Honda led the way in proactive environmental policies. In the 1970s, Honda became one of the first automotive companies to set up internal committees focused on pollution prevention and sustainable purchasing practices. This era saw the launch of the "New Honda Plan" in 1972, which revitalized Honda's corporate approach by placing a renewed emphasis on social and environmental contributions. The plan showcased Honda's dedication to corporate responsibility, emphasizing its role as a change agent in the industry. By the 1990s, Honda solidified its environmental commitment by publishing its first Environmental Annual Report, highlighting its dedication to transparency and accountability. Honda further aligned with the global environmental agenda by supporting the United Nations Earth Summit in 1992, reinforcing its commitment to sustainability on an international scale.

Third, Honda prioritized safety and community well-being as essential components of its social responsibility strategy. In 1970, Honda established the Safe Driving Promotion Headquarters, reflecting its dedication to promoting road safety. This initiative aimed to educate drivers on safe driving practices, helping to reduce accidents and foster responsible behavior on the road. Honda also demonstrated a strong commitment to local communities through projects like the "Hometown Forest" project in 1976, which involved planting trees around Honda facilities to enhance environmental conservation and green spaces. These early initiatives illustrated Honda's holistic approach to social responsibility, emphasizing the company's role in creating positive societal impact beyond manufacturing vehicles.

Fourth, Honda established the Honda Foundation in 1977, marking another significant step in its journey toward corporate social responsibility. The foundation was dedicated to promoting harmony between technology and the environment, aligning with Honda's mission of advancing sustainable innovation. Through grants and awards, the Honda Foundation supported research and projects focused on environmental protection and technological advancement. This initiative exemplified Honda's long-term perspective, investing in future generations and reinforcing its dedication to sustainability. By supporting projects that aligned with its values, the Honda Foundation symbolized Honda's commitment to fostering societal advancement through responsible technology.

Throughout the twentieth century, Honda's approach to sustainability was driven by a clear, top-down vision, led by its founder Soichiro Honda. This corporate strategy fostered a culture that prioritized environmental and social issues, distinguishing Honda from its competitors. The company's management consistently championed innovative technologies and corporate policies aimed at sustainability, guided by a philosophy of corporate responsibility. By proactively addressing environmental challenges and promoting community engagement, Honda established itself as a forward-thinking leader in corporate social responsibility.

After 2000: Shift Toward Formalization and Loss of Momentum

In the twenty-first century, Honda's sustainability efforts underwent a marked transformation. While the company continued to uphold its commitment to environmental and social responsibility, the nature of its approach shifted from a proactive, visionary strategy to a more formalized and segmented one. This change reflected broader industry trends and external pressures, including shareholder influence, regulatory requirements, and a heightened focus on compliance and management accounting. Unfortunately, this shift also led to a loss of the pioneering spirit that had once defined Honda's approach to sustainability.

First, Honda experienced increasing external pressures from stakeholders, including activist shareholders who prioritized financial performance and transparency. In response, Honda adopted a more segmented organizational structure, moving away from its unified, visionary approach. This shift resulted in the compartmentalization of environmental and social initiatives, which were now managed by specific departments rather than forming an integrated, company-wide vision. Although Honda continued to release annual sustainability reports and set ambitious targets, including goals for carbon neutrality, these initiatives often appeared to lack the concrete action and cohesive vision that had characterized Honda's earlier efforts. The rebranding of the "Environmental Annual Report" to a "CSR Report" in 2006 symbolized this shift, as Honda's sustainability communication became more compliance-oriented.

Second, Honda's organizational expansion led to a decentralized approach, resulting in what has been described as "partial optimization." As Honda expanded its global presence, individual departments became more focused on their metrics and objectives, with less alignment toward a cohesive sustainability vision. This decentralization resulted in fragmented environmental practices, with each department pursuing its own initiatives rather than working together toward unified goals. Honda's decentralization hindered its ability to respond holistically to global environmental challenges, as the absence of a unified approach made it difficult to implement consistent sustainability practices across regions. This fragmentation was evident in areas such as Scope 4 emissions reporting, where Honda struggled to maintain a cohesive and transparent approach.

Third, Honda increasingly relied on external consultants for strategic guidance, moving away from its internally driven, reflective decision-making process. This reliance on consultants led to a reduction in internal dialogue and innovation, as management frequently adopted consultant-driven strategies without thorough internal assessment. By relying on external recommendations, Honda's approach became more generic, lacking the distinctiveness that had once characterized its commitment to environmental and social responsibility. The reduction of internal discourse on sustainability issues contributed to an erosion of Honda's unique perspective, making its sustainability strategy less reflective of the company's core values.

Fourth, the strong top-down vision that had previously guided Honda's sustainability efforts began to weaken. Although Honda continued to set ambitious targets, such as carbon neutrality, these goals often lacked concrete plans and internal commitment. The company's original philosophy of "leaving blue skies for our children" became less prominent, as Honda struggled to differentiate itself in a market where many competitors adopted similar branding around sustainability. This loss of identity was further compounded by Honda's challenges in adapting its Japan-centric systems and methods to the needs of a global market. The environmental systems initially developed for the domestic market were not fully compatible with global standards, creating gaps in Honda's ability to implement effective sustainability strategies worldwide.

3.3.2 *Recent Triple Action to ZERO: A Circular Economy Framework*

Honda's "Triple Action to ZERO" framework forms the foundation of its circular economy approach, addressing three interconnected pillars: carbon neutrality, clean energy, and resource circulation. Instead of treating each of these goals in isolation, Honda recognizes their interdependence and aims to leverage synergies among them to create a sustainable, system-wide transformation.

Carbon Neutrality

To address the global challenge of climate change, Honda has set a goal to achieve carbon neutrality across its product lifecycle and corporate activities by 2050. Honda is committed to minimizing CO_2 emissions at each stage, from the manufacturing process to product disposal. In line with international climate targets to limit global temperature rise to 1.5 °C, Honda has pledged to have 100% of its automobile sales consist of electric vehicles (EVs) and fuel cell vehicles (FCVs) by 2040. By advancing electrification and alternative energy sources, Honda aims to significantly reduce the carbon footprint of the transportation sector.

Clean Energy

A critical component of Honda's "Triple Action to ZERO" initiative is the transition to 100% carbon-free energy across both corporate activities and product operations. Honda is working toward a carbon–neutral factory by 2025 at its Saitama plant, which will serve as a model for other production facilities worldwide. This initiative includes energy-efficient measures and a shift to renewable energy sources, thereby reducing Honda's reliance on fossil fuels and furthering its clean energy commitment.

Resource Circulation

Resource circulation is central to Honda's circular economy strategy, focusing on the reduction, reuse, and recycling of materials across its operations and product lifecycle. Recognizing the risks associated with resource scarcity, Honda has set an ambitious goal to achieve a 100% sustainable material utilization rate by 2050. This entails designing products for durability, disassembly, and recyclability to build a circular value chain. Honda is committed to reducing its consumption of finite resources and implementing a product lifecycle model that emphasizes resource efficiency.

3.3.3 *Circular Economy Strategies in Honda's Operations*

Honda's commitment to a circular economy is evident in its strategies to minimize waste, implement clean energy solutions, and lower CO_2 emissions across its operations. Honda has developed an integrated approach that combines lifecycle assessment (LCA), carbon–neutral production facilities, and innovative product design.

Lifecycle Assessment (LCA)

Honda utilizes Lifecycle Assessment (LCA) as a critical tool in its circular economy framework. LCA enables Honda to measure the environmental impact of its products across their entire lifecycle, from raw material extraction to disposal. By visualizing the CO_2 emissions associated with each stage, Honda can make informed decisions on how to reduce carbon emissions and improve resource efficiency during product development. This comprehensive approach ensures that environmental impact is minimized at every stage, aligning with Honda's CE goals.

Carbon–Neutral Production Facilities

Honda's Saitama factory serves as a model for achieving carbon neutrality in manufacturing. By incorporating renewable energy and advanced CO_2 reduction technologies, Honda aims for the Saitama factory to become carbon–neutral by 2025, with plans to replicate this model at its other global production sites. Through this initiative, Honda demonstrates how a scalable, low-carbon manufacturing approach can support broader environmental goals and help achieve carbon neutrality in its operations.

Electrification and Sustainable Product Design

A key strategy in Honda's circular economy framework is the electrification of its product lineup. Honda has set a target for all automobile products to be carbon-free by 2040, primarily through electrification and alternative energy solutions. In markets such as Asia, where motorcycles play a prominent role, Honda is committed to promoting electrification in the motorcycle business as well. By prioritizing product longevity, Honda's approach to product design emphasizes recyclability and disassembly, which aligns with the company's circular economy principles.

3.3.4 *Circular Resource Management*

Honda's circular economy strategy includes resource management initiatives that aim to reduce waste, promote recycling, and improve material efficiency. These initiatives span both corporate operations and product use, reflecting Honda's commitment to a resource-conserving approach.

Resource Reduction and Recycling in Manufacturing

Honda's manufacturing processes emphasize efficient use of resources, targeting a reduction in scrap and waste generation. Honda aims to decrease total waste output by 14.5% by 2030 (compared to business-as-usual scenarios), aligning with global sustainability targets. Additionally, Honda has implemented measures to conserve water resources, aiming to reduce total water withdrawal by 14.5% by 2030. Honda's efforts extend to compliance with international regulations such as the Basel Convention on hazardous waste, further reinforcing its commitment to environmental stewardship.

Sustainable Material Utilization

Honda's goal of using 100% sustainable materials by 2050 underpins its resource circulation strategy. To reduce the impact of resource depletion and secure a stable supply chain, Honda designs products that are easier to disassemble and recycle. This approach not only conserves resources but also enhances product longevity, allowing customers to continue benefiting from Honda's products while minimizing environmental impact. By stabilizing material procurement and utilizing recycled resources, Honda is building a circular value chain that maximizes resource efficiency.

Collaborative Partnerships and Innovation in Recycling Technology

Honda recognizes the importance of partnerships in achieving its resource circulation goals. Through collaborations with industry leaders, Honda is advancing recycling technology and establishing dismantling and recycling consortia. These partnerships enable Honda to secure a stable supply of recycled materials and reduce CO_2 emissions related to resource extraction. In doing so, Honda strengthens its position as a leader in the shift toward a circular economy.

3.3.5 *The Hydrogen Ecosystem: A Case for Clean Energy Innovation*

As part of its clean energy strategy, Honda has been at the forefront of hydrogen fuel cell technology since the 1990s. Its hydrogen initiatives are a crucial element of the "Triple Action to ZERO" framework, supporting clean energy and carbon neutrality.

Hydrogen as a Long-Term Energy Carrier

Honda sees hydrogen as a viable solution for long-term energy storage, particularly for island nations like Japan that lack natural resources. Unlike batteries, which are limited in storage capacity, hydrogen can be stored indefinitely, offering a sustainable energy solution. By converting surplus electricity into hydrogen, Honda contributes to a renewable energy cycle that reduces dependency on fossil fuels and aligns with its environmental goals.

Building Hydrogen Infrastructure

Honda's commitment to hydrogen extends to infrastructure development. In Japan, Honda has partnered with the Japan Hydrogen Station Network LLC to expand the hydrogen refueling infrastructure, supporting the adoption of hydrogen-powered vehicles. In North America, Honda collaborates with companies like Shell to create a network of hydrogen stations. These efforts contribute to the growth of a comprehensive hydrogen ecosystem, fostering the use of hydrogen as a clean energy source across various sectors.

3.3.6 *Addressing Resource Constraints and Environmental Risks*

Honda's circular economy approach is also influenced by its awareness of resource constraints and the associated environmental risks. The company recognizes that limited availability of essential resources, such as rare metals, poses risks to product manufacturing and long-term business sustainability. Honda's commitment to efficient resource use reflects its strategy to mitigate these risks and maintain continuity in its production processes.

Product-Centered Approach to Resource Efficiency

Honda's goal of achieving a 100% usage rate of sustainable materials by 2050 highlights its shift toward a circular value chain. Honda's product-centered approach focuses on creating products that are easier to disassemble and replace, allowing for reuse and recycling of components. This strategy not only minimizes waste but also increases product lifespan, creating value for customers while contributing to resource conservation.

Corporate Initiatives to Reduce Environmental Impact

In addition to product-centered strategies, Honda has implemented measures across its corporate operations to reduce waste and minimize environmental impact. Honda is actively working to reduce its water usage and incorporate the 3R (Reduce, Reuse, Recycle) principles across all business activities. Compliance with global environmental standards, such as the Montreal Protocol on ozone-depleting substances, further illustrates Honda's commitment to reducing its corporate environmental footprint.

3.3.7 Challenges and Future Directions

Honda's journey toward a circular economy is not without challenges. Transitioning to clean energy and sustainable materials entails significant costs, and the success of the hydrogen ecosystem depends on widespread infrastructure development and public acceptance. To address these challenges, Honda continues to invest in research and development, exploring broader applications of hydrogen fuel cells and expanding its circular value chain.

By fostering collaborative partnerships and leveraging its expertise in resource management, electrification, and hydrogen technology, Honda is well-positioned to lead the automotive industry toward a sustainable future. Honda's "Triple Action to ZERO" framework serves as a model for integrating environmental responsibility into corporate strategy, reflecting the company's commitment to achieving a zero-impact, circular economy by 2050.

3.4 Conclusion

Honda's approach to sustainability reflects two distinct eras, each shaped by unique strategies and outcomes. Before 2000, Honda was an industry leader in environmental and social responsibility, driven by founder Soichiro Honda's philosophy of making a positive societal impact. Through pioneering initiatives in pollution control, community engagement, and safety promotion, Honda set itself apart, taking a proactive approach well beyond regulatory requirements. Its early development of pollution-reducing technologies, such as the CVCC engine, and community-focused projects like the "Hometown Forest" initiative exemplified its commitment to long-term, holistic sustainability.

However, the new millennium brought changes. After 2000, external pressures such as shareholder influence and regulatory demands led Honda to adopt a more formalized, compartmentalized sustainability approach. This shift diluted the top-down vision that had previously unified Honda's environmental and social initiatives, replacing it with a compliance-driven structure that prioritized meeting regulatory standards. As Honda's global expansion increased decentralization, sustainability efforts became fragmented across regions, complicating its ability to respond effectively to global environmental challenges.

In recent years, Honda has sought to reframe its sustainability strategy through the "Triple Action to ZERO" approach, incorporating Circular Economy (CE) principles focused on carbon neutrality, clean energy, and resource circulation. This comprehensive framework represents an attempt to integrate sustainability across Honda's operations while addressing modern environmental concerns. Carbon neutrality is a central goal, with Honda aiming for all automobile sales to be electric or fuel cell vehicles by 2040. By adopting cleaner manufacturing practices, Honda aligns itself with broader global efforts to decarbonize and reduce greenhouse gas emissions.

Honda's clean energy initiatives focus on transitioning away from fossil fuels, with projects to create carbon–neutral factories and explore renewable energy solutions. These efforts contribute to global energy transition goals and demonstrate Honda's commitment to reducing its environmental footprint. Additionally, resource circulation emphasizes sustainable materials management, aiming to reduce waste and reliance on virgin resources. By promoting product durability, recyclability, and reuse, Honda is taking steps to build a circular value chain that conserves resources and minimizes waste.

Despite these ambitious goals, Honda faces challenges in fully realizing its CE strategy. The transition to sustainable materials and clean energy requires overcoming regulatory and logistical hurdles, as well as gaining public acceptance for new technologies like hydrogen fuel cells. Recognizing these challenges, Honda has pursued partnerships to support cross-sector collaboration in achieving its sustainability targets.

In conclusion, Honda's "Triple Action to ZERO" framework is a strategic effort to integrate CE principles into its core operations, reaffirming its commitment to responsible innovation. By reigniting its pioneering spirit and embracing modern sustainability practices, Honda can continue its mission to leave a positive legacy for future generations. This journey not only positions Honda as a leader in sustainable automotive practices but also serves as a model for the industry, demonstrating the potential to balance economic growth with environmental stewardship.

References

Ellen MacArthur Foundation. (2021). Circular economy: A transformative approach to business and society. Retrieved from https://ellenmacarthurfoundation.org.

Guarnieri, P., e Silva, L.C., Haleem, F., Bianchini, A., Rossi, J., Wæhrens, B.V., Farooq, S., Reyes, E., Jr., Reis, A.L.N., & Vieira, B.d.O. (2023). How Can We Measure the Prioritization of Strategies for Transitioning to a Circular Economy at Macro Level? A New Approach. Sustainability, 15(1), 680.

Park, Y. W., Sugie, R., & Mizuguchi, K. (2024). Circular Economy Strategy of Japanese Firms: A Comparative Study of Manufacturing and Other Industries. Communication of JIMA, 34(1), 15–22.

Patel, A., & Singh, S. (2023). Implementing circular economy strategies in the automobile industry–a step toward creating sustainable automobiles. Benchmarking: An International Journal, 30 (7), 2225–2233.

Shakhnoza, N. K., & Park, Y. W. (2023). Circular Economy in Automobile Industry: Literature Analysis. Management Review: An International Journal, 18(1), 83–113.

Chapter 4
CE Strategy in the Cosmetics Industry

Young Won Park and Yuki Nakano

4.1 Introduction

To examine the state of the Circular Economy (CE) in Japanese firms with a focus on R strategies, this study explores existing literature and case-specific insights. The CE framework has gained international attention for its promise to align economic, environmental, and social sustainability goals with the Sustainable Development Goals (SDGs) (Park et al. 2024). Transitioning from the traditional linear "take-make-dispose" model to a circular paradigm, CE seeks to create regenerative systems that enhance resource efficiency and reduce waste, addressing critical challenges such as resource scarcity and environmental degradation. This paradigm shift is underscored by frameworks such as the Ellen MacArthur Foundation's model, which emphasizes resource efficiency and waste minimization in modern business practices (Shakhnoza and Park 2023; Park et al. 2024).

Japan's manufacturing sector exemplifies CE practices, prominently employing the 3R strategy—Reduce, Reuse, Recycle—underpinned by robust regulatory frameworks such as the Basic Act for Promoting the Creation of a Recycling-Based Society and the Recycling Act (Ministry of Economy, Trade and Industry 2001). However, to address complex sustainability challenges comprehensively, an extended 9R framework is proposed. This framework includes Recycle, Remanufacture, Reuse, Refuse, Rethink, Reduce, Repair, Refurbish, and Repurpose (Park et al. 2024), offering a more nuanced approach to resource management.

Each strategy within the 9R framework plays a vital role in fostering sustainability. Recycling conserves resources and reduces energy use by reclaiming materials from end-of-life products (Guarnieri et al. 2023). Remanufacturing restores used products to their original condition, extending their life cycles and decreasing the need for raw materials. Reusing products delays new production and reduces waste generation. Refusing encourages conscious choices to avoid products contributing to waste, while Rethinking inspires innovation in production processes for sustainability. Reducing

Y. W. Park and K. Tamaki, *Circular Economy Strategy for SDG Business Management*,
https://doi.org/10.1007/978-981-96-4194-9_4

minimizes resource consumption and waste generation, while Repairing and Refurbishing extend product usability and functionality. Finally, Repurposing finds innovative new uses for end-of-life products, further minimizing waste and maximizing utility.

The adoption of the 9R framework not only addresses pressing environmental challenges but also offers significant economic and social advantages. By reducing raw material costs and waste disposal expenses, businesses can improve operational efficiency and foster deeper connections with sustainability-conscious consumers, enhancing brand value (Kirchherr et al. 2017). However, transitioning to a circular economy requires overcoming substantial challenges, including high initial investments, supply chain restructuring, and the development of new business models (Ness 2008; Ghisellini et al. 2016).

Technological innovation is essential in this transition. Advances in recycling technologies and resource efficiency processes are key enablers for businesses to maintain competitiveness while achieving sustainability goals (Geng et al. 2012). Moreover, successful implementation demands coordinated efforts across supply chains and stakeholder groups. This includes fostering consumer awareness and promoting behavioral changes to support circular practices (Hernández-Arzaba et al. 2022). Without such collaboration, efforts to achieve circularity may fall short.

Although extensive research exists on CE and 3R strategies, significant gaps remain concerning the competencies required for their effective implementation in Japanese manufacturing (Prieto-Sandoval et al. 2018; Geng et al. 2012). By integrating 9R strategies into CE frameworks, Japanese firms can unlock transformative opportunities to align economic growth with environmental sustainability. As this study explores CE strategies within the cosmetics industry, with a particular focus on Shiseido, it underscores the importance of a holistic approach that combines respect for sustainability with innovative practices. This analysis aims to provide actionable insights into overcoming challenges and capitalizing on opportunities in the journey toward a sustainable circular economy.

4.2 Circular Economy Strategy and Importance of 9R Strategies

To address our research questions—what is the current state of the Circular Economy in Japanese firms regarding R strategies, and how do Respect strategies contribute to fostering a Circular Economy within the cosmetic industry through case studies, we begin with a comprehensive literature review on the existing studies surrounding the Circular Economy (CE). The concept of the CE has emerged as a promising approach to achieving sustainability goals across economic, environmental, and social dimensions, gaining traction globally due to its alignment with Sustainable Development Goals (SDGs) (Park et al. 2024).

The transition from a linear 'take-make-dispose' model to a circular approach aims to create a regenerative system that maximizes resource efficiency and minimizes waste generation. This transformation is crucial in addressing the growing challenges of resource scarcity and environmental degradation. The framework introduced by the Ellen MacArthur Foundation (2015, 2024) serves as a cornerstone for understanding this transition, emphasizing the importance of resource efficiency and waste reduction in business practices (Shakhnoza and Park 2023; Park et al. 2024). By adopting CE principles, businesses not only reduce their environmental footprint but also unlock economic and social benefits.

4.2.1 9R Strategies in the Circular Economy

Among the various strategies that companies can implement within the framework of CE, the 3R (Reduce, Reuse, Recycle) strategy has gained significant importance, particularly in the context of Japanese manufacturing (Higo et al. 2020). Japan's regulatory framework, including the Basic Act for Promoting the Creation of a Recycling-Based Society and the Recycling Act, reinforces the centrality of these strategies in promoting sustainable practices within the manufacturing sector (Ministry of Economy, Trade and Industry 2001).

However, to further enhance the potential of CE, we propose extending the 3R strategy to the 9R strategy, which includes Recycle, Remanufacture, Reuse, Refuse, Rethink, Reduce, Repair, Refurbish, and Repurpose (Park et al. 2024). This expanded framework allows for a more comprehensive approach to resource management and waste reduction.

Recycle involves reclaiming materials from end-of-life products and reintroducing them into the production process, conserving natural resources and reducing energy consumption (Guarnieri et al. 2023). Remanufacture refers to restoring used products to their original condition, extending their lifespan and minimizing the need for new materials. Reuse encourages the repeated use of products, thereby delaying the need for new items and reducing waste generation. Refuse involves making conscious choices to avoid certain products or materials that may contribute to waste. Rethink encourages companies to reassess their production processes and product designs to enhance sustainability. Reduce focuses on minimizing resource consumption and waste production in manufacturing processes. Repair emphasizes the importance of fixing products to prolong their life cycle and reduce the consumption of new resources. Refurbish is similar to remanufacturing, as it involves updating or repairing products to return them to a like-new condition. Repurpose adapts products or components for entirely new uses. This strategy fosters creativity and innovation, as seen in the use of industrial waste for art or construction materials. Recycle remains a critical component of the framework, focusing on recovering materials to produce new products. However, the framework prioritizes recycling as a last resort, emphasizing its role only when higher-value strategies are not feasible.

These strategies collectively contribute to creating a circular economy by promoting sustainable consumption and production patterns while simultaneously addressing the pressing challenges of resource scarcity and environmental degradation.

4.2.2 Implementation of R Strategies

Implementing the 9R strategies offers a comprehensive approach to addressing the dual challenges of environmental sustainability and economic growth. Companies adopting CE principles can develop sustainable production systems that minimize raw material costs and reduce waste disposal expenses (Ness 2008). This approach not only fosters long-term relationships with consumers who prioritize sustainability but also enhances brand value (Kirchherr et al. 2017).

Technological innovation plays a crucial role in the successful implementation of these strategies. Advances in recycling technologies and the development of processes aimed at maximizing resource efficiency are vital for maintaining competitiveness in this rapidly evolving economic landscape (Geng et al. 2012). By transitioning to a circular model, companies can unlock new revenue streams by regenerating waste into valuable products while minimizing their overall resource consumption.

Over the past 10 years, the concepts and objectives of the circular economy have become increasingly detailed and have emerged as strategic issues within international, European, and national policies. Despite this progress, the transition to circular production models continues to face significant barriers. These include technological limitations, policy constraints, complex global supply chains, high initial investment costs, and the need for consumer behavior change. Ciliberto et al. (2021) examine the relationship between sustainable production and lean production, highlighting the need to invest in reverse logistics and Industry 4.0 systems to achieve CE targets. They propose a holistic approach, integrating lean methodology and Industry 4.0 technologies, to enhance sustainable development and competitiveness.

Digital technologies (DTs), such as the Internet of Things (IoT), big data, and data analytics, are essential enablers of the circular economy. However, there is limited guidance on how DTs can be applied to maximize circular strategies. Kristoffersen et al. (2020) propose the Smart CE framework, which translates circular strategies into actionable business analytics requirements for DTs. This framework helps organizations align their activities across disciplines and identify strategic initiatives to bridge gaps in circular economy implementation.

The integration of CE principles with Industry 4.0 technologies provides substantial opportunities for businesses to enhance their competitive edge while achieving sustainability. Manavalan and Jayakrishna (2019) emphasize the importance of 6R strategies (Recover, Reuse, Remanufacture, Recycle, Redesign, Reduce) within supply chain contexts to meet Industry 4.0 requirements. Their analysis demonstrates the potential of circular practices to improve social, economic, and environmental outcomes.

Despite these advancements, challenges persist. High upfront costs, regulatory barriers, and limited consumer acceptance of reused or remanufactured products hinder widespread adoption. Additionally, gaps in infrastructure and policy support exacerbate these issues. Murthy and Ramakrishna (2022) stress the importance of stakeholder awareness and robust governance frameworks to address these challenges, particularly in managing e-waste and ensuring transparency in recycling processes.

To overcome these barriers, collaborative efforts among governments, businesses, and consumers are essential. Policymakers must provide incentives and create supportive environments for CE initiatives, while businesses should invest in innovative technologies and sustainable practices. By fostering a culture of sustainability and leveraging digital advancements, Japanese firms can unlock the potential of the circular economy, contributing to a more sustainable future. Ongoing research and practical guidelines are critical for bridging the gap between theory and practice, enabling successful implementation of CE strategies and ensuring their long-term viability.

4.3 Methodology

This study utilizes a deep case study approach, centering on Shiseido, the leading company in Japan's cosmetics industry. To explore Shiseido's sustainability practices and its adoption of circular economy principles, we analyzed the company's sustainability reports spanning from 2019 to 2023. These reports serve as a primary source of data, offering detailed insights into Shiseido's initiatives, goals, and progress in integrating sustainability across its operations. The analysis of these reports allows us to track changes over time and assess the company's commitment to sustainable business practices, as well as its alignment with global environmental standards.

In addition to examining the sustainability reports, we applied text mining techniques to enhance our understanding of the recurring themes and strategies emphasized by Shiseido. Text mining is a valuable tool that enables the systematic analysis of large volumes of textual data. By processing and analyzing the language used in Shiseido's reports, we identified key terms, concepts, and patterns that reveal the company's focus areas in sustainability, such as waste reduction, packaging innovation, and carbon footprint management. This approach allowed us to uncover deeper insights into the company's priorities and strategic direction in relation to environmental and social sustainability.

The combination of document analysis and text mining provided a comprehensive methodological framework for this research. While the sustainability reports offer qualitative information on Shiseido's initiatives, the text mining approach enables a quantitative understanding of the emphasis placed on various aspects of sustainability. Together, these methods facilitate a thorough exploration of how Shiseido, as a major player in the Japanese cosmetics industry, is implementing and evolving its sustainability practices in response to growing environmental and consumer demands.

4.4 Case Study: Shiseido

Shiseido, a global leader in the cosmetics industry, has a rich history of innovation, sustainability, and strategic business evolution. In 2020, Shiseido introduced its packaging development policy known as the "Shiseido 5Rs," which embodies the company's commitment to sustainability and a circular economy. This policy is part of a broader mission to achieve 100% sustainable plastic containers by 2025, reflecting Shiseido's drive to reduce its environmental footprint and contribute to the global effort to mitigate climate change.

The "Shiseido 5Rs" framework is based on five core principles: Reduce, Reuse, Recycle, Replace, and Respect. These elements work together to minimize the environmental impact of the company's packaging and operations, while also fostering collaborations across industries to push sustainability forward. Shiseido's efforts are not only limited to packaging; the company's broader strategy includes enhancing the customer experience, digital transformation, and sustainable innovation across its product portfolio.

4.4.1 Shiseido's History of Innovation and Brand Strategy

Shiseido's sustainability journey is deeply rooted in its history of innovation and adaptability. Founded in 1872 by Arinobu Fukuhara, Shiseido began as a Western-style drugstore in Japan and quickly evolved into a leading cosmetics brand. Over the years, Shiseido expanded its product offerings, introducing new lines of beauty products and pioneering marketing strategies that set the company apart from its competitors.

In 1922, Shiseido established a system that allowed for efficient distribution and promotion of its products, including the introduction of beauty consultants and contracted retailers. By 1927, Shiseido had reorganized itself into Shiseido Co., Ltd., solidifying its position as a dominant force in Japan's cosmetics industry. Throughout the twentieth century, Shiseido continued to innovate, expanding its brand portfolio and diversifying into new product categories such as toiletries and pharmaceuticals.

The 1980s marked a period of global expansion for Shiseido, as the company entered markets in Asia, Europe, and the United States. However, the collapse of Japan's bubble economy in the 1990s presented significant challenges for the company. In response, Shiseido restructured its brand portfolio, focusing on its core strengths and consolidating its brands to improve cost efficiency and streamline operations.

In the early 2000s, Shiseido implemented a "market category strategy" that divided its brands into two categories: "customer contact expansion brands" and "customer contact deepening brands." This strategy allowed Shiseido to specialize and segment its offerings based on customer needs and preferences, ultimately leading to the consolidation of its brand portfolio.

Shiseido's commitment to innovation and customer engagement is further demonstrated by the launch of its e-commerce platform, "watashi+," in 2012. This platform serves as a comprehensive beauty hub that connects consumers with Shiseido products and services, fostering deeper relationships with customers through digital touchpoints.

4.4.2 The Shiseido 5Rs: A Circular Economy for Packaging

Shiseido's "5Rs" approach is a comprehensive strategy for addressing the environmental challenges posed by plastic packaging. Each of the five components—Reduce, Reuse, Recycle, Replace, and Respect—offers a distinct pathway toward sustainability, and together they form the foundation of the company's long-term vision for a more sustainable future (Fig. 4.1).

Reduce

The "Reduce" pillar of the Shiseido 5Rs focuses on minimizing the use of plastic in the company's packaging. This effort involves optimizing the size and weight of packaging materials to use fewer resources. Shiseido has been a pioneer in offering "refill and replacement" products since 1926, significantly reducing the need for single-use plastic packaging. The introduction of these products has made a profound

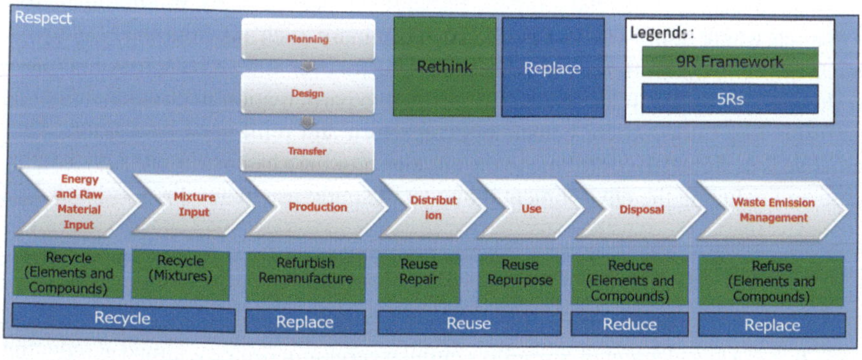

Fig. 4.1 Definition of 5Rs by 9R Framework

impact on the company's sustainability goals, and by 2022, Shiseido had launched over 770 SKUs across 30 brands globally under the refill and replacement model.

One of the most innovative applications of this principle is Shiseido's collaboration with AMCOR and Yoshino Kogyosho on LiquiForm® technology. This technology combines bottle manufacturing and liquid filling into a single step, thereby reducing the energy consumption and material waste associated with traditional packaging processes. By adopting this advanced technology, Shiseido has been able to produce refillable cosmetic containers that dramatically reduce the environmental burden.

Shiseido's "Reduce" strategy also extends beyond individual product packaging. The company is exploring ways to streamline its entire supply chain to further reduce plastic usage, such as developing mono-material packaging that is easier to recycle and optimizing its logistics to minimize the carbon footprint associated with transportation.

Reuse

The "Reuse" component focuses on encouraging the repeated use of packaging through refillable containers. Reusable packaging is central to Shiseido's sustainability strategy, as it reduces resource input, waste, and carbon emissions over the life cycle of a product. Shiseido offers refillable packaging across various product categories, including skincare, makeup, and personal care items. This approach not only benefits the environment by reducing plastic use but also appeals to eco-conscious consumers who are increasingly seeking sustainable alternatives.

One of the most notable successes in Shiseido's reuse strategy is the ELIXIR skincare brand, which introduced refillable packaging to the Japanese market in 2012. By promoting refillable containers, ELIXIR has reduced plastic use by approximately 85% compared to conventional packaging. Additionally, the brand's Life Cycle Assessment (LCA) methodology has shown that refillable packaging reduces carbon emissions by over 50% compared to regular packaging.

Shiseido has expanded the refillable packaging model globally, promoting its use in markets where refills were not previously customary, such as China and Singapore. In 2021, the company offered refillable packaging for over 800 SKUs across 33 brands worldwide. Shiseido's reuse efforts also extend to participation in circular shopping platforms like Loop, where consumers can return and refill used packaging. This initiative is designed to contribute to the circular economy by encouraging packaging reuse and reducing the environmental impact of single-use materials.

Recycle

Recycling is a key element of Shiseido's circular economy strategy, aimed at reducing the use of single-use plastics and promoting the reuse of materials. To support recycling, Shiseido is developing packaging that is easier to disassemble and recycle after use. This includes creating mono-material packaging and packaging that can be easily refilled without compromising the product's design or functionality.

Shiseido's recycling efforts are closely tied to its partnerships with industry leaders. The company has collaborated with Sekisui Chemical Co. and Sumitomo Chemical Co. to build an innovative recycling system for cosmetic containers since 2022. This joint initiative involves collecting used plastic containers from stores, recycling them into raw materials, and reusing them to produce new containers. The process begins with Shiseido collecting the used packaging, which is then gasified by Sekisui Chemical using a cutting-edge ethanol recycling technology. Sumitomo Chemical subsequently converts the ethanol into ethylene, which is used to produce recycled polyolefins. These polyolefins match the quality of those made from conventional fossil resources, effectively closing the recycling loop.

Shiseido has also implemented in-store collection programs to encourage consumers to return used packaging for recycling. The skincare brand IPSA introduced a recycling initiative in China, Hong Kong, and Taiwan in 2021. The program was highly successful, with over 9,000 participants and more than 20,000 cosmetic containers collected within six months. These efforts reflect Shiseido's commitment to not only recycling materials but also educating and engaging consumers in sustainable practices.

Replace

The "Replace" pillar of the 5Rs strategy focuses on finding alternatives to conventional plastic materials. Shiseido is actively researching and developing new packaging materials that are more environmentally friendly, such as biodegradable plastics and biomass-based materials. These alternative materials are designed to minimize the environmental impact of packaging, particularly in terms of reducing marine plastic pollution.

In its quest to develop sustainable alternatives, Shiseido has explored various options, including biodegradable resins and packaging made from renewable resources. The company is committed to introducing more sustainable materials into its packaging designs without compromising the quality or performance of its products.

By integrating these new materials into its product lines, Shiseido aims to reduce its reliance on fossil fuels and contribute to the global effort to reduce plastic waste. Shiseido is also collaborating with external partners to accelerate the development and commercialization of these materials, reinforcing its commitment to sustainability through innovation.

In 2022, Shiseido announced that they will replace all packages made by plastics to sustainable packages by 2025. Recent result is 69% achieved in 2023. In addition, they are dealing not only with packages but also marketing tools. In 2022, they replaced their visual merchandize tool to 100% recycled material and started changing promotion materials such as sales stands at pharmacies to paper,which used to be all plastics,to reduce usage of single-used plastic.

Respect

The "Respect" element of the 5Rs strategy goes beyond the physical aspects of packaging and focuses on Shiseido's core values of respect for people, society, and the environment. This principle reflects the company's dedication to creating products that are loved by consumers and developed with care for the world around them.

According to Shihori Oyama of Shiseido's Brand Value Development Institute, respect in the context of packaging development means crafting products that customers can continue to use with love, while also respecting the planet. This holistic approach to sustainability emphasizes the importance of considering the broader social and environmental impacts of packaging decisions, ensuring that Shiseido's products align with both consumer values and ecological responsibility.

Respect is also about building lasting relationships with customers by offering products that meet their needs while minimizing environmental harm. This customer-centric approach is evident in Shiseido's ongoing efforts to enhance product usability, quality, and design, all while maintaining a focus on sustainability.

4.4.3 Shiseido's Recent Strategic Focus

In 2023, Shiseido introduced its medium-term management strategy, "SHIFT 2025 and Beyond," which focuses on achieving a core operating profit of over 50 billion yen by 2025 in Japan. This strategy is built on three pillars:

- Business Structure Transformation: Shiseido aims to transform its business structure for profitable growth. This includes strategic price increases for prestige brands like "SHISEIDO" and strengthening self-sales capabilities for premium brands such as "Maquillage." The company also leverages data-driven insights to optimize its product offerings and enhance customer value.
- Rationalization of Fixed Costs: To streamline operations, Shiseido is improving its transportation logistics and reducing the costs of promotional materials. The company is also exploring digital solutions to enhance efficiency in staffing and store operations.
- Organizational Culture Reform: Shiseido is working to foster an innovative culture by encouraging top-down decision-making and promoting a mindset of self-innovation. This cultural shift aims to accelerate product development and enhance organizational agility.

4.4.4 Sustainability Initiatives: Premium/Sustainability Pillar

Shiseido's sustainability efforts extend beyond packaging. The company's research and development philosophy, "Dynamic Harmony," seeks to balance the creation of new beauty solutions with respect for people, society, and the environment. Under the "Premium/Sustainability" pillar, Shiseido has made sustainability an integral part of its product development process. The company is working on reducing its environmental footprint through innovations in both packaging and raw materials.

- Sustainable Packaging: As part of its 5Rs strategy, Shiseido is committed to sustainable packaging solutions, aiming for 100% sustainable packaging by 2025. By 2021, approximately 65% of Shiseido's packaging in Japan was classified as sustainable. This includes the development of lighter, refillable, and recyclable packaging solutions that reduce plastic use and minimize waste.

  For example, Shiseido's skincare brand, ELIXIR, introduced refillable packaging in 2012. The shift to refillable solutions has resulted in an 85% reduction in plastic use and a 50% reduction in carbon footprint compared to regular packaging, based on Life Cycle Assessment (LCA) methodology.
- Recycling and Collaboration: To further enhance recycling efforts, Shiseido has implemented in-store collection programs. The skincare brand IPSA launched a recycling initiative in China, Hong Kong, and Taiwan in 2021, successfully collecting over 20,000 cosmetics containers in just six months. Shiseido collaborates with industry partners, including Aeon Retail Co. and TerraCycle Japan, to support these initiatives.
- Developing Alternatives: Shiseido is also engaged in the development of alternative materials to replace conventional plastics. This includes biodegradable and biomass-based plastics that have lower environmental impacts.

4.4.5 Looking Ahead: Innovation and Sustainability as Core Drivers

Shiseido's sustainability journey is a testament to its dedication to creating beauty products that not only serve customers but also contribute to the well-being of the environment. By integrating innovative packaging solutions and adopting a holistic approach to sustainability, Shiseido has positioned itself as a leader in the global cosmetics industry.

The company's strategic initiatives, including the "Shiseido 5Rs" and the "SHIFT 2025 and Beyond" plan, underscore its commitment to evolving with consumer needs while respecting the planet. With ongoing investments in sustainable packaging, raw materials, and digital solutions, Shiseido continues to balance tradition and innovation in its mission to deliver beauty with integrity.

In conclusion, Shiseido's approach to sustainability—through the 5Rs framework, circular economy collaborations, and brand strategies—reflects a comprehensive and future-forward vision. By addressing the environmental challenges of the twenty-first century, Shiseido not only preserves its rich legacy but also ensures that its products and practices remain relevant and responsible in an ever-changing world.

4.5 Implications of Respect Among 5Rs

The principle of "Respect" within Shiseido's "Shiseido 5Rs" framework is multi-faceted, going beyond environmental sustainability to embody a broader philosophy of valuing the interconnectedness of people, society, and the planet. The "Respect" component has profound implications for Shiseido's brand ethos, customer relations, and long-term sustainability goals. Based on the provided context, here are several key implications of this principle, as shown in Fig. 4.2.

4.5.1 Respect for the Environment and Future Generations

The foundation of the "Respect" principle is deeply rooted in Shiseido's commitment to environmental stewardship. By incorporating sustainable practices into its packaging development, product design, and broader business operations, Shiseido is signaling a long-term commitment to reducing its ecological footprint. The company's efforts to introduce biodegradable and biomass-based plastics, as well as its emphasis on refillable and recyclable packaging, are direct manifestations of this respect for nature.

This approach suggests that Shiseido is thinking beyond short-term gains and is focused on preserving the environment for future generations. The decision to reduce reliance on conventional plastics and minimize the impact on marine ecosystems is a clear indication that Shiseido acknowledges its role as a global corporate citizen and is dedicated to contributing positively to global sustainability efforts.

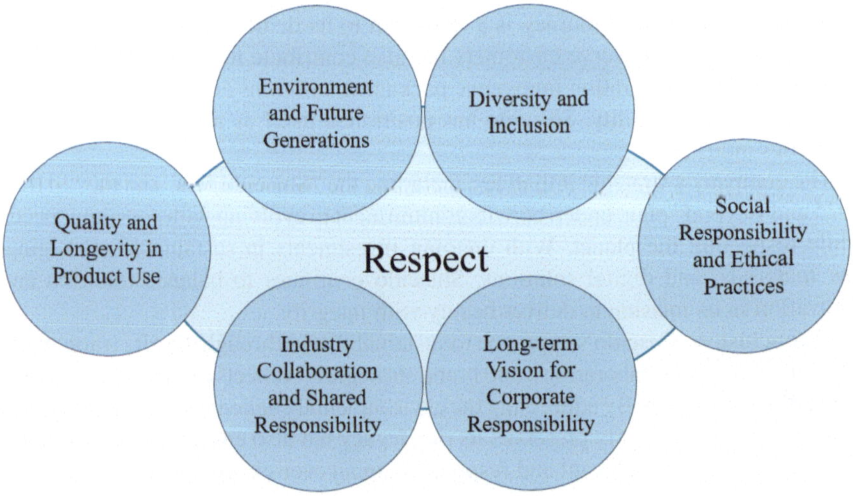

Fig. 4.2 Key implications of Shiseido's Respect

Shiseido's focus on environmental respect strengthens its brand image as a responsible and ethical company, enhancing its appeal to eco-conscious consumers who prioritize sustainability in their purchasing decisions. By aligning its packaging and products with global efforts to combat climate change and environmental degradation, Shiseido not only builds consumer trust but also contributes to a more sustainable beauty industry.

4.5.2 Respect for Consumers: Quality and Longevity in Product Use

"Respect" in the context of Shiseido's 5Rs framework also applies to the company's relationship with its customers. By creating products that are designed to last, with refillable and sustainable packaging options, Shiseido fosters a sense of loyalty and trust among its consumers. The emphasis on product longevity allows consumers to continue using their favorite products without the guilt of contributing to waste.

Shihori Oyama from Shiseido's Brand Value Development Institute highlighted that the "Respect" principle means crafting products that customers can "continue to use with love." This reflects the company's deep understanding of consumer values and their desire for products that not only perform well but also align with their ethical and environmental beliefs.

Shiseido's consumer-centric approach, which emphasizes product usability and sustainability, enhances the overall customer experience. By respecting customer values and offering products that meet high standards of quality and environmental responsibility, Shiseido strengthens its brand loyalty and fosters long-term relationships with its customers. Additionally, this approach positions Shiseido as a leader in ethical consumerism, appealing to a growing demographic of consumers who demand transparency and responsibility from the brands they support.

4.5.3 Respect for Diversity and Inclusion

In the context of a global company like Shiseido, "Respect" also has implications for diversity and inclusion. Shiseido operates in multiple regions and serves a diverse consumer base, which necessitates a nuanced understanding of different cultural values, preferences, and beauty standards. By respecting these differences, Shiseido ensures that its products and sustainability efforts resonate with a broad range of consumers.

For instance, the expansion of refillable packaging to markets like China and Singapore demonstrates Shiseido's respect for regional preferences while also introducing sustainable practices that may not have been customary in those regions. This approach signifies a willingness to learn from and adapt to different markets, while also promoting universal values such as environmental responsibility.

Shiseido's respect for cultural diversity enhances its global brand presence and allows the company to build deeper connections with consumers across different regions. This inclusivity not only broadens Shiseido's market reach but also reinforces its commitment to social responsibility by acknowledging and celebrating the diverse needs and values of its customer base.

4.5.4 Respect for Industry Collaboration and Shared Responsibility

The "Respect" pillar also implies a collaborative approach to sustainability, recognizing that meaningful progress toward a circular economy cannot be achieved in isolation. Shiseido's partnerships with companies such as AMCOR, Yoshino Kogyosho, Sekisui Chemical Co., and Sumitomo Chemical Co. demonstrate a commitment to working with industry leaders to drive innovation in sustainable packaging and recycling.

By collaborating with external partners, Shiseido not only accelerates the development of sustainable solutions but also contributes to a broader industry movement toward reducing plastic waste and promoting the circular economy. This collaborative spirit is rooted in the belief that respect for the environment requires collective action and shared responsibility.

Shiseido's collaborative approach enhances its reputation as a thought leader in sustainability. By actively engaging with other industry players, Shiseido contributes to the development of best practices and innovative technologies that can be adopted across the cosmetics and packaging industries. This not only amplifies the company's impact on environmental sustainability but also positions Shiseido as a key player in driving industry-wide change.

4.5.5 Respect for Social Responsibility and Ethical Practices

Beyond environmental concerns, the "Respect" pillar reflects Shiseido's broader commitment to social responsibility. As a company with a rich history and global influence, Shiseido has a responsibility to contribute positively to society, both through its business practices and its interactions with communities.

Shiseido's respect for social responsibility is evident in its efforts to create a positive impact on both local and global communities. This includes ethical sourcing of ingredients, ensuring fair labor practices, and promoting gender equality and diversity within its workforce. By embedding respect for human rights and ethical practices into its operations, Shiseido demonstrates that it values not only its customers but also the broader society in which it operates.

Shiseido's commitment to ethical practices enhances its brand credibility and strengthens its corporate social responsibility (CSR) profile. As consumers become increasingly concerned with the social and ethical impact of the brands they support, Shiseido's respect for human rights, fair labor, and community well-being will likely resonate with socially conscious consumers and stakeholders. This can lead to stronger customer loyalty, increased investor confidence, and improved stakeholder relations.

4.5.6 Respect as a Long-Term Vision for Corporate Responsibility

Finally, the "Respect" principle has long-term implications for Shiseido's overall corporate vision. By embedding respect into its sustainability strategy, Shiseido is not only addressing immediate environmental challenges but also positioning itself for future success in a rapidly evolving industry. The company's goal of achieving 100% sustainable plastic containers by 2025 is a testament to its long-term commitment to reducing its environmental impact and contributing to the global effort to combat climate change.

Shiseido's respect for long-term sustainability reflects its understanding of the interconnectedness of environmental, social, and economic factors. By prioritizing respect for the planet and its inhabitants, Shiseido is building a business model that is resilient, adaptable, and aligned with global sustainability goals.

Shiseido's long-term focus on respect and sustainability positions the company as a forward-thinking leader in the beauty industry. As consumers, investors, and regulators increasingly prioritize sustainability, Shiseido's proactive approach will likely result in competitive advantages, including enhanced brand loyalty, regulatory compliance, and greater market share in an eco-conscious global market.

In conclusion, the "Respect" principle in Shiseido's 5Rs strategy encompasses more than just environmental sustainability. It reflects a holistic approach to corporate responsibility that values consumers, society, and the planet. Through its innovative packaging solutions, ethical business practices, and commitment to long-term sustainability, Shiseido is setting a high standard for the cosmetics industry. This respect-based approach not only enhances Shiseido's brand value but also ensures that the company remains relevant and responsible in a rapidly changing world. As Shiseido continues to evolve, its dedication to respect will likely serve as a cornerstone of its success in the future.

4.6 Conclusion

The exploration of Circular Economy (CE) strategies within Japanese firms, particularly in the cosmetic industry through the lens of Shiseido, reveals a critical intersection of sustainability, innovation, and economic viability. The transition from a linear economic model to a circular one is a fundamental shift necessary for addressing pressing global challenges such as resource depletion and environmental degradation. Implementing the 9R strategies—Recycle, Remanufacture, Reuse, Refuse, Rethink, Reduce, Repair, Refurbish, and Repurpose—provides a comprehensive framework that encourages businesses to rethink their production and consumption patterns, ultimately fostering a more sustainable future.

Shiseido serves as an illustrative example of how a traditional company can successfully navigate the complexities of integrating CE principles into its business model. By adopting the "Shiseido 5Rs" framework, which emphasizes the importance of Respect alongside the 4Rs, the company demonstrates a holistic approach to sustainability that considers environmental, social, and ethical dimensions. Furthermore, the principle of "Respect" within the 5Rs framework underscores the importance of holistic corporate responsibility. This principle extends beyond environmental stewardship to encompass respect for consumers, diversity, and social responsibility. Shiseido's commitment to ethical sourcing, gender equality, and community engagement reflects a broader understanding of the interconnectedness between business success and societal well-being. This multifaceted strategy positions Shiseido as a leader in the cosmetic industry and as a model for other firms seeking to embark on their own circular economy journeys.

The analysis highlights the vital role of technological innovation in achieving ambitious sustainability goals. Advances in recycling technologies and collaborations across industries exemplify how innovative practices can significantly improve resource efficiency and waste management. For instance, Shiseido's partnerships with Sekisui Chemical and Sumitomo Chemical to create a closed-loop recycling system for plastic cosmetic containers illustrate the potential for cross-industry collaboration to yield tangible results.

However, the transition to a circular economy is fraught with challenges. Substantial initial investments to develop new technologies and reconfigure supply chains can deter firms from fully committing to CE strategies. Effective implementation requires collaboration among various stakeholders, including suppliers, customers, and governmental bodies, emphasizing the importance of a coordinated approach to overcome barriers and align efforts toward common sustainability objectives.

To facilitate this transition, companies must prioritize education and engagement initiatives that foster a culture of sustainability among consumers and employees. Building awareness and understanding of CE principles is critical in driving behavioral changes that support sustainable consumption and production patterns. Shiseido's efforts to engage customers reflect a growing recognition of the importance of customer involvement in the sustainability journey.

As consumer awareness of sustainability issues continues to grow, Shiseido's approach positions it favorably in an increasingly eco-conscious marketplace. The company's forward-thinking strategies not only align with global sustainability goals but also set a benchmark for the cosmetics industry and beyond.

In summary, the integration of Circular Economy principles and the implementation of 9R strategies present transformative opportunities for Japanese firms, particularly in the cosmetic industry. By embracing sustainability as a core tenet of their business models, companies can reduce their environmental footprint and enhance their competitiveness in a rapidly evolving market. The journey toward a circular economy requires collaboration, innovation, and commitment from all stakeholders involved. As exemplified by Shiseido, success in this endeavor will ultimately depend on balancing economic growth with social responsibility and environmental stewardship. Through continued research and practical applications, Japanese firms can lead the way in redefining industry standards and contributing to a more sustainable global economy.

References

Ciliberto, C., Szopik-Depczyńska, K., Tarczyńska-Łuniewska, M., Ruggieri, A., & Ioppolo, G. (2021). Enabling the Circular Economy transition: A sustainable lean manufacturing recipe for Industry 4.0. Business Strategy and the Environment, 30(7), 3255–3272.

Ellen Mac Arthur Foundation. (2015). Towards the circular economy. Journal of Industrial Ecology, 2(1), 23–44 Available at: https://www.werktrends.nl/app/uploads/2015/06/Rapport_McKinsey-Towards_A_Circular_Economy.pdf.

Ellen MacArthur Foundation. (2024). Circular economy principles and practices: Shaping the future of sustainable business. Retrieved from https://ellenmacarthurfoundation.org/

Geng, Y., Fu, J., Sarkis, J., & Xue, B. (2012). Towards a national circular economy indicator system in China: An evaluation and critical analysis. Journal of Cleaner Production, 23(1), 216–224.

Ghisellini, P., Cialani, C., & Ulgiati, S. (2016). A review on circular economy: The expected transition to a balanced interplay of environmental and economic systems. Journal of Cleaner Production, 114, 11–32.

Guarnieri, P., Bianchini, A., Rossi, J., e Silva, LC., Trojan, F., Lizot, M., & de Oliveira Vieira, B. (2023). Transitioning towards a circular economy under a multicriteria and the new institutional theory perspective: A comparison between Italy and Brazil. Journal of Cleaner Production, 409, 137094.

Hernández-Arzaba, J. C., Nazir, S., Leyva-Hernández, S. N., & Muhyaddin, S. (2022). Stakeholder Pressure Engaged with Circular Economy Principles and Economic and Environmental Performance. Sustainability, 14(23), 16302.

Higo, M., Tsunoo, S., & Tanaka, J. (2020). The impact of the circular economy and the direction of Japanese companies: Transition from a mass consumption society to a circular society in the manufacturing industry. Knowledge Creation and Integration, 28(12), 20–33.

Kirchherr, J., Reike, D., & Hekkert, M. (2017). Conceptualizing the circular economy: An analysis of 114 definitions. Resources, Conservation, and Recycling, 127, 221–232.

Kristoffersen, E., Blomsma, F., Mikalef, P., & Li, J. (2020). The smart circular economy: A digital-enabled circular strategies framework for manufacturing companies. Journal of Business Research, 120, 241–261.

Manavalan, E., & Jayakrishna, K. (2019). An analysis on sustainable supply chain for circular economy. Procedia Manufacturing, 33, 477-484.

Ministry of Economy, Trade, and Industry (METI). (2001). Basic Act for Promoting the Creation of a Recycling-Based Society. Retrieved from https://www.meti.go.jp.

Murthy, S., & Ramakrishna, S. (2022). A review on global E-waste management: urban mining towards a sustainable future and circular economy. Sustainability, 14(2), 647.

Ness, D. (2008). Sustainable urban infrastructure in China: Towards a factor 10 improvement in resource productivity through integrated infrastructure systems. International Journal of Sustainable Development and World Ecology, 15, 288–301.

Park, Y. W., Sugie, R., & Mizuguchi, K. (2024). Circular Economy Strategy of Japanese Firms: A Comparative Study of Manufacturing and Other Industries. Communication of JIMA, 34(1), 15–22.

Prieto-Sandoval, V., Jaca, C., & Ormazabal, M. (2018). Towards a consensus on the circular economy. Journal of Cleaner Production, 179, 605–615.

Shakhnoza, N. K., & Park, Y. W. (2023). Circular Economy in Automobile Industry: Literature Analysis. Management Review: An International Journal, 18(1), 83–113.

Chapter 5
CE Strategy in the Multifunction Printer Industry

Young Won Park, Sugie Ryosuke, Kakeru Mizuguchi, and Jinyao Mao

5.1 Introduction

In recent years, the circular economy (CE) has gained significant traction among companies and policymakers as a transformative business model aimed at achieving sustainable economic growth. Unlike the conventional linear economy, where resources are extracted, products are manufactured, used, and ultimately disposed of in a one-way trajectory, the CE seeks to establish a circular process that maximizes resource efficiency and minimizes waste generation. This paradigm shift not only promises to mitigate environmental impacts but also presents vast potential for companies to create economic value. The CE model has been recognized as a key strategy for achieving several of the United Nations Sustainable Development Goals (SDGs), particularly those related to responsible consumption and production, climate action, and industry innovation (Schroeder et al. 2019).

Academic research on CE has been progressing rapidly, emphasizing the construction of sustainable business models that prioritize efficient resource use and waste reduction (Ghisellini et al. 2016). Organizations that implement CE strategies can expect enhanced competitiveness through lower resource costs and the creation of new business opportunities (Ness 2008). Furthermore, improving product durability and cultivating long-term relationships with consumers are critical for increasing brand value and achieving sustainable growth. The CE framework highlights the possibility of these efforts contributing to improved environmental quality while ensuring economic development (Kirchherr et al. 2017).

However, challenges persist in realizing the full potential of CE strategies to enhance corporate profitability. The initial investments required for the transition to CE can be substantial, and the time required to see a return on these investments often poses a barrier. Additionally, cooperation throughout the supply chain, along with consumer education and awareness initiatives, can be costly and resource-intensive for companies. Moreover, the transition to a CE requires a systemic change that goes beyond individual firm strategies. It necessitates the reconfiguration of entire value

Y. W. Park and K. Tamaki, *Circular Economy Strategy for SDG Business Management*,
https://doi.org/10.1007/978-981-96-4194-9_5

chains and the development of new business ecosystems (Konietzko et al. 2020a, 2020b).

Building specific capabilities to monetize CE strategies has emerged as a crucial challenge for organizations. In the context of the Japanese manufacturing industry, where effective resource utilization and environmental protection strategies are prevalent, many companies have struggled to translate these strategies into profitable ventures. This difficulty is often attributed to strict regulations and trade restrictions that inhibit successful monetization efforts (Higo et al. 2020). A notable factor contributing to this struggle is a lack of understanding of the specific capabilities necessary to implement CE strategies effectively.

While prior studies have highlighted various initiatives related to CE strategies, there has been limited concrete analysis of the essential capabilities and the pathways for developing these capabilities (Prieto-Sandoval et al. 2018; Geng et al. 2012). Ghisellini et al. (2016), Senoo (2019), and Shakhnoza and Park (2023) have underscored the 3Rs—Reduce, Reuse, Recycle—as central pillars of CE strategies, particularly in the manufacturing sector. However, the practical implementation of these strategies and the development of necessary capabilities remain underexplored, especially in the Japanese context.

This study aims to address these research gaps by investigating the capabilities needed for Japanese manufacturing companies to implement the 3Rs effectively. It also explores how these companies can develop and build the requisite capabilities through an in-depth analysis of the CE strategy employed by Japanese manufacturing companies. The insights gained from this study aim to provide concrete guidelines for implementing CE strategies, thereby establishing a competitive advantage for Japanese manufacturing firms.

A compelling example of effective CE implementation is found in Fujifilm Business Innovation Corp. (formerly Fuji Xerox, hereafter referred to as Fujifilm BI), which underwent a transformative journey in the 1990s, driven by innovative leadership and a forward-thinking vision. Fujifilm BI's leadership recognized the increasing consumer demand for sustainability and the necessity of aligning environmental management with the company's operational goals of reducing costs and enhancing profit margins.

Fujifilm BI's recycling efforts are integral to its closed-loop system, significantly enhancing resource utilization and minimizing environmental impacts throughout the product lifecycle. By successfully implementing these strategies, Fujifilm BI exemplifies the potential of a circular economy, demonstrating that sustainability and profitability can coexist and thrive. Through its innovative approaches, Fujifilm BI serves as a model for Japanese manufacturing firms, illustrating how effective capabilities in the 3Rs can lead to competitive advantages and long-term sustainability in the ever-evolving landscape of global business.

5.2 The Emergence of Circular Economy (CE) and 3R Trend of Japanese Manufacturing Industry

The concept of the Circular Economy (CE) has gained prominence as a transformative business model aimed at transitioning from the traditional linear economy, characterized by a "take-make-dispose" approach, toward a more sustainable and regenerative system. Kirchherr et al. (2017) conducted an extensive analysis of 114 CE definitions, concluding that CE is an "economic system that replaces the 'end-of-life' concept with reducing, alternatively reusing, recycling and recovering materials in production/distribution and consumption processes." CE focuses on optimizing resource use across a product's entire lifecycle, minimizing waste, and promoting the reuse and recycling of materials. This model is particularly significant in addressing the growing environmental, economic, and social challenges associated with resource scarcity, environmental degradation, and the need for sustainable development.

5.2.1 *The Role of CE in Enhancing Business Competitiveness and Challenges*

One of the primary benefits of adopting CE strategies is the potential for companies to enhance their competitiveness. CE strategies provide a comprehensive approach to managing resource flows, reducing waste, and addressing environmental challenges, all while creating new business opportunities. By embracing CE principles, companies can reduce costs associated with raw materials and waste management, improve resource efficiency, and enhance their long-term sustainability.

For example, CE enables businesses to develop more durable products, extend product lifecycles through repair and reuse, and foster stronger relationships with consumers by offering sustainable solutions (Kirchherr et al. 2017). This approach not only contributes to environmental sustainability but also enhances brand value and customer loyalty, which are critical factors in maintaining competitiveness in a rapidly changing market.

Moreover, the successful implementation of CE strategies requires technological innovation. Advances in recycling technologies, the development of resource-efficient processes, and the adoption of new business models are key to ensuring that CE strategies are effective and contribute to maintaining or improving corporate competitiveness (Geng et al. 2012). By leveraging CE, businesses can simultaneously address environmental and economic challenges, positioning themselves for long-term success in a more sustainable global economy.

Despite the numerous advantages of CE, implementing circular strategies presents several challenges. These include technological limitations, policy constraints, complex global supply chains, high initial investment costs, and the need for consumer behavior change. Logistical difficulties in recycling and remanufacturing, along with regulatory barriers, further complicate the transition to CE practices. Overcoming these challenges requires innovative solutions and cross-sectoral collaboration. (Korhonen et al. 2018).

To better understand these challenges, several researchers have conducted in-depth analyses of CE implementation issues. Govindan and Hasanagic (2018) provide a systematic review from a supply chain perspective, highlighting the intricate nature of global supply networks, particularly in industries like automotive and multifunction printer manufacturing. Their work underscores how the interconnectedness of stakeholders in these sectors complicates the effective implementation of CE practices.

Building on this, Kalmykova et al. (2018) offer a comprehensive review of CE theories, practices, and implementation tools. Their research emphasizes that successful CE implementation extends beyond technological innovations, requiring significant changes in consumer behavior, business models, and policy frameworks. This multifaceted approach highlights the need for a holistic strategy in addressing CE challenges.

Furthermore, regulatory constraints and logistical challenges, particularly in recycling and remanufacturing, further complicate the adoption of circular practices (Shakhnoza and Park 2023; Generowicz et al. 2011). Additionally, transportation requirements for recycling materials are often costly and energy-intensive, contributing to increased carbon emissions (Alamerew and Brissaud 2020). These factors add another layer of complexity to the implementation of CE strategies, emphasizing the need for innovative solutions that address both environmental and economic concerns.

Addressing these complex issues requires a multi-level approach, as suggested by Ghisellini et al. (2016). This involves coordinating efforts at the micro-level (companies and consumers), meso-level (eco-industrial parks), and macro-level (cities, regions, and nations). For instance, investments in research and development can advance recycling technologies and sustainable production methods. Furthermore, governments play a crucial role in incentivizing CE adoption through supportive regulatory frameworks and financial mechanisms.

In conclusion, while CE offers significant potential for enhancing business competitiveness and addressing environmental challenges, its implementation is not without obstacles. Success in transitioning to a circular economy will depend on overcoming technological, economic, and social barriers through innovation, collaboration, and supportive policy frameworks. The following sections will explore how the Japanese manufacturing industry, with its focus on efficiency and innovation, is positioned to lead in this transition, offering valuable insights into the practical application of CE principles, particularly through the 3R (Reduce, Reuse, Recycle) strategy, in a highly developed industrial context.

5.2.2 3R Strategies and Circular Economy in Japan's Manufacturing Sector

The 3R strategies (Reduce, Reuse, Recycle) form the cornerstone of CE and are particularly relevant in manufacturing industries producing complete products. These strategies aim to minimize resource use, extend product lifecycles, and reintroduce waste materials into the production process. The 3R framework offers multiple benefits, including improved resource efficiency, reduced environmental impact, and enhanced corporate sustainability (Östlin et al. 2009; Geng et al. 2012).

- Reduce: The "Reduce" strategy focuses on minimizing resource use at the design and production stages. This can be achieved through innovations in product design, which prioritize resource efficiency and waste reduction. By reducing the amount of raw materials used in production, companies can lower costs and decrease their environmental impact.
- Reuse: The "Reuse" strategy involves extending the lifecycle of products by enabling them to be used multiple times. This can be achieved through repair, refurbishment, or repurposing of products, which reduces the need for new materials and contributes to resource conservation.
- Recycle: The "Recycle" strategy focuses on reclaiming materials from end-of-life products and reintroducing them into the production process. Recycling not only reduces waste but also lowers the demand for virgin materials, thereby conserving natural resources.

In the context of the manufacturing industry, the 3R strategies are essential for reducing environmental impact and enhancing resource efficiency. By adopting these strategies, automotive companies can reduce their reliance on finite resources, lower costs associated with raw materials, and minimize waste generation throughout the product lifecycle (Shakhnoza and Park 2023).

In particular, the manufacturing sector in Japan has been at the forefront of implementing 3R strategies as part of broader CE efforts. Japan's resource limitations, coupled with its stringent environmental regulations, have made the adoption of CE strategies particularly relevant. The country's Basic Law for Establishing a Recycling-Based Society and the Recycling Law promote the implementation of 3R strategies across industries, with a strong emphasis on reducing waste and promoting recycling (Higo et al. 2020; Senoo 2019).

The manufacturing industry in Japan has responded to these regulatory frameworks by adopting various CE practices aimed at reducing resource use and minimizing waste. For example, the automotive industry has implemented recycling systems for end-of-life vehicles, enabling the recovery of valuable materials like metals and plastics. Additionally, innovations in product design have reduced the amount of raw materials used in manufacturing, further contributing to resource conservation.

Despite these efforts, the implementation of 3R strategies in Japan's manufacturing sector is not without challenges. Many companies face difficulties in ensuring profitability while adhering to CE principles. For instance, the costs associated with recycling can be high, particularly when the quality of recycled materials is inconsistent. Furthermore, market acceptance of reused or remanufactured products is often low, making it difficult for companies to achieve profitability (Higo et al. 2020).

While significant progress has been made in understanding the potential of CE to promote sustainability, several research gaps remain. One key area that requires further exploration is the development of capabilities needed for effective CE implementation. Specifically, more research is needed to understand how companies can develop and build the necessary capabilities to effectively implement and monetize circular economy strategies, particularly in the context of the 3Rs (Reduce, Reuse, Recycle) in manufacturing.

Building on the literature review presented earlier, several key insights emerge regarding the implementation of circular economy (CE) strategies within the manufacturing sector. While research indicates that CE can significantly enhance business competitiveness through increased resource efficiency and waste reduction (Kirchherr et al. 2017), companies encounter substantial hurdles in its execution. These challenges include high initial investment costs, the complexities of supply chain coordination, and the need for developing specific capabilities (Korhonen et al. 2018). Although the 3R principles (Reduce, Reuse, Recycle) form the foundational pillars for successful CE strategies in manufacturing (Ghisellini et al. 2016; Senoo 2019), many companies struggle to achieve profitability while applying these principles (Higo et al. 2020).

To systematically assess how companies can overcome these challenges and implement CE strategies effectively, this study proposes a framework that explores the connection between implementation capabilities and strategic integration. This framework is composed of two main dimensions:

The first dimension, "CE Implementation Capabilities," refers to the practical skills and resources companies require to carry out CE initiatives. These capabilities encompass effective resource management across the product lifecycle, sustainable production competencies, and logistics expertise to ensure efficient material flow and recovery. Possessing these capabilities is essential for companies to manage their circular economy efforts successfully.

The second dimension, "3R Strategy Integration Level," assesses how comprehensively a company has adopted CE practices, ranging from basic recycling initiatives to advanced closed-loop systems.

Combining these dimensions yields a matrix that identifies four distinct strategic positions:

- "Circular Economy Leaders": companies that exhibit both high implementation capabilities and full 3R integration, showcasing advanced execution and efficient closed-loop systems.
- "Strategy-Oriented": organizations with well-developed 3R planning but limited practical implementation capabilities.
- "Initial Stage": firms primarily focused on basic recycling with limited capabilities and no systematic approach.

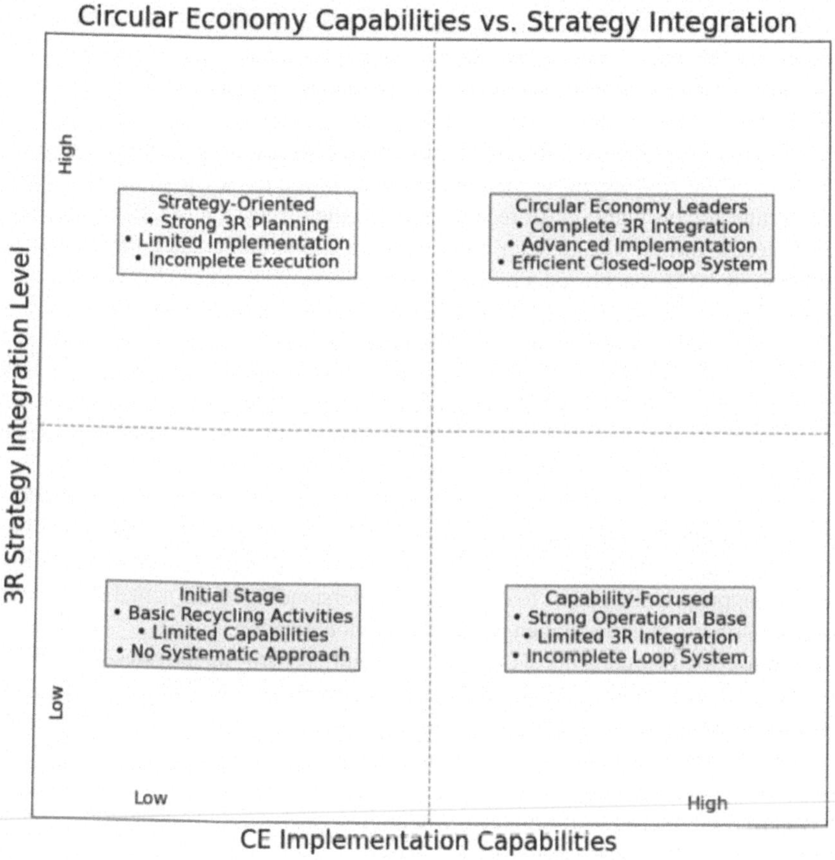

Fig. 5.1 CE Implementation Capability-Integration Matrix. *Source* Authors

- "Capability-Focused": companies that possess strong operational capabilities but have yet to achieve full 3R integration or develop closed-loop systems.

This framework will be utilized to analyze Fujifilm BI's CE strategy development, examining how the company has built the necessary capabilities and progressed its 3R integration. The analysis will provide insights into the practical requirements for effective CE implementation in the manufacturing industry (Fig. 5.1).

5.3 Methodology

In this study, we adopted a case study to analyze the capacity building for the profitability of CE strategy. The reasons for using case study are: (1) the accumulation of cases on the capacity building of CE strategy in Japanese companies has not progressed sufficiently, and (2) it is suitable for the research question of "how the capacity has been built" (Yin 1994). By grasping these actual situations historically, we conducted an exploratory study to find important findings and future research topics.

In this study, we targeted Fujifilm BI, a Japanese manufacturing company. Fujifilm BI is one of the first Japanese manufacturers to introduce a CE strategy and has been aiming for profitability. In recent years, as the discussion of CE strategy has accelerated, Fujifilm BI has been working on a CE strategy since the 1990s. In particular, in 2000, it achieved a recycling rate of over 99%. Such characteristics of the company are considered to be suitable for the research question of this study.

The case study used primary and secondary data. Primary data was obtained through interviews. The interviews were conducted twice between June and July 2024, lasting between 1.5 and 2 h. The interviews were conducted in a semi-structured format, in which participants responded to questions prepared in advance, and flexible questions were asked according to the progress of the dialogue.

In addition, we had the opportunity to actually observe the manufacturing process of recycled products. We interviewed manufacturing personnel about any questions that arose during the tour, and collected detailed information from an on-site perspective. This approach allowed us to deepen our understanding of the actual state of the recycling process and the challenges facing its monetization.

We transcribed the contents of the interviews and asked the interviewees to confirm them in order to eliminate any discrepancies in perception. In addition, if any additional questions arose in the course of the research, we asked additional questions via email. As secondary data, we also used materials such as company news releases, securities reports, and company histories. These materials were used to supplement the interview content and confirm factual relationships that could not be fully grasped through limited interviews alone.

5.4 Case Study

5.4.1 Overview of Circular Economy

In the early 1990s, Fujifilm BI found itself at a crucial juncture in its business strategy, particularly regarding its shift toward a circular economy (CE). This pivotal change was brought about by the visionary leadership of the company's top executives. At the time, Fujifilm BI's management visited an advanced factory in Europe that had already incorporated recycling as a central element of its manufacturing process. They observed firsthand how deeply embedded the idea of recycling was within European society, where customers were beginning to demand environmentally conscious practices from businesses.

Inspired by this visit, the leadership of Fujifilm BI recognized the growing importance of sustainability and the potential for linking environmental management with traditional business goals such as cost reduction and profit margin improvement. Specifically, the company's top management became intrigued by the prospect of building a profitable recycling business. Their thinking was that if the company could reuse at least 30% of the parts from collected products, it would not only make the recycling process economically viable but also reduce the environmental impact of their operations. This would, in turn, create a virtuous cycle where environmental and business benefits would reinforce each other.

The company's leadership acted swiftly, setting out a new direction for the entire organization. They gave instructions to develop a comprehensive recycling system with the following three objectives:

- Building new manufacturing through company-wide cooperation: The first goal was to link the newly established recycling system to the overall improvement of the company's constitution. This required collaboration across various departments, from design to manufacturing, logistics, and customer service.
- Renewing the image of the factory: Historically, factories had a reputation for being "3K" (an abbreviation in Japanese for kitsui, kitanai, and kiken, meaning "hard, dirty, and dangerous"). Fujifilm BI's goal was to eliminate this outdated perception by transforming its factories into cleaner, safer, and more comfortable working environments. The shift in factory operations would not only improve working conditions but also align with the company's broader sustainability objectives.
- Maintaining customer satisfaction: Even though the company would be using recycled materials and components in its products, the management emphasized that the quality, service, and pricing should match that of new products. This goal was crucial for ensuring customer trust and satisfaction in the long term.

By 1995, Fujifilm BI officially began its efforts to build a resource recycling system. This ambitious project was driven by the top management's commitment to achieving "zero waste" and promoting the reuse of materials wherever possible. The company's resource circulation system was built on three foundational pillars:

- Closed-loop system: The closed-loop system envisioned a cycle where products that had reached the end of their lifecycle would be collected, disassembled, and the usable parts reused to manufacture new products. This system would drastically reduce waste and minimize the need for virgin materials.
- Inverse manufacturing: To support the closed-loop system, Fujifilm BI adopted a practice known as "inverse manufacturing," which involves designing products with their future recycling and reuse in mind. From the initial planning stages, products were designed to be easily disassembled and their components reused or recycled.
- Zero emissions: Finally, the company set a bold goal of achieving zero waste by ensuring that all materials used in the production process would either be reused or recycled. Any waste that could not be directly reused would be processed through recycling or thermal recovery (i.e., converting waste to energy).

Fujifilm BI's resource recycling system was notably different from conventional refurbishing models. Instead of simply refurbishing used products to give them a second life, Fujifilm BI developed a process that disassembled products down to the component level. The components were then meticulously cleaned, inspected, and sorted. Only those parts that passed rigorous quality checks were reused in new products, ensuring that the reliability and performance of products made from recycled parts matched those made from entirely new materials.

The reuse rate became a critical factor in determining the economic feasibility of the system. For Fujifilm BI, ensuring that parts could be reused required thoughtful product design from the outset. To support this, the company developed a series of design guidelines aimed at extending the lifespan of parts, improving the durability of components, and making products easier to disassemble. For example, components that could not be reused were separated by material type, allowing for more efficient recycling.

In Japan, Fujifilm BI classified materials into as many as 44 categories, while in Asia, materials were divided into up to 70 categories. These detailed classifications helped ensure that as many materials as possible were recycled. Components that could not be recycled were sent for thermal recycling, contributing to the company's "zero waste" objective.

By 2000, Fujifilm BI had successfully achieved zero waste in Japan. This was a major milestone, as it went beyond merely collecting and recycling valuable materials. The company had committed itself to the much more difficult challenge of eliminating all waste from its production process and ensuring that even non-valuable materials were properly disposed of or reused.

In parallel with its environmental goals, Fujifilm BI was also focused on making its recycling business profitable. For the company, sustainability was not just about environmental stewardship; it was also about creating a stable and sustainable business model. To that end, the company worked to expand its reuse design, develop new technologies, and improve the efficiency of its production processes. These efforts, which included automation and improved productivity, enabled Fujifilm BI to make its recycling business profitable by 2003.

Fujifilm BI's resource circulation system achieved what is known as a "closed-loop system," where products are collected, reused, and recycled in a continuous cycle. The success of this system hinged on the company's effective integration of the 3R principles: Reduce, Reuse, and Recycle. By linking these initiatives together, Fujifilm BI was able to meet its dual objectives of "zero waste" and a profitable recycling business. The following sections provide a detailed exploration of how Fujifilm BI implemented these principles in its operations.

Figure 5.2 shows the closed-loop system of Fujifilm BI. Within the system, the flow of materials and information are separate. The solid lines indicate the flow of materials, and the dotted lines indicate the flow of information.

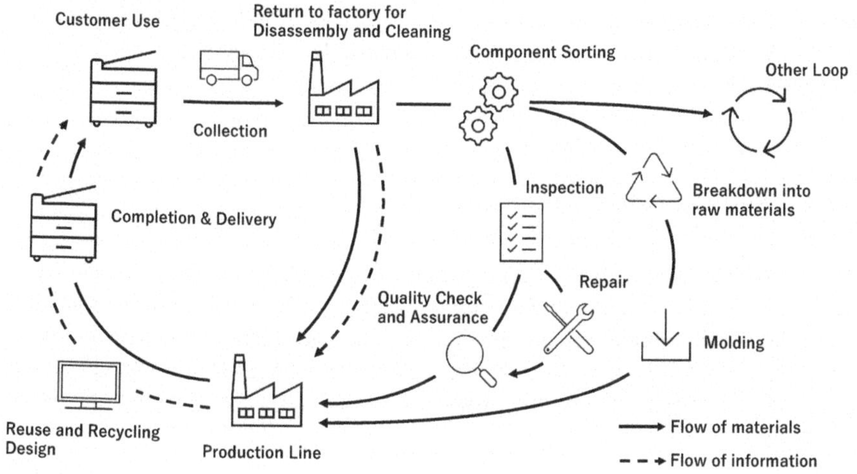

Fig. 5.2 Fujifilm BI's Closed-loop System. *Source* Authors, based on Fuji Xerox Co., Ltd. (2013)

5.4.2 Reduce-Related Initiatives

In line with its circular economy strategy, Fujifilm BI has been particularly focused on initiatives aimed at reducing the environmental impact of its products. One of the key strategies the company pursued was making its products smaller and lighter, thereby reducing the amount of raw materials needed for production and lowering the overall environmental footprint.

One example of this strategy can be seen in Fujifilm BI's work on multifunction devices and printers. In a recent model, the company was able to reduce the number of parts used, optimize the design layout, and achieve significant reductions in both weight and volume. Specifically, the company reduced the weight of the product by 30% and the volume by 40% compared to previous models. These changes not only made the products easier to transport and more efficient to manufacture but also helped reduce CO2 emissions during both the production process and the logistics chain.

Additionally, Fujifilm BI has placed a strong emphasis on recycling plastic resources. The company uses recycled plastics in the production of certain components, thus reducing the need for virgin plastic materials. Beyond this, Fujifilm BI has been exploring new, environmentally friendly materials for its products. For instance, the company has introduced flame-retardant bio-based plastic parts made from cellulose, a natural material derived from wood. This innovation helps reduce the environmental impact of plastic use while maintaining the performance and safety standards required in its products.

Fujifilm BI is also making strides in addressing the growing problem of marine plastic pollution. Starting in February 2024, the company plans to use plastics sourced from marine plastic waste as raw materials for the main parts of its multifunction devices. This initiative is an important step toward both reducing plastic pollution in the oceans and promoting the circular economy by turning waste materials into valuable resources.

5.4.3 *Reuse-Related Initiatives*

Fujifilm BI has been actively working on reusing products and parts as part of its broader sustainability and circular economy strategy. Since 1995, the company has established design guidelines and procurement policies focused on reuse and recycling. These guidelines have been deployed company-wide and are essential in structuring product design with resource efficiency in mind. The core principles of Fujifilm BI's design for reuse include:

- Long-life design: Products are engineered to extend the lifespan of parts so they can be reused multiple times.
- Separate design: Products are designed to facilitate easy separation of short-life components from long-life ones, enabling more efficient reuse of the durable parts.
- Strength design: Special attention is given to the strength and durability of parts to minimize damage during usage, recovery, and recycling processes.
- Disassembly design: Products are constructed to be easily disassembled, simplifying the separation of materials and components for reuse or recycling.
- Use of reusable materials: Wherever possible, recyclable and reusable materials are chosen to facilitate rematerialization and to ensure they can be reintegrated into new products.
- Design standardization: The company aims to standardize parts across different product lines, allowing components to be reused in other models or future versions of the same product.

These guidelines enable Fujifilm BI to design products that are structured for reuse after collection, ensuring the efficient use of resources throughout the product lifecycle. By considering reuse during the design phase, the company maximizes the potential for extending the value of materials and components, reducing the need for raw materials, and minimizing waste.

In addition to its design principles, Fujifilm BI has implemented a reverse logistics system that further supports its reuse efforts. This system is triggered when a product is returned or collected, with a "recycling judgment system" automatically classifying products based on their eligibility for reuse or recycling. The system is integrated into the company's core operational processes, ensuring a smooth and efficient flow of collected products through either the reuse or recycling streams.

Once used products are collected, they are transported to designated reuse facilities where they undergo a detailed disassembly process. Each part is diagnosed by the company's "usage history information system," which evaluates the condition and potential for reuse. Parts deemed reusable are cleaned and restored using advanced cleaning and blasting technologies. After refurbishment, the parts are reassembled into products, which undergo the same rigorous inspection and adjustment processes as new products. This ensures that products made with reused parts meet the same high standards for quality and performance.

One of the key technologies developed by Fujifilm BI is a specialized cleaning process that uses reduced water with high cleaning power to remove oil-based stains from parts. This process effectively restores parts to a reusable state without compromising quality. Additionally, the company introduced blasting technology, which addresses the issue of exterior plastic components yellowing due to aging. By removing the yellowing through blasting, the company has increased the reuse rate of exterior parts from 50 to 80%, significantly improving the sustainability of its products.

In terms of consumables, Fujifilm BI has been proactive in reusing materials such as toner cartridges and toner recovery bottles. Since the 1990s, the company has implemented a collection and reuse program for these items, reducing the need for new resources and lowering the environmental burden. This initiative complements the company's broader reuse strategy by incorporating consumable products into the circular economy.

5.4.4 Recycle-Related Efforts

Fujifilm BI's recycling process is a meticulous system that involves the thorough disassembly, cleaning, and sorting of products to recover as many reusable components as possible. One of the key aspects of this process is the removal of exterior covers and other parts that need to be replaced or cleaned. The company's in-house developed system plays a critical role in determining whether each part can be reused. This system reads detailed information from components, such as power-on time and operational history, to make precise decisions about the reusability of parts.

Once products have been classified through the recycling judgment system, those deemed recyclable are sent to Fujifilm BI's recycling centers. At these centers, the products are further disassembled in cooperation with recycling partners who utilize the latest recycling technologies. This collaborative approach ensures that the products are processed into a state where they can be reused as raw materials or components. Through these efforts, Fujifilm BI achieved a remarkable recycling rate of over 99.9% (zero waste) in Japan by 2000, a milestone the company has maintained ever since.

The company's recycling system goes beyond simply refurbishing parts—it involves a complete breakdown of products into their fundamental components. This comprehensive approach to recycling ensures that materials are either reused in new products or processed into raw materials that can be reintegrated into the manufacturing cycle. Fujifilm BI also leverages a nationwide network of recycling partners to manage the recycling process. This network not only ensures access to cutting-edge recycling technology but also reduces transportation distances, thereby minimizing the company's overall carbon footprint.

If a part is found to be reusable, Fujifilm BI subjects it to a rigorous inspection and repair process. Each part is carefully tested for functionality, and repairs are made as necessary. For large assemblies, only the necessary components are replaced, reducing waste and improving efficiency. If a part contains sensitive customer information, it is either replaced or the data is completely erased to protect customer privacy. Once parts have been inspected and repaired, they are reassembled into refurbished products.

The final stage of the recycling process involves assembling refurbished and new parts on the production line according to established procedures. For exterior covers, Fujifilm BI typically replaces the front cover with a new one for aesthetic reasons, but the sides and back covers are often made from refurbished components. These refurbished machines are subjected to the same rigorous adjustment and inspection processes as new products, ensuring that they meet the company's high standards for quality and performance.

One of the key indicators of the success of Fujifilm BI's recycling efforts is the fact that refurbished products demonstrate failure rates that are comparable to, or even lower than, those of new products. This is largely due to the fact that refurbished devices have already been in operation and have demonstrated stable performance. As a result, they are less likely to experience the initial failures often seen in new products, particularly in terms of electrical issues.

These recycling efforts form a crucial part of Fujifilm BI's closed-loop system. By thoroughly reusing and recycling parts and materials, the company significantly improves resource utilization efficiency and reduces its environmental impact. This comprehensive approach to recycling and reuse is central to Fujifilm BI's commitment to sustainability and circular economy principles, ensuring that its products contribute to a greener future throughout their entire lifecycle.

5.5 Key Findings on 3R Strategy Capabilities and Implementation

5.5.1 *Identification of Capabilities Necessary for Effective Implementation of the 3R Strategy*

Through case analysis, it is clear that building a closed-loop system is crucial for the effective execution of the 3R (Reduce, Reuse, Recycle) strategy. A core aspect of this system is Fujifilm BI's "Control over Arterial and Venous Logistics." This control optimizes the logistics flow from product recovery to reuse, serving as a key factor for successful recycling. Studies by Govindan et al. (2015) highlight the importance of logistics in managing the entire resource recovery and reuse process. For example, real-time monitoring and optimization of logistics flows are essential to increase product recovery rates and secure a stable supply of reusable materials. Fujifilm BI's implementation of this logistical control plays a pivotal role in system efficiency, supporting the success of its recycling operations.

Moreover, Fujifilm BI has introduced systems that evaluate the lifespan and quality of parts in real-time, determining whether components can be reused. This capability, termed "Parts Sorting," plays a critical role in the recycling process. Masoudipour et al. (2017) and Taleizadeh et al. (2019) emphasized that predicting the quality of recovered products and designing supply chains accordingly enhance the potential for reuse. Fujifilm BI's systems minimize waste and ensure optimal resource utilization.

The company has also adopted reverse manufacturing, designing products to retain high recyclability even after use. This approach, termed "Recycling Design," contributes significantly to environmentally friendly product development. Bocken et al. (2016) and den Hollander et al. (2017) emphasize that considering recyclability at the product design stage is crucial for sustainable product development. By considering factors like ease of recycling and selecting materials that facilitate reuse during the initial design phase, companies can ensure easier resource recovery at the disposal stage, significantly enhancing recycling efficiency.

Fujifilm BI has also developed proprietary cleaning and blasting technologies, which restore reusable parts to a suitable condition for reuse. This "Cleaning Technology Capability" contributes to improving reuse rates. Studies by Kassab et al. (2023) and Asaba (2001) show how advanced cleaning technologies help maintain product quality in recycling processes, supporting both environmental and economic sustainability.

Finally, Fujifilm BI utilizes automation to enhance productivity, making recycled products as profitable as new ones. Since each recovered product varies in wear and usage, producing high-quality recycled items requires sophisticated manufacturing capabilities. Fujifilm BI's traditional "Manufacturing Capabilities," a hallmark of Japanese manufacturing, are essential in ensuring that diverse product conditions are consistently processed into high-quality recycled items. Östlin et al. (2009) and Ghisellini et al. (2016) underscore the importance of balancing sustainability and productivity for successful recycling operations.

In conclusion, these capabilities enable Japan's manufacturing industry to implement the 3R strategy effectively and build a closed-loop system. Fujifilm BI's case provides a concrete example of the capabilities necessary for the successful execution of the 3R strategy, offering valuable insights for realizing sustainable resource circulation.

Summary of 3R Implementation Capabilities

- Control of Arterial and Venous Logistics: Optimizes the flow from product recovery to reuse, supporting efficient recycling and reuse.
- Parts Sorting Capability: Assesses the quality of recovered parts in real-time to determine their reusability.
- Recycling Design Capability: Ensures recyclability throughout the product's lifecycle.

- Cleaning Technology Capability: Restores reusable parts to high quality, enhancing reuse rates.
- Manufacturing Capability: Achieves the same profitability for recycled products as for new ones through advanced manufacturing.

5.5.2 *Development and Building Process of Capabilities Needed for the 3R Strategy*

Case studies on Fujifilm BI reveal the critical role of "Leadership" in developing and building the capabilities necessary to implement the 3R strategy. In the 1990s, top management at Fujifilm BI successfully linked environmental management with corporate challenges after observing recycling facilities in Europe. This leadership drove the company's efforts to build an effective recycling system, laying the foundation for developing 3R-related capabilities.

The significance of leadership in driving transformation is widely acknowledged in prior research. Kirkman et al. (2009) showed that transformational leadership promotes sustainable innovation in businesses. Transformational leaders articulate a shared vision of the future, intellectually stimulate subordinates, provide individual support, and set high expectations. For example, recycling-conscious product design requires guidance and strategies to direct designers in conceptualizing and materializing these designs (den Hollander et al. 2017). Fujifilm BI's leadership successfully presented these guidelines and strategies, facilitating the company's circular economy (CE) strategy.

Additionally, Fujifilm BI's top management recognized the necessity of "Company-Wide Cooperation" in building the recycling system. This aligns with studies on the importance of internal integration and collaboration with suppliers in supply chain management (Wong et al. 2011). To establish new manufacturing systems, top management at Fujifilm BI directed company-wide improvements, strengthening organizational cooperation. Moreover, efforts to refresh factory environments and make them conducive to productive work were essential in promoting effective recycling activities. This helped create a corporate culture where employees actively participated in recycling efforts, playing a crucial role in achieving sustainability goals (Jabbour and de Sousa Jabbour 2016).

Fujifilm BI also focused on developing technical capabilities necessary for the 3R strategy. For example, the adoption of reverse manufacturing and the establishment of design guidelines enabling reuse reflect an approach that considers the entire product lifecycle. Enhancing these technical capabilities can improve the effectiveness of recycling throughout a product's lifecycle (Geyer and Jackson 2004). The company also introduced innovations such as in-house cleaning technologies and blasting techniques, highlighting how "Technological Innovation" contributes to improving recycling outcomes (Geng et al. 2012; Kassab et al. 2023; Asaba 2001).

Collaboration with recycling partners is another essential element of Fujifilm BI's 3R strategy. By strengthening "Partnerships with External Partners," the company has introduced advanced recycling technologies, facilitating efficient resource circulation. Dyer and Singh (1998) discuss the strategic value of inter-firm cooperation, noting that collaborating allows companies to share unique resources and capabilities that they cannot achieve alone. Fujifilm BI's effective cooperation with recycling partners demonstrates how this collaboration enables the execution of efficient circular economy strategies.

In summary, Fujifilm BI's 3R strategy involves the development and construction of capabilities through leadership, company-wide cooperation, technological innovation, and partnerships with external partners. These processes have enabled Fujifilm BI to establish an effective closed-loop system, supporting the implementation of its 3R strategy.

5.6 Conclusion

In conclusion, the transition to a circular economy (CE) presents both opportunities and challenges for companies, particularly within the manufacturing sector. The case of Fujifilm BI serves as a compelling illustration of how a strategic commitment to the principles of the CE can yield substantial economic and environmental benefits. By embracing the 3Rs—Reduce, Reuse, and Recycle—Fujifilm BI has not only enhanced its operational efficiency but has also positioned itself as a leader in sustainability within the Japanese manufacturing landscape.

The initial steps taken by Fujifilm BI highlight the importance of visionary leadership and a clear strategy in implementing CE practices. Their journey underscores the need for companies to align their operational goals with sustainability objectives, demonstrating that the adoption of environmentally friendly practices can lead to significant cost reductions and new revenue streams. The company's focus on creating a closed-loop system has enabled it to minimize waste, optimize resource use, and ultimately transform waste into valuable resources. This not only mitigates the environmental impact of production but also enhances the company's competitiveness in a market increasingly driven by sustainability.

Moreover, the robust recycling system established by Fujifilm BI illustrates the necessity of investing in infrastructure and capabilities that support sustainable practices. Their meticulous approach to disassembly, cleaning, and sorting showcases how effective resource management can significantly increase reuse rates and contribute to a circular economy. The company's initiatives, such as the design of smaller, lighter products and the incorporation of recycled materials, reflect a forward-thinking approach that prioritizes both environmental responsibility and consumer satisfaction.

However, it is crucial to acknowledge the broader challenges that many companies face when adopting CE strategies. The initial investment and time required for implementation can deter organizations from fully committing to sustainable practices. Furthermore, the need for cooperation across the supply chain and consumer education emphasizes the complexity of the transition to a circular economy.

In light of these considerations, it is evident that developing specific capabilities to effectively implement the 3Rs is essential for the success of CE strategies. Companies must invest in the necessary infrastructure, foster innovation, and cultivate a culture of sustainability to overcome these challenges. By learning from the experiences of Fujifilm BI and others, Japanese manufacturing firms can establish competitive advantages and contribute to a more sustainable future. Ultimately, the path to a circular economy not only enhances profitability but also fosters environmental stewardship, ensuring that economic growth does not come at the expense of the planet.

References

Alamerew, Y. A., & Brissaud, D. (2020). Modelling reverse supply chain through system dynamics for realizing the transition towards the circular economy: A case study on electric vehicle batteries. Journal of Cleaner Production, 254, 120025.

Asaba, F. (2001). Technological development toward "Bottle to Bottle" for PET bottles. Environmental Technology, 30(10), 797–804.

Bocken, N. M. P., de Pauw, I., Bakker, C., & van der Grinten, B. (2016). Product design and business model strategies for a circular economy. Journal of Industrial and Production Engineering, 33(5), 308–320.

den Hollander, M. C., Bakker, C. A., & Hultink, E. J. (2017). Product design in a circular economy: Development of a typology of key concepts and terms. Journal of Industrial Ecology, 21(3), 517–525.

Dyer, J. H., & Singh, H. (1998). The relational view: Cooperative strategy and sources of interorganizational competitive advantage. Academy of Management Review, 23(4), 660–679.

Fuji Xerox Co., Ltd.(2013). Fuji Xerox 50-Year History 1962–2012.

Generowicz, A., Kowalski, Z., & Kulczycka, J. (2011). Planning of waste management systems in urban area using multi-criteria analysis. Journal of Environmental Protection, 2(6), 736–743.

Geng, Y., Fu, J., Sarkis, J., & Xue, B. (2012). Towards a national circular economy indicator system in China: An evaluation and critical analysis. Journal of Cleaner Production, 23(1), 216–224.

Geyer, R., & Jackson, T. (2004). Supply loops and their constraints: The industrial ecology of recycling and reuse. California Management Review, 46(2), 55–73.

Ghisellini, P., Cialani, C., & Ulgiati, S. (2016). A review on circular economy: The expected transition to a balanced interplay of environmental and economic systems. Journal of Cleaner Production, 114, 11–32.

Govindan, K., & Hasanagic, M. (2018). A systematic review on drivers, barriers, and practices towards circular economy: A supply chain perspective. International Journal of Production Research, 56(1–2), 278–311.

Govindan, K., Soleimani, H., & Kannan, D. (2015). Reverse logistics and closed-loop supply chain: A comprehensive review to explore the future. European Journal of Operational Research, 240(3), 603–626.

Higo, M., Tsunoo, S., & Tanaka, J. (2020). The impact of the circular economy and the direction of Japanese companies: Transition from a mass consumption society to a circular society in the manufacturing industry. Knowledge Creation and Integration, 28(12), 20–33.

Jabbour, C. J. C., & de Sousa Jabbour, A. B. L. (2016). Green human resource management and green supply chain management: Linking two emerging agendas. Journal of cleaner production, 112, 1824–1833.

Kalmykova, Y., Sadagopan, M., & Rosado, L. (2018). Circular economy–From review of theories and practices to development of implementation tools. Resources, conservation and recycling, 135, 190–201.

Kassab, A., Al Nabhani, D., Mohanty, P., Pannier, C., & Ayoub, G. Y. (2023). Advancing plastic recycling: Challenges and opportunities in the integration of 3d printing and distributed recycling for a circular economy. Polymers, 15(19), 3881.

Kirchherr, J., Reike, D., & Hekkert, M. (2017). Conceptualizing the circular economy: An analysis of 114 definitions. Resources, Conservation and Recycling, 127, 221–232.

Kirkman, B. L., Chen, G., Farh, J. L., Chen, Z. X., & Lowe, K. B. (2009). Individual power distance orientation and follower reactions to transformational leaders: A cross-level, cross-cultural examination. Academy of Management Journal, 52(4), 744–764.

Konietzko, J., Bocken, N., & Hultink, E. J. (2020a). Circular ecosystem innovation: An initial set of principles. Journal of Cleaner Production, 253, 119942.

Konietzko, J., Bocken, N., & Hultink, E. J. (2020b). A tool to analyze, ideate and develop circular innovation ecosystems. Sustainability, 12, 417.

Korhonen, J., Honkasalo, A., & Seppälä, J. (2018). Circular economy: the concept and its limitations. Ecological economics, 143, 37–46.

Masoudipour, E., Amirian, H., & Sahraeian, R. (2017). A novel closed-loop supply chain based on the quality of returned products. Journal of Cleaner Production, 151, 344–355.

Ness, D. (2008). Sustainable urban infrastructure in China: Towards a Factor 10 improvement in resource productivity through integrated infrastructure systems. The International Journal of Sustainable Development & World Ecology, 15(4), 288–301.

Östlin, J., Sundin, E., & Björkman, M. (2009). Product life-cycle implications for remanufacturing strategies. Journal of Cleaner Production, 17(11), 999–1009.

Prieto-Sandoval, V., Jaca, C., & Ormazabal, M. (2018). Towards a consensus on the circular economy. Journal of Cleaner Production 179, 605–615.

Schroeder, P., Anggraeni, K., & Weber, U. (2019). The relevance of circular economy practices to the Sustainable Development Goals. Journal of Industrial Ecology, 23, 77–95.

Senoo, K. (2019). From New Production and Sales Doctrine to Existing Product Continued Use Doctrine: A Consideration on the Deconstruction of the 3Rs in Response to the Circular Economy. Proceedings of the Annual Conference of the Japan Society for Research Policy and Innovation Management, 34, 7–10.

Shakhnoza, N. K & Park, Y. W. (2023). Circular Economy in Automobile Industry: Literature Analysis. Management Review: An International Journal, 18(1), 83–113.

Taleizadeh, A. A., Alizadeh-Basban, N., & Niaki, S. T. A. (2019). A closed-loop supply chain considering carbon reduction, quality improvement effort, and return policy under two remanufacturing scenarios. Journal of Cleaner Production, 232, 1230–1250.

Wong, C. Y., Boon-Itt, S., & Wong, C. W. (2011). The contingency effects of environmental uncertainty on the relationship between supply chain integration and operational performance. Journal of Operations management, 29(6), 604–615.

Yin, R. K. (1994). Case study research: Design and methods. SAGE Publications.

Chapter 6
CE Strategy in the Food Industry

Young Won Park

6.1 Introduction

The food industry is at a pivotal juncture, facing numerous challenges that threaten its sustainability and ability to meet the growing demands of a global population. Central among these challenges are food waste, inefficient resource utilization, and environmental degradation, which together undermine the resilience of food systems. To address these issues, the circular economy (CE) has emerged as a transformative framework. By prioritizing resource optimization, waste minimization, and sustainable production and consumption, CE offers a regenerative model that shifts away from the linear 'take-make-dispose" system, presenting a pathway for the food industry to align with global sustainability goals and enhance its long-term viability.

Food waste is a significant concern within the food industry, with global estimates suggesting that approximately one-third of all food produced—equivalent to 1.3 billion tons annually—goes to waste. In Japan, the Ministry of Agriculture, Forestry, and Fisheries (MAFF) reported that food waste reached 25.5 million tons in 2020. This waste is not only an ethical issue, considering the persistent challenges of food insecurity, but also an environmental and economic problem. Disposed food contributes significantly to greenhouse gas emissions, particularly methane, when it decomposes in landfills. Additionally, the cost of managing this waste, coupled with the limited capacity of landfill sites, creates financial and logistical pressures for businesses and municipalities. Adopting CE principles provides a solution by transforming food waste into valuable resources, such as compost or bioenergy, and fostering practices that close the loop within the food supply chain.

The pervasive use of single-use plastics in food packaging represents another challenge. Plastic packaging, while integral to food preservation and safety, accounts for approximately one-third of global plastic production and contributes significantly to environmental pollution. Japan has taken initial steps, such as implementing mandatory charges for plastic bags in 2020, to address the issue. However, the food industry continues to search for sustainable alternatives that maintain the functional benefits of plastic while reducing its environmental footprint. CE-driven solutions, such as

Y. W. Park and K. Tamaki, *Circular Economy Strategy for SDG Business Management*,
https://doi.org/10.1007/978-981-96-4194-9_6

the development of biodegradable and recyclable materials or reusable packaging systems, can help alleviate the industry's reliance on plastics. These strategies also align with consumer expectations for sustainability and offer businesses opportunities to enhance their reputation and gain a competitive edge in the market.

The inefficiencies in resource use within the food industry extend beyond waste management to agricultural practices. Agriculture, as a resource-intensive sector, heavily depends on chemical fertilizers, pesticides, and water, often leading to soil degradation, water scarcity, and biodiversity loss. In a country like Japan, where agricultural land is limited, maximizing resource efficiency is imperative. CE practices, such as utilizing organic waste as compost to improve soil health, can reduce the dependency on chemical inputs, foster environmental conservation, and contribute to sustainable agricultural productivity. This approach supports a stable food supply chain and reduces environmental impact, ensuring the long-term viability of the sector.

Technological advancements play a critical role in enabling the food industry's transition to CE. Tools such as artificial intelligence (AI) and blockchain technology have been instrumental in addressing inefficiencies. AI-powered demand forecasting, for instance, can minimize overproduction and reduce food waste, while blockchain technology enhances traceability within supply chains, ensuring safety and reducing losses. Additionally, innovations in recycling processes allow for the transformation of food by-products—such as coffee grounds, eggshells, and fruit peels—into high-value products like bioplastics, animal feed, or bioenergy (Levidow et al. 2012). These technologies exemplify how integrating CE principles can create new opportunities for sustainability and innovation within the industry.

Beyond environmental benefits, CE practices present significant economic opportunities. By turning waste into valuable resources and optimizing input use, businesses can achieve cost savings and generate new revenue streams. For example, reusing food waste for energy production or creating secondary products reduces disposal costs and opens up profitable avenues. Moreover, circular practices enhance brand image and consumer trust by aligning with growing expectations for sustainability. Companies such as Mizkan and Starbucks Japan have demonstrated leadership by repurposing waste into new products or incorporating sustainable materials into their operations. These efforts not only reduce environmental impact but also enhance market competitiveness in an increasingly eco-conscious business landscape.

The alignment of CE principles with the United Nations Sustainable Development Goals (SDGs) further highlights its relevance. SDG 12, which focuses on responsible consumption and production, is particularly pertinent to the food industry. By adopting CE practices, businesses can contribute to achieving these global objectives and demonstrate leadership in sustainability. Additionally, this alignment opens opportunities for partnerships with governmental and non-governmental organizations, facilitating broader adoption and scaling of circular practices.

However, the transition to CE within the food industry is not without its challenges. Existing regulatory frameworks, market dynamics, and consumer behaviors often hinder the widespread adoption of circular practices. Current regulations may lack sufficient incentives for waste reduction or resource optimization, while market structures can disincentivize investments in CE infrastructure due to perceived risks. Consumer engagement is equally critical; encouraging behaviors such as purchasing surplus food, separating waste for recycling, or using reusable packaging requires targeted education and incentives. Overcoming these barriers will require a collaborative approach involving governments, businesses, academia, and civil society to create an enabling environment for CE.

In Japan, cultural values such as "mottainai" (a sense of regret over waste) provide a unique advantage in advancing CE initiatives. This ethos aligns naturally with CE principles and can be leveraged to foster public acceptance and support for sustainable practices. Additionally, Japan's strong technological foundation and innovation capacity position the country as a leader in developing and implementing CE solutions. These cultural and technical strengths enable Japan to set an example for other nations in adopting circular practices.

The urgency of addressing food industry challenges has never been greater. Climate change, resource depletion, and population growth underscore the need for a paradigm shift in how food is produced, consumed, and disposed of. CE provides a comprehensive framework to meet these challenges by fostering sustainable practices that balance environmental stewardship, economic viability, and social responsibility. The food industry, by embracing CE principles, has the potential to lead by example, demonstrating how innovation and collaboration can drive resilience and sustainability.

This chapter explores the application of CE principles within the food industry, focusing on Japan. It examines the current trends, challenges, and opportunities while highlighting successful case studies and initiatives. By showcasing the operationalization of the 9R framework, this chapter aims to inspire stakeholders across the industry to adopt circular practices, contributing to a sustainable and equitable future for the global food system.

6.2 Circular Economy Trend in the Food Industry

6.2.1 Literature Review of Circular Economy (CE) in the Food Industry and EC Platforms

Circular Economy in the Food Industry: Frameworks, Innovations, and Challenges

The concept of the Circular Economy (CE) has gained global traction as industries seek sustainable solutions to environmental challenges (Korhonen et al. 2018; Park et al. 2024). In the food industry, CE addresses pressing concerns such as resource inefficiency, food waste, and the environmental impacts of production. Pagotto and Halog (2016) highlighted the inefficiencies in Australian agri-food systems, including excessive water consumption, greenhouse gas emissions, and waste generation. Their study underscored the importance of transitioning from linear production systems to circular models that maximize resource efficiency. By employing input–output analysis and material flow analysis, their research revealed the potential of CE to reduce environmental burdens while maintaining competitiveness.

In European contexts, Genovese et al. (2017) demonstrated the benefits of integrating CE principles into food supply chains. Their analysis compared traditional and circular production systems, showing that circular approaches significantly reduced lifecycle emissions and increased resource recovery rates. This aligns with global initiatives such as the United Nations' Sustainable Development Goals (SDGs), particularly Goal 12, which emphasizes responsible consumption and production.

Key innovations driving CE adoption in the food industry include advancements in bioplastics, sustainable packaging, and food waste valorization (Levidow et al. 2012; Kaur et al. 2018; Rosenboom et al. 2022). Rosenboom et al. (2022) explored the role of bioplastics in reducing the carbon footprint of packaging. Derived from renewable materials, bioplastics offer compatibility with existing recycling systems and biodegradability under controlled conditions. However, their large-scale adoption faces challenges, including high costs and potential conflicts with food production.

Geueke et al. (2018) focused on the chemical safety of recycled food packaging, emphasizing the importance of designing materials that balance environmental benefits with consumer safety. Their research highlighted that recycled materials, while environmentally beneficial, can sometimes introduce hazardous chemicals. Addressing this requires redesigning packaging materials to minimize contamination risks.

Food waste valorization is another cornerstone of CE. Principato et al. (2019) examined the pasta supply chain in Italy, emphasizing how CE practices minimized losses. For example, straw from wheat harvests was repurposed as animal feed, while waste from pasta production was recycled into other products. This closed-loop system illustrates the potential for resource recovery to create economic and environmental value.

Despite these innovations, challenges persist in achieving systemic CE adoption. Jurgilevich et al. (2016) explored the socio-technical transitions required to implement CE principles in food systems. Their research emphasized the importance of local "niches"—protected spaces for experimentation and learning. These niches allow stakeholders to develop and test innovative solutions before scaling them across the value chain. However, transitioning to CE requires more than isolated experiments; it demands systemic change supported by robust policies and consumer engagement.

For example, the circular food system must address inefficiencies at various stages of the value chain, from production to consumption. Jurgilevich et al. (2016) noted that inefficiencies in nutrient flow during production and high rates of food waste during consumption are critical areas for intervention. They proposed that socio-technical innovations, such as demand forecasting tools and waste reduction strategies, could bridge these gaps.

Role of Digital Platforms and Collaborative Models in Advancing CE

Digital platforms have emerged as transformative tools in operationalizing CE within the food industry. These platforms leverage technology to enhance resource recovery, reduce waste, and connect stakeholders across the value chain. Ciulli et al. (2020) introduced the concept of "circularity brokers"—digital platforms that act as intermediaries to bridge "circularity holes" in food supply chains. These brokers perform six key roles: connecting, informing, protecting, mobilizing, integrating, and measuring. By facilitating the transfer of surplus food from waste generators to potential users, these platforms reduce inefficiencies and promote circularity.

The rise of food-sharing platforms exemplifies how digital technology supports CE. Michelini et al. (2018) categorized these platforms into three models: sharing for money, sharing for charity, and sharing for the community. Platforms like food banks and social supermarkets have transitioned into the digital space, enabling wider reach and greater efficiency. For instance, digital marketplaces connect businesses with surplus food to consumers and charitable organizations, ensuring that excess resources are repurposed rather than discarded.

One notable example is food-sharing apps like OLIO and Too Good To Go, which allow consumers to purchase surplus food at discounted prices. These platforms not only reduce food waste but also provide economic benefits to users and vendors. Additionally, they foster a sense of community by connecting individuals who share a common goal of sustainability.

E-commerce platforms have also played a pivotal role in advancing CE principles. For example, platforms such as "TABETE" and "Kuradashi" in Japan focus on redistributing surplus food. TABETE connects users with stores and restaurants that have unsold food, offering consumers high-quality products at lower prices while reducing food waste (Kuradashi 2024). Similarly, Kuradashi collaborates with manufacturers to sell surplus goods online, providing consumers with discounted items and reducing the environmental impact of waste disposal.

Collaboration is another key element of CE implementation. Public–private partnerships and cross-industry collaborations enable the development of robust infrastructures for waste management and recycling. Muscio and Sisto (2020) emphasized the importance of aligning research and innovation agendas with CE principles. They argued that collaborative models, involving governments, businesses, and NGOs, are essential for scaling CE practices. For example, partnerships between municipalities and private companies have facilitated the development of waste-to-energy systems, converting organic waste into biogas for renewable energy production.

Technology also enhances transparency and efficiency in CE practices. Blockchain systems provide traceability across supply chains, ensuring that surplus food is redistributed safely and efficiently. AI-powered demand forecasting tools help businesses optimize inventory management, reducing overproduction and minimizing waste.

Consumer engagement is equally critical in advancing CE through digital platforms. Educational campaigns and incentives encourage individuals to adopt sustainable behaviors, such as purchasing surplus food or using reusable packaging. Loyalty programs and discounts for eco-friendly actions further motivate consumers to participate in CE initiatives.

Despite their potential, digital platforms face challenges in scaling CE practices. Ciulli et al. (2020) noted that successful implementation requires overcoming barriers such as inadequate infrastructure, regulatory constraints, and limited consumer awareness. To address these issues, policymakers must support digital innovation through funding, subsidies, and streamlined regulations.

In conclusion, digital platforms and collaborative efforts are transforming the food industry by advancing CE principles. They address critical inefficiencies in waste management, foster community engagement, and promote sustainable practices. By integrating technology and collaboration, these platforms empower stakeholders to transition toward a more sustainable and circular food system.

6.2.2 CE Trends in the Japanese Food Industry

The Japanese food industry grapples with multifaceted challenges, including high food waste volumes, dependence on plastic packaging, and low food self-sufficiency. CE offers innovative pathways to address these issues.

Driving Forces Behind CE in the Japanese Food Industry

Japan faces mounting challenges in achieving sustainability within its food industry. Issues such as food loss, limited natural resources, and environmental degradation have prompted the adoption of Circular Economy (CE) principles. The Ministry of the Environment and related agencies have actively promoted food recycling legislation, establishing a robust framework for waste management and resource recovery. By implementing the Food Recycling Law, the government has outlined ambitious targets to reduce food waste and transform waste streams into valuable resources. This legislation encourages collaboration among producers, distributors, and consumers, creating a circular ecosystem within the industry.

Additionally, Japan's CE initiatives align with global movements such as the UN Sustainable Development Goals (SDGs), particularly Goal 12, which focuses on responsible consumption and production. With increasing public awareness and government support, businesses are integrating CE principles into their operations, recognizing their potential to reduce costs, enhance brand image, and contribute to a sustainable society. Moreover, advancements in technology, such as AI-driven demand forecasting and innovative recycling solutions, have catalyzed progress in achieving a circular food system.

Policies like the "3Rs" (Reduce, Reuse, Recycle) and the Basic Environmental Plan serve as guiding principles for businesses and municipalities. These initiatives encourage resource efficiency, promote composting, and incentivize innovation in packaging design to reduce environmental impact. For example, subsidies and tax benefits have been provided to companies investing in recycling technologies or waste reduction strategies. Such frameworks are instrumental in driving CE adoption in Japan's food industry, making it a model for integrating circularity in developed economies.

Innovations and Practices Driving CE Adoption

Food loss reduction is a cornerstone of CE in Japan. The "1/3 Rule," which governs food distribution, has historically contributed to significant food waste. However, reforms are underway to relax these strict guidelines and enable better inventory management. Companies are also leveraging technology to optimize production and minimize waste. AI-driven systems predict demand more accurately, while blockchain ensures traceability, reducing losses along the supply chain.

Major retail chains, such as Lawson and AEON, have implemented strategies to sell products nearing expiration dates at discounted prices, encouraging consumers to purchase items that might otherwise go to waste. Additionally, initiatives like "mottainai campaigns" foster consumer awareness about the environmental and social costs of food waste. These campaigns have proven effective in shifting societal attitudes and promoting sustainable consumption patterns.

The recycling of food waste into animal feed, fertilizer, and bioenergy exemplifies CE in action. Companies like Nichirei and Kirin Brewery are repurposing waste materials into new products, transforming a liability into a revenue stream. Nichirei processes leftover food from production lines into livestock feed, ensuring that valuable nutrients are not wasted (Nichirei Corporation 2024). Similarly, Kirin utilizes spent grain from beer production to create high-protein animal feed, reducing dependency on imported feed ingredients.

Composting initiatives have also gained traction, with municipalities and private firms collaborating to convert organic waste into nutrient-rich fertilizers. These fertilizers are then supplied to local farmers, closing the nutrient loop and supporting sustainable agriculture. Such practices demonstrate how CE principles can create synergies between different sectors, reducing environmental impact while generating economic benefits.

Then, packaging waste remains a critical issue in Japan, particularly due to the reliance on single-use plastics. The introduction of biodegradable and reusable packaging has become a priority for many food companies. For example, Suntory and Asahi Breweries have pioneered plant-based plastics, reducing their environmental footprint while meeting consumer demands for sustainable products(Suntory Holdings 2024). Moreover, initiatives like the "Bring Your Own Bag" campaign and the implementation of plastic bag fees have successfully curbed the use of disposable packaging.

Efforts to standardize packaging materials for recyclability have also been instrumental. Collaboration between manufacturers, retailers, and waste management companies ensures that packaging can be easily sorted and processed. Innovations such as mono-material packaging and smart labeling systems further enhance the recyclability of materials, promoting a circular economy in the food packaging sector.

Collaborative Efforts for CE Implementation

Collaboration between government bodies, corporations, and NGOs has been vital in scaling CE practices. Public–private partnerships have facilitated the development of infrastructure for waste collection, processing, and recycling. For example, the Kyoto Food Waste Reduction Network brings together local governments, businesses, and citizens to implement city-wide initiatives for reducing food waste. This network has successfully decreased waste sent to landfills while promoting community engagement and awareness.

Next, cross-sectoral collaboration is another pillar of CE in Japan. Companies from diverse industries are pooling resources and expertise to create innovative solutions. For instance, beverage manufacturers and logistics providers have joined forces to establish closed-loop systems for packaging. By recovering and reprocessing used materials, they ensure that resources are reused rather than discarded. Similarly, partnerships between food producers and energy firms are transforming organic waste into biogas, providing renewable energy and reducing greenhouse gas emissions.

Then, consumer participation is essential for the success of CE initiatives. Education campaigns and awareness programs have been rolled out to inform the public about the importance of reducing waste and supporting sustainable practices. Supermarkets and restaurants are also incentivizing consumers through loyalty programs and discounts for eco-friendly behavior, such as bringing reusable containers or purchasing "ugly" produce. These efforts are gradually reshaping consumer habits, making sustainability a mainstream priority.

Japan's progress in implementing CE principles offers valuable lessons for other nations. The integration of advanced technologies, supportive policies, and collaborative frameworks demonstrates the potential of CE to address pressing environmental and social challenges. As global interest in CE grows, Japan's food industry serves as a benchmark for innovation and sustainability. By sharing best practices and fostering international collaboration, Japan can contribute to the global transition toward a circular economy.

The transition to a Circular Economy in Japan's food industry is driven by a combination of regulatory support, technological innovation, and collaborative efforts. By addressing food loss, enhancing recycling practices, and promoting sustainable packaging, the industry is making significant strides toward reducing its environmental footprint. However, challenges remain, including the need for greater consumer engagement and the development of scalable solutions.

As Japan continues to refine its approach to CE, its food industry exemplifies the transformative potential of circular practices. By fostering innovation and collaboration, the industry not only contributes to national sustainability goals but also sets a global example for achieving a more sustainable and resilient future.

6.2.3 The 9R Framework

The integration of the 9R framework—Refuse, Rethink, Reduce, Reuse, Repair, Refurbish, Remanufacture, Repurpose, and Recycle—provides a comprehensive structure for aligning Circular Economy (CE) principles with the operational realities of the food industry (Park et al. 2024). This section builds upon the global and Japanese trends outlined earlier, connecting their practices and innovations to each of the 9R strategies.

The literature review of CE in the food industry highlighted key global frameworks and innovations, emphasizing the need for systemic shifts to address inefficiencies in food systems. For instance, Pagotto and Halog (2016) revealed the potential for circular models to mitigate resource-intensive practices, while Genovese et al. (2017) demonstrated how integrating CE into supply chains significantly reduces lifecycle emissions and resource waste. These insights resonate with the 9R strategies, particularly in the areas of Reduce, Recycle, and Repurpose. Practices such as bioplastics development and food waste valorization align with recycling and repurposing strategies, as illustrated by the efforts of Rosenboom et al. (2022) and Principato et al. (2019).

In Japan, where CE trends are shaped by cultural values such as "mottainai" and regulatory support for sustainable practices, the 9R framework finds a natural application. The country's innovative use of AI-driven forecasting, blockchain for supply chain transparency, and the promotion of sustainable packaging exemplifies the principles of Refuse, Rethink, and Reduce. For instance, initiatives like the relaxation of the "1/3 Rule" for food distribution address the Reduce strategy by minimizing unnecessary food loss through smarter inventory management. Similarly, Suntory and Asahi Breweries' adoption of plant-based plastics reflects a commitment to Refuse unsustainable materials in favor of environmentally friendly alternatives.

The Reuse and Repair strategies are evident in Japan's focus on recycling food waste into valuable resources. Companies like Nichirei and Kirin Brewery transform food production byproducts into animal feed and fertilizer, aligning with the Reuse principle. Meanwhile, rethink-focused initiatives, such as modular product design and community composting programs, underscore the importance of keeping materials and products in use for as long as possible.

Refurbish, Remanufacture, and Repurpose strategies find practical applications in Japan's collaborative CE efforts. Cross-industry partnerships, such as those between beverage manufacturers and logistics providers, establish closed-loop systems that embody these strategies. For instance, repurposing spent grain into biogas or protein supplements demonstrates how food industry byproducts can be reintegrated into other sectors, creating multi-functional uses for materials that would otherwise be discarded.

The Recycle strategy in Japan goes beyond traditional recycling to include advanced innovations such as mono-material packaging and the use of smart labeling systems to enhance material recoverability. Public–private collaborations, like the

Kyoto Food Waste Reduction Network, further amplify recycling efforts by fostering community engagement and infrastructure development.

The 9R framework also bridges technological and collaborative models discussed before. Digital platforms such as TABETE and Kuradashi operationalize strategies like Refuse and Rethink by enabling surplus food redistribution and aligning consumer behavior with CE principles. These platforms also support the Reuse and Recycle strategies by ensuring surplus food and packaging materials are effectively utilized rather than discarded. Moreover, these platforms serve as circularity brokers, integrating supply chain actors to close the loop and reduce inefficiencies.

In conclusion, the 9R framework offers a cohesive lens through which the global and Japanese approaches to CE can be assessed and applied. It encapsulates the critical innovations, policies, and collaborative models discussed earlier while emphasizing the need for holistic and integrated strategies. By addressing every stage of a product's lifecycle—from design and production to consumption and disposal—the 9R framework underscores the transformative potential of CE in reshaping the food industry for a sustainable future. As Japan and the global community continue to refine their CE practices, the 9R framework remains a valuable tool for achieving systemic sustainability.

6.3 Case Studies

6.3.1 Food Loss Reduction Cases

The issue of food loss has become a pressing global concern, particularly in regions with industrialized food production systems. Food loss, which refers to edible food discarded at various stages of production and consumption, contributes significantly to environmental degradation through greenhouse gas emissions and resource wastage. In Japan, initiatives aimed at reducing food loss have taken center stage in addressing these environmental and societal challenges. These case studies illustrate innovative strategies employed by companies and municipalities to tackle food loss effectively.

One prominent example is the collaboration between municipalities and large food manufacturers, such as the partnership between Kyoto City and Mizkan Group. Mizkan, a leading producer of condiments and sauces, has undertaken initiatives to address food loss through product innovation and community collaboration. In partnership with Kyoto City, Mizkan developed a series of recipes designed to make use of often-discarded food parts, such as vegetable peels and stems. For instance, the "Mottainai Nabe" ("Nothing-Wasted Hotpot") and "Mottainai Pickles" recipes aim to educate consumers on minimizing waste while enjoying nutritious meals. By showcasing these recipes on their official website and social media platforms, Mizkan effectively engages households and encourages sustainable consumption practices (Mizkan Group 2024).

Starbucks Japan provides another compelling example. The company has implemented a robust recycling program that repurposes coffee grounds, a major byproduct of its operations, into agricultural compost (Starbucks Japan 2024). This compost is used to grow vegetables and other crops, which are subsequently reintegrated into the Starbucks supply chain. For example, sandwiches and baked goods in select Starbucks outlets feature ingredients grown using this recycled compost. By doing so, Starbucks not only reduces its environmental footprint but also creates a circular model that integrates waste management and food production.

Another notable effort is seen in food waste management systems adopted by restaurants and dining chains. Ume-no-Hana, a popular chain specializing in tofu-based cuisine, utilizes food waste from its central kitchens to produce organic fertilizers. This practice exemplifies a "food loop" model, where waste generated during meal preparation is reinvested into agricultural production. This closed-loop system minimizes disposal costs, reduces greenhouse gas emissions, and supports local farmers by providing high-quality fertilizers.

Japan's Ministry of Agriculture, Forestry, and Fisheries (MAFF) has also been proactive in promoting food loss reduction through regulatory measures and public awareness campaigns (MAFF 2024). For instance, the "One-Third Rule" governing food distribution has been relaxed to prevent premature disposal of unsold items. The revised regulation allows retailers to extend the sale period for perishable goods, encouraging better inventory management and reducing waste at the distribution level.

Educational initiatives also play a significant role in food loss reduction. Organizations such as the "Food Bank Japan" facilitate the redistribution of surplus food to those in need. By partnering with retailers and food manufacturers, these food banks ensure that consumable goods nearing their expiration dates are distributed to charitable organizations and low-income households rather than being discarded. Such practices exemplify the potential of community-driven solutions to address food insecurity while reducing waste.

Finally, technology-driven solutions have emerged as a key driver of food loss reduction. For instance, artificial intelligence (AI) and machine learning algorithms are being deployed to optimize supply chain logistics and demand forecasting. These technologies enable producers and retailers to align supply with demand more accurately, minimizing surplus inventory and reducing waste. Companies such as Lawson, a leading convenience store chain in Japan, use AI-powered systems to predict demand for bento boxes and ready-to-eat meals, ensuring that production and stock levels are closely aligned with consumer behavior.

Through these diverse approaches, Japan demonstrates a commitment to tackling food loss through innovative, collaborative, and technology-enabled strategies. By engaging stakeholders across the supply chain, from producers to consumers, these initiatives highlight the potential for systemic change in reducing food waste and promoting sustainability.

6.3.2 Food E-commerce Platform Cases

E-commerce has emerged as a transformative platform for addressing food loss by enabling efficient distribution, promoting food-sharing models, and fostering direct connections between producers and consumers. Several innovative e-commerce platforms in Japan have been instrumental in minimizing food waste while supporting sustainable food systems. Below, we explore key cases illustrating the integration of circular economy principles in the food e-commerce sector.

One notable example is TABETE, a pioneering food-sharing application. TABETE connects users with businesses that have surplus food, such as bakeries, supermarkets, and restaurants (TABETE 2024). Through the app, businesses list items that are safe to consume but at risk of being discarded due to low demand or approaching expiration dates. Consumers can browse available items, purchase them at discounted rates, and pick them up at designated locations. By creating this direct link, TABETE significantly reduces food waste while providing affordable meal options for consumers. As of 2022, TABETE boasted over 520,000 registered users and 2,100 partner businesses, including major retail chains and local eateries. This model not only addresses food loss but also strengthens community ties and promotes environmental consciousness.

Kuradashi, another impactful platform, operates as a "social good marketplace" with a focus on reducing food waste (Kuradashi 2024). Kuradashi collaborates with manufacturers to sell surplus or near-expiration products at heavily discounted prices. The platform's unique value proposition includes donating a portion of its sales revenue to social and environmental causes. For example, funds generated through Kuradashi's operations have supported food bank initiatives and environmental conservation projects. By aligning economic incentives with social responsibility, Kuradashi exemplifies how e-commerce can drive sustainable practices in the food industry.

WakeAi is yet another e-commerce model designed to mitigate food loss while supporting local producers and small businesses. Originally launched during the COVID-19 pandemic to address supply chain disruptions, WakeAi has evolved into a socially conscious marketplace where consumers can purchase surplus food products at discounted prices. The platform's unique feature lies in its support for food bank programs, ensuring that unsold items reach vulnerable populations. WakeAi's model demonstrates the potential of e-commerce platforms to act as intermediaries between surplus and need, effectively reducing waste while promoting social equity.

The case of rebake highlights the potential for specialized e-commerce platforms to target niche markets. Focused on artisanal baked goods, rebake connects bakeries with surplus inventory to consumers seeking high-quality, affordable products. Consumers can purchase "lost bread" or surplus baked goods at discounted prices, which are then delivered to their homes. This platform not only reduces waste but also provides an additional revenue stream for small businesses while introducing consumers to unique culinary experiences.

Tabechoku, an innovative direct-to-consumer platform, addresses food loss by connecting consumers with local producers. Unlike traditional e-commerce platforms, Tabechoku emphasizes the importance of "local-to-local" transactions, reducing the need for extensive logistics and packaging. Farmers and producers can list their fresh produce, often including imperfect or surplus items, which consumers purchase directly (Tabechoku 2024). This model reduces waste by creating a market for products that might otherwise be discarded due to cosmetic imperfections or overproduction. Moreover, Tabechoku enhances transparency and trust between producers and consumers, fostering a sense of shared responsibility for sustainable food systems.

Several factors contribute to the success of these platforms. Firstly, technological innovation plays a pivotal role in facilitating real-time inventory management and customer engagement. AI-driven analytics and user-friendly interfaces allow platforms to match supply with demand effectively. Secondly, these platforms leverage social and environmental incentives to attract users, aligning consumer values with sustainable practices. Lastly, collaboration with stakeholders across the supply chain, including producers, retailers, and consumers, ensures the scalability and sustainability of these initiatives.

The economic impact of food e-commerce platforms extends beyond waste reduction. By creating new markets for surplus goods, these platforms enhance the profitability of producers and retailers while offering cost savings to consumers. Furthermore, they contribute to job creation in logistics, technology development, and customer service, illustrating the broader economic benefits of integrating circular economy principles into e-commerce.

In conclusion, food e-commerce platforms such as TABETE, Kuradashi, WakeAi, rebake, and Tabechoku exemplify innovative solutions to food loss. By combining technology, social responsibility, and economic incentives, these platforms redefine the relationship between food production and consumption. As the e-commerce sector continues to evolve, its role in addressing food loss and promoting sustainability will likely expand, offering valuable insights for other industries seeking to adopt circular economy practices.

6.3.3 *Case Analysis with 9R Framework*

The comparison of the case studies within the framework of the 9R principles—Recycle, Remanufacture, Reuse, Refuse, Rethink, Reduce, Repair, Refurbish, and Repurpose—reveals the diverse ways circular economy principles are implemented in addressing food loss and promoting sustainability in the food industry. Recycling is prominently demonstrated in food loss reduction cases such as Starbucks Japan's transformation of coffee grounds into agricultural compost and Ume-no-Hana's use of food waste for organic fertilizers. In contrast, food e-commerce platforms indirectly contribute to recycling by preventing surplus food from entering waste streams, reducing reliance on conventional waste management processes.

Remanufacturing finds expression in Mizkan's development of recipes like "Mottainai Pickles," where vegetable peels and stems are turned into consumable products. Food e-commerce platforms like Tabechoku align with remanufacturing by creating markets for imperfect produce that might otherwise be discarded. Reuse is exemplified in Starbucks Japan's circular model, which integrates compost-grown produce back into its supply chain, and in TABETE's redistribution of surplus food to consumers, ensuring its primary purpose of consumption is fulfilled.

Refusing unnecessary waste practices is evident in the regulatory changes, such as Japan's relaxation of the "One-Third Rule," which allow perishable goods to stay in circulation longer, while e-commerce platforms like rebake refuse to let artisanal bread go to waste by ensuring surplus inventory is sold. Rethinking consumption and distribution models is reflected in food loss reduction campaigns like "Mottainai," which encourage households to rethink food usage, and WakeAi's redesign of supply chain dynamics to connect surplus producers with consumers and food banks through technology.

Reducing waste is actively pursued in both cases. AI-powered demand forecasting used by companies like Lawson minimizes overproduction, while platforms such as TABETE and Kuradashi efficiently manage surplus inventory, directly addressing overproduction and underutilization. Repair, though less applicable to food systems, is analogous in food loss reduction cases where resources like food waste are "repaired" into compost or animal feed for environmental use, whereas in e-commerce platforms, this principle is less prominently featured.

Refurbishing is reflected in Mizkan's repurposing of discarded food parts into new recipes and rebake's creative approach to selling surplus artisanal baked goods, ensuring these products find new markets. Repurposing is strongly demonstrated in Ume-no-Hana's transformation of kitchen waste into fertilizers and Starbucks Japan's use of coffee grounds for compost, as well as in Kuradashi and WakeAi's innovative strategies to repurpose surplus food into discounted sales items or donations for social initiatives.

6.4 Conclusion

The focus on reducing food loss and integrating circular economy principles into food systems, as demonstrated in the case studies and applications discussed, signals a transformative shift in how the food industry approaches sustainability. The challenges of food waste, resource inefficiency, and environmental degradation are formidable; yet, they are met with innovative strategies and collaborative efforts that underscore the potential for systemic change. This chapter has provided insights into the implementation of circular economy strategies through diverse initiatives, revealing their capacity to create environmental, economic, and social value.

The overarching theme of this chapter emphasizes the critical role of the 9R framework—Recycle, Remanufacture, Reuse, Refuse, Rethink, Reduce, Repair, Refurbish, and Repurpose—as a guiding structure for fostering sustainability in the food industry. This framework serves as a comprehensive approach to addressing waste and inefficiency at various stages of the food value chain, from production to consumption. By comparing case studies such as food loss reduction initiatives and food e-commerce platforms, it becomes evident that the principles of circularity are not only viable but also adaptable across different operational contexts and stakeholder groups.

Key takeaways from the analysis illustrate that recycling and repurposing, while central to many initiatives, are most impactful when integrated with other elements of the 9R framework. For instance, the efforts of Starbucks Japan to recycle coffee grounds into agricultural compost and reintegrate them into their supply chain highlight the importance of creating closed-loop systems that maximize resource efficiency. Similarly, e-commerce platforms such as TABETE and Kuradashi demonstrate the power of digital innovation in enabling reuse by connecting surplus food with consumers and organizations that need it. These practices not only reduce waste but also generate economic benefits and foster social equity.

Another crucial insight is the value of rethinking and refusing traditional models of production and consumption. The relaxation of Japan's "One-Third Rule" exemplifies how policy changes can reduce waste by encouraging better inventory management and reducing premature disposal. At the same time, the consumer-focused campaigns, such as the "Mottainai" movement, inspire individuals to rethink their relationship with food and adopt more sustainable consumption habits. These behavioral changes are critical in complementing technological and operational advancements, ensuring the longevity and scalability of circular practices.

The integration of technology, particularly through digital platforms and artificial intelligence, emerges as a transformative force in operationalizing circular economy principles. AI-driven demand forecasting, as seen in Lawson's operations, minimizes overproduction and aligns supply with actual consumer demand. Meanwhile, digital platforms like WakeAi and rebake provide innovative solutions for surplus food redistribution, reducing waste and creating new markets for undervalued goods. These examples underscore the importance of leveraging technology not just as a tool for efficiency but as a catalyst for systemic change in food systems.

Collaboration stands out as a recurring theme in the successful implementation of circular economy initiatives. Public–private partnerships, cross-industry collaborations, and community-driven efforts form the backbone of many successful strategies. For example, the partnership between Kyoto City and Mizkan Group illustrates how municipalities and businesses can work together to create educational programs and innovative products that reduce waste while fostering community engagement. Similarly, food banks and food-sharing platforms demonstrate the potential of grassroots and organizational collaborations in addressing food insecurity and reducing waste simultaneously.

Despite the progress highlighted in these case studies, challenges remain. Regulatory frameworks need to evolve further to incentivize circular practices and eliminate barriers to innovation. Market structures must adapt to prioritize long-term sustainability over short-term gains, and businesses need to overcome perceived risks associated with investing in circular infrastructure. Moreover, consumer education and engagement remain critical, as the success of many initiatives depends on individuals adopting sustainable behaviors, such as separating waste for recycling, purchasing surplus food, or using reusable packaging.

In the context of Japan, cultural values such as "mottainai" provide a unique advantage in fostering public acceptance and participation in circular economy initiatives. By aligning circular practices with these deeply ingrained cultural principles, stakeholders can effectively mobilize societal support for sustainability efforts. Furthermore, Japan's technological expertise and innovative capacity position it as a global leader in developing and implementing circular solutions, particularly in addressing food loss and waste.

Looking ahead, the potential for scaling and replicating these initiatives across global contexts presents a significant opportunity. Japan's progress offers valuable lessons for other countries seeking to adopt circular economy principles in their food systems. The integration of advanced technologies, supportive policies, and collaborative frameworks demonstrated in these case studies provides a blueprint for tackling similar challenges in diverse settings. By sharing best practices and fostering international collaboration, Japan can contribute to the global transition toward a more sustainable and resilient food industry.

In conclusion, the application of the 9R framework within the food industry exemplifies the transformative potential of the circular economy. By addressing food loss, enhancing recycling and reuse practices, and fostering innovation and collaboration, stakeholders are not only reducing environmental impacts but also creating economic opportunities and social benefits. The case studies explored in this chapter highlight the multidimensional advantages of circular practices, demonstrating that sustainability and profitability can coexist. As the food industry continues to evolve, embracing the principles of circularity will be essential for building a future that balances ecological integrity, economic viability, and social well-being. Through sustained effort and collaboration, the transition to a circular economy in the food sector holds the promise of a more sustainable and equitable world.

References

Ciulli, F., Kolk, A., & Boe-Lillegraven, S. (2020). Circularity Brokers: Digital Platform Organizations and Waste Recovery in Food Supply Chains. Journal of Business Ethics, 167(2), 299–331. https://doi.org/10.1007/s10551-019-04160-5.

Genovese, A., Acquaye, A. A., Figueroa, A., & Koh, S. C. L. (2017). Sustainable Supply Chain Management and the Transition Towards a Circular Economy: Evidence and Some Applications. Omega, 66, Part B, 344–357. https://doi.org/10.1016/j.omega.2015.05.015.

Geueke, B., Groh, K., & Muncke, J. (2018). Food Packaging in the Circular Economy: Overview of Chemical Safety Aspects for Commonly Used Materials. Journal of Cleaner Production, 193, 491–505. https://doi.org/10.1016/j.jclepro.2018.05.005.

Jurgilevich, A., Birge, T., Kentala-Lehtonen, J., Korhonen-Kurki, K., Pietikäinen, J., Saikku, L., & Schösler, H. (2016). Transition Towards Circular Economy in the Food System. Sustainability, 8(1), 69. https://doi.org/10.3390/su8010069.

Kaur, G., Uisan, K., Ong, K. L., & Lin, C. S. K. (2018). Recent Trends in Green and Sustainable Chemistry & Waste Valorisation: Rethinking Plastics in a Circular Economy. Current Opinion in Green and Sustainable Chemistry, 9, 30–39. https://doi.org/10.1016/j.cogsc.2017.11.003.

Korhonen, J., Honkasalo, A., & Seppälä, J. (2018). Circular Economy: The Concept and Its Limitations. Ecological Economics, 143, 37–46. https://doi.org/10.1016/j.ecolecon.2017.06.041.

Kuradashi. (2024). Social Good Marketplace for Surplus Food. Retrieved from https://www.kuradashi.jp.

Levidow, L., Birch, K., & Papaioannou, T. (2012). Divergent Paradigms of European Agro-Food Innovation: The Knowledge-Based Bio-Economy (KBBE) as an R&D Agenda. Science, Technology, & Human Values, 38(1), 94–125. https://doi.org/10.1177/0162243912438143.

MAFF. (2024). Food Loss and Recycling Policies in Japan. Ministry of Agriculture, Forestry, and Fisheries of Japan, Retrieved from https://www.maff.go.jp.

Michelini, L., Principato, L., & Iasevoli, G. (2018). Understanding Food Sharing Models to Tackle Sustainability Challenges. Ecological Economics, 145, 205–217. https://doi.org/10.1016/j.ecolecon.2017.11.006.

Mizkan Group. (2024). Official Website. Initiatives on Food Waste Reduction. Retrieved from https://www.mizkan.com.

Muscio, A., & Sisto, R. (2020). Are Agri-Food Systems Really Switching to a Circular Economy Model? Implications for European Research and Innovation Policy. Sustainability, 12(14), 5554. https://doi.org/10.3390/su12145554.

Nichirei Corporation (2024). Recycling Food Waste into Livestock Feed. Retrieved from https://www.nichirei.co.jp.

Pagotto, M., & Halog, A. (2016). Towards a Circular Economy in Australian Agri-food Industry: An Application of Input-Output Oriented Approaches for Analyzing Resource Efficiency and Competitiveness Potential. Journal of Industrial Ecology, 20(5), 1176–1186 https://doi.org/10.1111/jiec.12373.

Park, Y.W., Sugie, R., & Mizuguchi, K. (2024). Circular Economy Strategy of Japanese Firms: A Comparative Study of Manufacturing and Other Industries. Communication of JIMA, 34(1), 15–22.

Principato, L., Ruini, L., Guidi, M., & Secondi, L. (2019). Adopting the Circular Economy Approach on Food Loss and Waste: The Case of Italian Pasta Production. Resources, Conservation and Recycling, 144, 82–89. https://doi.org/10.1016/j.resconrec.2019.01.025.

Rosenboom, J. G., Langer, R., & Traverso, G. (2022). Bioplastics for a Circular Economy. Nature Reviews Materials, 7, 117–137. https://doi.org/10.1038/s41578-021-00350-8.

Starbucks Japan. (2024). Recycling Coffee Grounds for Sustainable Agriculture. Retrieved from https://www.starbucks.co.jp.

Suntory Holdings. (2024). Bioplastics Innovation in Packaging. Retrieved from https://www.suntory.com

TABETE. (2024). Food Sharing Platform for Surplus Food Reduction. Retrieved from https://www.tabete.me.

Tabechoku, (2024). Mottainai Mikan. Retrieved from https://www.tabechoku.com/products/123587?srsltid=AfmBOop1MWfWxBP16EaLWDZl6Gc_LqfgQFiJVX3MMCQ93ATTZQ5NGoeA.

Chapter 7
CE Strategy in the Electric Vehicle Batteries Industry

Young Won Park and Shota Inoue

7.1 Introduction

The global movement toward sustainability has spurred a paradigm shift, with the Circular Economy (CE) emerging as a cornerstone for aligning industrial practices with the goals of the Sustainable Development Goals (SDGs). This transformative framework prioritizes reducing waste, optimizing resource use, and fostering sustainable consumption and production patterns. The automotive sector, particularly electric vehicle batteries (EVBs), has become a critical focus within this transition, driven by evolving technological advancements and innovative recycling strategies.

The journey toward achieving a CE model highlights the interconnected benefits of environmental preservation, resource security, and economic growth. However, the path is fraught with challenges, including technological limitations, regulatory gaps, consumer behavior complexities, and the need for significant industrial restructuring. Overcoming these obstacles requires multi-sectoral collaboration, emphasizing collective efforts to navigate the transition successfully.

The EVB market has undergone profound changes, fueled by the global surge in electric vehicle (EV) adoption. This growth has reshaped market dynamics, shifting global shares among countries and manufacturers. Technological advancements, particularly the evolution from traditional lithium-ion batteries to solid-state batteries, underscore progress in safety, energy density, and lifecycle longevity.

This study delves into global EVB recycling strategies through comprehensive case studies. While prior research on CE trends in EVBs often focuses on specific technologies or single-country initiatives (Rönkkö et al. 2024), this study provides a broader comparative analysis. By examining pioneering recycling strategies in Europe, China, and Japan, it identifies diverse approaches, technologies, and focal points, offering valuable insights into overcoming recycling challenges. This work highlights the potential for CE practices to transform the automotive sector, contributing to a more sustainable future aligned with the SDGs.

Y. W. Park and K. Tamaki, *Circular Economy Strategy for SDG Business Management*,
https://doi.org/10.1007/978-981-96-4194-9_7

7.2 Trends in the Circular Economy of Electric Vehicle Batteries (EVBs)

The circular economy (CE) has emerged as a compelling strategy to achieve sustainability across economic, environmental, and social dimensions. By aligning with the Sustainable Development Goals (SDGs), CE promotes minimizing waste, optimizing resource efficiency, and encouraging sustainable consumption and production patterns (Shakhnoza and Park 2023; Park et al. 2024). In response to global challenges such as resource scarcity, waste generation, and environmental degradation, the shift from a linear "take-make-dispose" model to a circular system offers a regenerative solution that maximizes resource use while minimizing environmental impacts.

Electric vehicle batteries (EVBs) lie at the heart of this transition, driven by the global acceleration toward electric vehicles (EVs) as a means to reduce greenhouse gas emissions and combat climate change (Deveci et al. 2021; Elgowainy et al. 2018; Roy et al. 2022). The increasing adoption of EVs highlights the need for sustainable management practices throughout the lifecycle of EVBs (Bonsu 2020). These practices are essential not only for minimizing environmental damage but also for addressing the significant resource requirements associated with battery production.

Recent years have witnessed rapid growth in the global EV market, spurred by advancements in technology, government incentives, and rising consumer demand for cleaner transportation options. Circular economy principles provide a framework for enhancing the value and longevity of EVBs while reducing their environmental footprint (Albertsen et al. 2021; Jaffe 2017; Rönkkö et al. 2024). However, EVB production is highly energy-intensive, and its environmental and social implications include resource extraction challenges and human rights concerns (Albertsen et al. 2021; Deng 2015).

Managing EVBs at the end of their lifecycle presents complex challenges. The batteries' composition, which includes hazardous materials, poses environmental risks, while their recyclability remains limited due to technological and economic constraints (Olsson et al. 2018; Saxena et al. 2015). Nevertheless, circular economy practices such as reuse, repurposing, and recycling offer substantial opportunities for improving sustainability in EVB management (Saxena et al. 2015; Harper et al. 2019). The development and implementation of robust policy and regulatory frameworks are critical for driving this transition (European Commission 2020).

7.2.1 *Research and Innovations in EVB Circular Economy Practices*

Recent studies have explored various facets of EVB management within the CE framework, providing insights into emerging trends, challenges, and innovations. Groenewald et al. (2017) introduced a novel method to accelerate the testing of lithium-ion cells, significantly reducing the time required for battery characterization while maintaining measurement accuracy. This advancement facilitates the assessment of EVBs for second-life applications, supporting the broader goals of a circular economy.

Reinhardt et al. (2019) examined sustainable business models (SBMs) in the battery second-use (B2U) industry. Their research emphasized a network-centric design involving multiple stakeholders, promoting sustainability in both the EV industry and the emerging B2U market. By integrating environmental, economic, and social considerations, this approach seeks to address current unsustainable practices while accelerating the adoption of CE principles.

Recycling technology has also seen significant advancements. Mossali et al. (2020) reviewed existing methods for recycling lithium-ion batteries, focusing on processes for battery disassembly, material recovery, and securing hazardous components. Their analysis highlighted technological solutions proposed by research projects and industrial initiatives, identifying critical gaps and areas for improvement. Similarly, Velázquez-Martínez et al. (2019) evaluated emerging technologies from a CE perspective, emphasizing the importance of robust recycling processes to recover all components effectively.

In the regulatory domain, Neumann et al. (2022) provided an overview of existing policies and proposed new directives for EVB recycling. Their work covered practices in material collection, sorting, transportation, handling, and recycling, underscoring the importance of comprehensive regulatory frameworks in advancing CE objectives. Baars et al. (2021) conducted a material flow analysis focusing on cobalt embedded in EVBs across the European Union. Their findings emphasized strategies to reduce cobalt dependency and enhance recycling efficiency, demonstrating the potential for ambitious CE strategies to address resource challenges.

Other notable advancements include innovations in State of Health (SoH) estimation techniques for EVBs. Basia et al. (2021) proposed a feature-based classification system to improve SoH estimation accuracy, facilitating the repurposing of end-of-life EVBs. This development aligns with CE principles by enabling better utilization of EVBs in secondary applications.

7.2.2 *Opportunities and Challenges*

Despite significant progress, numerous challenges hinder the full realization of CE practices in EVB management. Manual disassembly and labor-intensive recycling processes remain significant barriers, as do challenges in automating these tasks due to the complex and variable designs of EVBs (Albertsen et al. 2021; Harper et al. 2019). The lack of standardization across battery types exacerbates these issues, making it difficult to develop scalable and efficient recycling systems (Ai et al. 2019; Olsson et al. 2018).

The economic viability of recycling networks is another critical concern. Building the necessary infrastructure involves high upfront costs, and the unpredictable volume of end-of-life (EOL) batteries further complicates investment decisions (Fallah et al. 2021; Hu et al. 2022). Moreover, the low cost of virgin materials often undermines the financial attractiveness of recycling, necessitating stronger regulatory and financial incentives (Helbig et al. 2018).

Environmental and safety risks associated with EVB transportation and recycling are additional obstacles. Strict regulations governing hazardous materials, while essential for safety, can increase logistical complexities and costs (Ai et al. 2019; Wegener et al. 2015). Furthermore, the rapid evolution of battery technologies creates challenges in designing recycling systems that can accommodate changes in battery chemistry and materials (Yanamandra et al. 2022).

Collaboration among stakeholders is vital for overcoming these challenges. Effective partnerships between automakers, battery manufacturers, policymakers, and recyclers can drive the development of more efficient and sustainable recycling systems. Alamerew and Brissaud (2020) emphasized the importance of shared understanding and collaborative decision-making in achieving CE objectives, particularly in the context of reverse logistics for EOL batteries.

7.2.3 Circular Economy Strategies for EVBs

To address the multifaceted challenges of EVB management, researchers and practitioners have proposed comprehensive CE strategies. Richa et al. (2017) introduced a waste management hierarchy inspired by CE principles, emphasizing reuse and cascaded use to minimize environmental impacts and maximize economic benefits. Their lifecycle eco-efficiency metrics provide a valuable framework for evaluating the trade-offs associated with different management practices.

The "9R" strategies—Recycle, Remanufacture, Reuse, Refuse, Rethink, Reduce, Repair, Refurbish, and Repurpose—offer a holistic approach to CE implementation (Park et al. 2024). These strategies encompass the entire EVB lifecycle, from production and usage to EOL management. By integrating these principles into industry practices, companies can unlock significant economic, environmental, and social benefits.

The circular economy of electric vehicle batteries presents a transformative opportunity to reduce resource consumption, minimize waste, and promote sustainability throughout the EVB lifecycle. While significant challenges remain, advancements in technology, policy, and stakeholder collaboration offer promising pathways for progress. Emerging innovations, robust regulatory frameworks, and the adoption of comprehensive CE strategies are essential for driving meaningful change and realizing the full potential of a circular economy in the automotive sector. By embracing these principles, the industry can contribute to a greener, more sustainable future, aligning with global sustainability goals and addressing the pressing challenges of our time.

7.3 Methodology

This research explores the integration of Circular Economy (CE) principles with advancements in electric vehicle (EV) battery technology and recycling strategies. It employs a comprehensive literature review to examine the transition to a CE framework aligned with the Sustainable Development Goals (SDGs). This review focuses on identifying challenges and innovations within the automotive battery market and technological advancements shaping the industry's evolution.

To provide a nuanced understanding, the study incorporates detailed case studies of global initiatives in EV battery recycling. These case studies span multiple regions and companies, offering a comparative perspective on diverse approaches and strategies in addressing sustainability challenges in the battery sector. This methodology enables the identification of best practices and insights for fostering resource efficiency, waste reduction, and environmental stewardship in line with CE principles.

7.4 EV Battery Recycling Case Studies

7.4.1 Case Studies in the European Union (EU)

In the dynamic landscape of electric vehicles and renewable energy, the demand for high-performance batteries has surged, positioning Northvolt as a leading innovator in the industry. Founded in 2016 by Peter Carlsson and Paolo Cerruti, former Tesla executives, Northvolt's mission has been to address the growing need for sustainable energy solutions. The Swedish battery manufacturer places circular economy principles at the core of its operations, emphasizing resource efficiency, waste reduction, and environmental stewardship. Northvolt's holistic approach to battery production integrates the use of renewable materials, sustainable sourcing practices, and advanced recycling methods, minimizing waste and environmental impact throughout the battery lifecycle.

Northvolt prioritizes sustainability-focused research and development, continually exploring innovative technologies and materials to enhance battery performance while reducing their environmental footprint. By doing so, the company advances the circular economy agenda in the battery industry. Northvolt's expansion strategies include plans to open additional battery plants across Europe and North America, leveraging renewable energy sources and eco-friendly manufacturing processes. These expansions align with Northvolt's commitment to sustainable growth and its vision of a circular economy framework.

Collaboration is a cornerstone of Northvolt's strategy. By partnering with automotive manufacturers, technology companies, and government agencies, Northvolt fosters innovation and knowledge-sharing in circular battery production. These collaborations have facilitated the development of sustainable materials, cutting-edge recycling technologies, and closed-loop systems. The company ensures the longevity and recyclability of its products through rigorous quality assurance and lifecycle management practices. By optimizing battery design and maintenance, Northvolt extends product lifespan and minimizes resource consumption.

In addition to producing batteries for electric vehicles, Northvolt explores opportunities in renewable energy storage, grid stabilization, and consumer electronics. This diversification enhances resource efficiency and resilience within the circular economy framework. Northvolt also emphasizes transparency and communication, fostering trust and engagement through sustainability reports and stakeholder initiatives. These efforts contribute to its reputation as a leader in advancing circular economy principles.

Northvolt's commitment to circularity profoundly impacts the electric vehicle market and the renewable energy sector. By championing resource efficiency, waste reduction, and environmental stewardship, Northvolt drives positive change across the battery value chain. Its innovative solutions to environmental challenges associated with battery manufacturing set a compelling example for the industry, inspiring collective action toward a greener future.

Umicore, a Belgium-based multinational materials technology company, is another key player in advancing circular economy principles in the battery industry. With roots dating back to the Union Minière du Haut-Katanga in 1906, Umicore has evolved into a technology-focused business specializing in refining, recycling, and producing precious metals and specialty materials. The company has pioneered battery recycling technologies, leveraging its expertise to address sustainability challenges in the electric vehicle sector.

Umicore's approach centers on a closed-loop recycling model fortified by proprietary technology. By reprocessing used batteries to extract metals such as copper, cobalt, nickel, and lithium, Umicore transforms them into high-quality materials for new battery production. This closed-loop system minimizes waste and conserves resources, reducing reliance on primary extraction while promoting sustainable supply chains. Umicore's advanced recycling technologies achieve recovery rates exceeding 95%, underscoring its commitment to resource conservation and environmental sustainability.

Collaboration plays a significant role in Umicore's strategy. The company partners with automotive manufacturers, battery producers, and other stakeholders to scale recycling efforts and accelerate the adoption of circular economy practices. A notable partnership with Volkswagen's subsidiary PowerCo exemplifies Umicore's dedication to advancing sustainable solutions within the electric vehicle industry. Furthermore, Umicore invests heavily in research and development, driving continuous innovation in separation techniques, refining processes, and material characterization methods to enhance recycling efficiency.

Umicore's efforts have positioned it as a global leader in sustainable resource management. By closing the materials loop and promoting the reuse of valuable metals, the company significantly contributes to the transition toward a low-carbon future. Its focus on innovation and collaboration ensures that it remains at the forefront of addressing environmental and resource challenges in the battery industry.

BASF, a German chemical company, is renowned for its innovative recycling methodologies and commitment to circular economy principles. BASF specializes in converting metals sourced from used batteries into cathode materials for new battery production, emphasizing the reuse of recovered elements. This approach not only improves resource efficiency but also underscores BASF's dedication to sustainability and circularity within the battery ecosystem.

BASF supplies core materials for lithium-ion batteries, including cathode materials and electrolytes. By handling rare metals like nickel cobalt aluminum oxide and nickel cobalt manganese oxide, the company ensures that its products meet diverse application requirements for energy density, lifetime, and safety. BASF's recycling initiatives gained significant momentum with the 2024 opening of a metal refining facility at its Schwarzheide plant. This facility—the first of its kind in Europe—focuses on upcycling rare metals such as lithium, nickel, cobalt, manganese, and copper recovered from used batteries. These materials are then integrated with virgin resources to produce new cathode materials, enabling sustainable production practices.

The Schwarzheide plant demonstrates BASF's ability to innovate within the circular economy framework, reducing waste while enhancing the value of recovered materials. Supported by EUR 175 million in funding from the European Project of Common Interest (IPCEI), the facility exemplifies how public–private partnerships can drive progress in battery recycling. BASF also participates in the Battery Pass Consortium, contributing to the specification of the EU Battery Passport. This initiative aims to establish standardized carbon footprint calculations for battery production, distribution, usage, and recycling.

Through these efforts, BASF aspires to become a European leader in material refining, recovery, and recycling. Its focus on sustainability and innovation underscores the importance of robust recycling systems for the circular economy of batteries. By integrating advanced recycling processes into its operations, BASF ensures that valuable materials are effectively repurposed, supporting the transition to a more sustainable energy landscape.

Northvolt, Umicore, and BASF exemplify diverse approaches to advancing circular economy principles in the battery industry. While Northvolt focuses on holistic production and lifecycle management, Umicore emphasizes closed-loop systems and advanced recycling technologies. BASF's commitment to upcycling and material innovation further illustrates the versatility of strategies within the circular economy framework. Together, these companies contribute significantly to the global effort to create a sustainable, resource-efficient future.

7.4.2 Comparison of European, Chinese and Japanese Firms in Circular Battery Recycling

Comparison of Chinese and European Firms in Circular Battery Recycling

Leading Chinese companies BRUNP, NIO, and CATL are at the forefront of advancing circular economy (CE) principles in battery recycling, addressing the dual challenges of resource scarcity and environmental sustainability. As the global demand for electric vehicles (EVs) and rechargeable batteries continues to grow, these firms are pioneering innovative approaches to reshape the battery industry while promoting a more sustainable future.

BRUNP exemplifies an integrative approach by seamlessly incorporating battery manufacturing, consumption, and recycling into its operational framework. Using proprietary technologies, BRUNP maximizes yields and resource efficiency across the entire battery lifecycle. This comprehensive strategy not only reduces waste but also conserves valuable materials such as lithium, nickel, and cobalt. BRUNP has ambitious plans to construct a large-scale recycling facility by 2027, signaling a significant investment in recycling infrastructure. This facility will bolster the company's ability to manage end-of-life batteries, reflecting its commitment to sustainability and circularity. By merging manufacturing, consumption, and recycling, BRUNP sets a high standard for the battery industry, demonstrating how a holistic approach can drive innovation and sustainability.

NIO adopts a similarly comprehensive strategy by collaborating with solar energy providers to enhance its battery recycling initiatives. Central to NIO's approach is the development of battery exchange stations, which promote the sustainable use of batteries by enabling swift and efficient swapping. These stations serve as vital infrastructure for sustainable mobility, reducing downtime for EV users while extending the lifecycle of batteries. NIO's integration of solar energy into this infrastructure underscores its commitment to reducing carbon emissions and fostering environmentally responsible practices. This synergy between battery swapping and renewable energy demonstrates a holistic approach to CE principles, advancing the company's broader environmental objectives and setting a benchmark for other firms.

CATL, China's leading automotive battery manufacturer, focuses on creating circular value chains for EV batteries. Through strategic collaborations and acquisitions, CATL has established itself as a leader in optimizing resource utilization and minimizing waste throughout the battery lifecycle. The company's emphasis on sustainable management practices encompasses every stage of battery production, from sourcing raw materials to recycling spent batteries. CATL's initiatives include the development of closed-loop systems that ensure valuable materials are recovered and reused, reducing reliance on finite natural resources. By prioritizing collaboration with other industry stakeholders, CATL exemplifies how partnerships can amplify efforts to build a more circular and sustainable economy within the automotive sector.

Together, BRUNP, NIO, and CATL illustrate the growing momentum toward CE principles in the battery industry. Their advanced recycling technologies, integrative approaches, and focus on collaboration demonstrate the potential of CE to address critical environmental and resource challenges. As the demand for EVs and energy storage solutions continues to rise, the leadership of these companies in promoting resource efficiency and sustainability will play a pivotal role in shaping the future of the global battery ecosystem.

While Chinese and European firms share a common commitment to CE principles, their approaches and strategies reflect distinct regional priorities and operational models. For instance, both BRUNP and Northvolt, a Swedish battery manufacturer, prioritize CE principles by emphasizing resource efficiency and waste reduction. Both companies invest significantly in research and development (R&D) to drive sustainability and innovation within their operations. Furthermore, they collaborate extensively with industry stakeholders to foster innovation, share knowledge, and develop circular solutions across supply chains. By prioritizing transparency and stakeholder engagement, both BRUNP and Northvolt build trust and drive collective progress within the CE ecosystem.

Despite these similarities, their strategies differ significantly. BRUNP's integrative approach combines manufacturing, consumption, and recycling within a unified operational framework. This model allows BRUNP to address the entire battery lifecycle, from production to disposal, with a focus on infrastructure development, such as battery exchange stations. In contrast, Northvolt's efforts center on high-performance lithium-ion battery production and recycling, emphasizing sustainable R&D and expansion strategies. Northvolt's approach reflects a focus on innovation in battery design and manufacturing, leveraging renewable energy sources to further its sustainability goals.

These differences highlight how regional contexts and market dynamics shape corporate strategies. BRUNP's approach reflects the rapid expansion and industrial integration characteristic of China's battery market, while Northvolt's focus aligns with Europe's regulatory environment and emphasis on renewable energy adoption. Despite their distinct methodologies, both companies make significant contributions to advancing CE principles within their respective regions.

The comparison extends beyond BRUNP and Northvolt to include other leading firms such as NIO, CATL, Umicore, and BASF. NIO's emphasis on integrating battery swapping infrastructure with renewable energy highlights its unique approach to sustainable mobility. Similarly, CATL's circular value chain initiatives underscore its focus on optimizing resource utilization and minimizing waste. European firms like Umicore specialize in closed-loop recycling systems, achieving industry-leading recovery rates for critical materials. BASF, on the other hand, innovates in recycling methodologies, focusing on upcycling metals into cathode materials for new battery production. These varied approaches reflect the diversity of strategies employed globally to advance CE principles in the battery industry.

In summary, Chinese firms like BRUNP, NIO, and CATL lead the way in advancing CE principles by adopting integrative, innovative, and collaborative approaches to battery recycling. Their efforts underscore the importance of addressing the entire battery lifecycle, from production to disposal, while emphasizing resource efficiency and waste reduction. By fostering partnerships and investing in infrastructure and technology, these companies set a benchmark for sustainability and circularity in the global battery ecosystem. The unique strategies of these firms, combined with the complementary approaches of European and other international players, contribute to the collective progress toward a more sustainable future for the planet.

Comparison of Japanese and European Firms in Circular Battery Recycling

In Japan, Panasonic and Toyota demonstrate a comprehensive approach to circular economy principles within the automotive industry, particularly focusing on battery technology and end-of-life management. Their collaboration in establishing Panasonic EV Energy Co., Ltd. reflects their shared commitment to advancing battery technology for electric vehicles (EVs). By combining their expertise in battery development and automotive manufacturing, these companies have significantly contributed to the widespread adoption of hybrid electric vehicles (HEVs) and EVs, thereby promoting sustainable mobility solutions. Examining their strategies provides valuable insights into how Japanese firms are navigating the transition toward a circular economy, especially in comparison with European firms.

Panasonic, a leading electronics company, has actively incorporated circular economy principles across its operations, encompassing product development, manufacturing, and environmental sustainability. Established in 1996 in partnership with Toyota, Panasonic EV Energy Co., Ltd. focuses on developing nickel-metal hydride batteries for EVs. Over the years, Panasonic has made significant advancements in battery technology, including lithium-ion and thin lithium polymer batteries, catering to applications in HEVs, EVs, and consumer electronics. Notable products such as the Eneloop rechargeable nickel-metal hydride batteries and the Evolta line of alkaline and rechargeable batteries underscore Panasonic's commitment to energy efficiency and durability.

To meet the growing global demand for EVs, Panasonic has been expanding its production capacity for lithium-ion batteries, aiming to achieve a global production capacity of 200 GWh by 2030. This expansion aligns with the company's strategic goals to address the increasing need for sustainable energy storage while supporting the transition to electric mobility. Panasonic has also enhanced productivity and cost efficiency at its battery manufacturing facilities in Nevada, Kansas, and other locations through automation, process optimization, and advanced manufacturing technologies.

Panasonic's supply chain strategies further underscore its commitment to resilience and sustainability. By diversifying sourcing, localizing procurement, and forming strategic partnerships, the company ensures a stable raw material supply while reducing carbon emissions. Collaborations with recycling companies like Redwood Materials Inc. have fostered the development of closed-loop systems for recycling primary and secondary batteries, promoting resource circularity and minimizing environmental impact.

Aligned with its long-term vision, "Panasonic GREEN IMPACT," the company aims to reduce CO2 emissions by approximately 100 million tons by 2030. Panasonic has already achieved carbon neutrality in several of its facilities through renewable energy procurement and energy efficiency improvements. Additionally, the company's initiatives in battery recycling include reprocessing used primary batteries into materials for new battery production. This commitment to sustainability also extends to emerging markets such as energy storage systems for data centers and home use, as well as the electrification of construction machinery and motorcycles. By strategically diversifying its business, Panasonic aims to double its sales revenue from industrial and consumer businesses by 2030, delivering innovative solutions characterized by reliability, safety, and sustainability.

Panasonic's circular economy strategy is a testament to its ability to thrive in a rapidly evolving market while minimizing its environmental footprint and contributing to a more sustainable future. Its efforts encompass product innovation, optimization of manufacturing processes, and active participation in environmental sustainability initiatives.

Toyota, as an original equipment manufacturer (OEM), has also shown a strong commitment to circular economy principles, particularly in the collection and recycling of nickel-metal hydride (NiMH) batteries used in hybrid vehicles. The company's emphasis on NiMH batteries stems from its pioneering role in popularizing hybrid technology globally. As the manufacturer of iconic hybrid models like the Prius, Toyota has developed a significant fleet of vehicles equipped with these batteries.

Recognizing the importance of responsible end-of-life management for these batteries, Toyota has established dedicated centers for their collection and recycling. These facilities serve as hubs for receiving used batteries, dismantling them, and extracting valuable materials such as nickel, cobalt, and rare earth elements. By ensuring efficient and environmentally responsible recycling processes, Toyota reduces the demand for virgin resources and mitigates the environmental impacts associated with battery disposal.

Toyota's recycling initiatives align with broader circular economy goals, emphasizing resource recovery and waste reduction. By repurposing recovered materials into new batteries or other applications, Toyota demonstrates how end-of-life management can support sustainability. The company has also formed partnerships with local and global recycling entities to enhance its recycling capabilities and create robust closed-loop systems.

Toyota's strategic focus on hybrid vehicle batteries underscores its broader commitment to sustainability and resource management. Through partnerships and collaborations, Toyota continues to address the challenges of battery recycling while promoting innovation in resource management. These efforts set a benchmark for the industry, showcasing how circular economy principles can be effectively integrated into automotive practices.

When comparing the strategies of Japanese firms like Panasonic and Toyota with European firms such as Northvolt, Umicore, and BASF, both similarities and differences become apparent. Both Japanese and European firms emphasize sustainable battery production through the adoption of circular economy principles. Panasonic and Toyota focus on developing advanced battery technologies for EVs while integrating environmental sustainability into their operations. Similarly, Northvolt, Umicore, and BASF prioritize sustainable battery manufacturing and recycling, leveraging renewable materials and closed-loop systems to minimize waste and environmental impact.

Collaboration with industry stakeholders is a shared priority for Japanese and European firms. Panasonic's partnerships with recycling companies like Redwood Materials and Toyota's alliances with global recycling entities reflect a commitment to fostering innovation and knowledge-sharing across the battery value chain. European firms such as Northvolt and Umicore adopt similar collaborative approaches, working with automakers and technology companies to advance circular solutions in battery production and recycling.

Both Japanese and European firms prioritize resource efficiency and recycling in their circular economy strategies. Panasonic's efforts to reprocess used batteries into new materials align with BASF's focus on upcycling metals for cathode production. Both regions employ advanced recycling technologies to recover critical materials, reducing reliance on primary resource extraction and supporting circular economy goals.

Exploration of product diversification and innovation beyond electric vehicle batteries is another area of alignment. Panasonic's strategic expansion into energy storage and industrial electrification parallels Northvolt's efforts to develop batteries for renewable energy storage and consumer electronics. Similarly, Toyota's focus on hybrid technology reflects the innovative approaches of European firms like BASF, which emphasize material traceability and recycling methodologies.

Both Japanese and European firms emphasize transparency and stakeholder engagement to foster trust and collaboration within the circular economy ecosystem. Panasonic and Toyota share insights into their sustainability practices through reports and initiatives, encouraging collective action toward shared goals. European firms like Northvolt and Umicore adopt similar strategies to promote accountability and drive progress in sustainability.

Despite these similarities, regional differences influence the strategic priorities of Japanese and European firms. Japan's focus on precision and efficiency in resource recovery reflects its industrial strengths and cultural emphasis on innovation. In contrast, European firms often operate within stringent regulatory frameworks, such as the EU Battery Passport initiative, which enhances traceability and compliance. Northvolt's emphasis on renewable energy integration and Umicore's industry-leading recovery rates highlight Europe's regulatory-driven approach to circular economy practices. Meanwhile, Toyota's extensive experience with hybrid technology positions it uniquely to address the challenges of NiMH battery recycling.

Panasonic and Toyota exemplify a comprehensive commitment to circular economy principles through innovative practices in battery technology, recycling, and end-of-life management. Their efforts align closely with those of leading European firms, underscoring the global importance of sustainability and resource efficiency in the battery industry. By prioritizing collaboration, innovation, and environmental stewardship, these companies contribute to the development of a more sustainable and circular economy. As global demand for EVs and sustainable energy solutions continues to grow, the strategies employed by Japanese and European firms will play a crucial role in shaping a greener future.

7.4.3 Comparison of Case Studies

The activities of the eight companies, categorized into three from Europe, three from China, and two from Japan, illustrate distinct strategies aligned with the 9R framework of circular economy principles. The framework includes strategies such as Repair, Refurbish, Remanufacture, Reuse, Refuse, Rethink, Reduce, Repurpose, and Recycle. These companies adopt different approaches based on their geographic, operational, and industrial contexts.

Chinese companies like CATL, NIO, and Japanese company Toyota exhibit a vertically integrated value chain that spans from battery production to after-sales services and the recycling of electric vehicles (EVs). This integration enables these companies to implement strategies such as "Repair" and "Refurbish," allowing for the direct management of the entire lifecycle of their products. This vertical integration not only optimizes resource use but also ensures streamlined processes for extending the life of batteries and vehicles.

In contrast, European firms operate within a more segmented value chain where battery material suppliers and automotive original equipment manufacturers (OEMs) are distinct entities. This separation allows material suppliers to specialize in other aspects of the 9R framework. For instance, companies like Northvolt focus on "Rethink" and "Repurpose" by developing innovative methods to enhance the performance of storage batteries. Meanwhile, BASF emphasizes "Remanufacture" and "Reuse" through upcycling discarded batteries, transforming them into high-value materials for new applications. Umicore, another European firm, aligns its efforts with "Remanufacture" and "Reduce" by refining raw materials in an energy-efficient manner to achieve high-value battery materials that are not easily replicated by OEMs alone.

In terms of battery packaging, companies such as Northvolt in Europe, CATL in China, and Panasonic in Japan engage in manufacturing solutions that are often subject to cost pressures within the automotive supply chain. To mitigate this dependence, these companies are diversifying their applications by repurposing batteries for non-automotive uses, including grid storage and industrial machinery. This strategy aligns with the "Repurpose" principle of the 9R framework and represents an effort to expand beyond automotive applications while maintaining profitability and sustainability.

The concept of "Refuse," which focuses on avoiding the use of conflict minerals and ensuring compliance with human rights standards, varies across regions due to differing regulatory environments. For example, companies from Europe (like Northvolt and BASF) and Japan (like Panasonic and Toyota) implement strict controls to maintain traceability in their supply chains. These measures include using proof-of-origin documentation and disposal manifests to meet corporate social responsibility (CSR) objectives. The expansion of cross-border trade in finished EVs and semi-finished storage batteries underscores the importance of traceability; companies that fail to meet these standards risk being excluded through non-tariff barriers.

Building a comprehensive battery value chain that incorporates the full spectrum of the 9R framework requires addressing gaps in existing capabilities. For instance, areas such as "Repurpose" and "Remanufacture" may require collaboration with material manufacturers and packaging companies, as these aspects are challenging for vehicle OEMs to manage independently. Cross-sector partnerships and innovative collaborations are essential to cover these gaps, fostering a more holistic and efficient approach to the circular economy within the battery industry.

7.5 Conclusion

The transition toward a Circular Economy (CE) for electric vehicle batteries (EVBs) is a pivotal element in achieving sustainability goals, addressing the pressing challenges of environmental preservation, resource security, and economic growth. This study has highlighted the diverse strategies employed by companies across Europe, China, and Japan, showcasing how the CE principles are operationalized within different industrial and regulatory contexts.

In Europe, companies such as Northvolt, Umicore, and BASF demonstrate a segmented approach where battery material suppliers and automotive OEMs operate independently but collaboratively within the CE framework. These firms excel in strategies like "Rethink," "Repurpose," and "Remanufacture," focusing on enhancing battery performance, upcycling discarded materials, and refining raw materials in energy-efficient ways. This specialization enables European companies to leverage advanced recycling technologies and closed-loop systems, addressing critical challenges like resource dependency and waste reduction.

Chinese firms, including BRUNP, NIO, and CATL, adopt a vertically integrated approach that encompasses manufacturing, consumption, and recycling. This integration allows them to directly address "Repair" and "Refurbish" strategies, optimizing the entire battery lifecycle. Their efforts in developing large-scale recycling facilities and innovative infrastructure, such as battery exchange stations integrated with renewable energy, underscore their commitment to sustainability and circularity. By focusing on holistic value chains and strategic collaborations, these companies set a benchmark for innovation in the global battery ecosystem.

Japanese companies Panasonic and Toyota showcase a hybrid approach that combines vertical integration with collaborative strategies. Panasonic's emphasis on

"Recycle," "Repurpose," and supply chain resilience aligns with its broader sustainability goals, including carbon neutrality and resource circularity. Toyota's initiatives in recycling nickel-metal hydride batteries demonstrate its leadership in "Repair" and "Refurbish," reflecting its legacy in hybrid technology and end-of-life management. Both companies highlight the importance of technological advancements and stakeholder engagement in achieving CE objectives.

A comparative analysis reveals both commonalities and regional distinctions. European firms operate within stringent regulatory frameworks, prioritizing compliance, traceability, and renewable energy integration. Chinese firms leverage rapid industrial growth and infrastructure development to implement comprehensive CE strategies. Japanese firms emphasize precision and efficiency, reflecting their industrial strengths and cultural focus on innovation.

The collective insights from these case studies underscore the need for a comprehensive approach to CE implementation, integrating the 9R principles—Recycle, Remanufacture, Reuse, Refuse, Rethink, Reduce, Repair, Refurbish, and Repurpose. Building a robust and holistic battery value chain requires addressing gaps in capabilities through cross-sector partnerships and innovative collaborations. Effective policy frameworks, technological advancements, and stakeholder cooperation are critical to overcoming challenges such as resource scarcity, regulatory compliance, and economic viability.

In conclusion, the journey toward a CE model for EVBs is both a challenge and an opportunity for the global automotive sector. Companies like Northvolt, Umicore, BASF, BRUNP, NIO, CATL, Panasonic, and Toyota exemplify the transformative potential of CE principles, offering innovative solutions to pressing environmental and resource challenges. By embracing these strategies and fostering international collaboration, the industry can contribute significantly to a sustainable, resource-efficient future aligned with the Sustainable Development Goals (SDGs).

References

Ai, N., Zheng, J., & Chen, W. Q. (2019). US end-of-life electric vehicle batteries: Dynamic inventory modeling and spatial analysis for regional solutions. Resources, Conservation and Recycling, 145, 208–219.

Alamerew, Y. A., & Brissaud, D. (2020). Modelling reverse supply chain through system dynamics for realizing the transition towards the circular economy: A case study on electric vehicle batteries. Journal of Cleaner Production, 254, 120025.

Albertsen, L., Richter, J. L., Peck, P., Dalhammar, C., & Plepys, A. (2021). Circular business models for electric vehicle lithium-ion batteries: An analysis of current practices of vehicle manufacturers and policies in the EU. Resources, conservation and recycling, 172, 105658.

Baars, J., Domenech, T., Bleischwitz, R., Melin, H. E., & Heidrich, O. (2021). Circular economy strategies for electric vehicle batteries reduce reliance on raw materials. Nature Sustainability, 4(1), 71–79.

Basia, A., Simeu-Abazi, Z., Gascard, E., & Zwolinski, P. (2021). Review on State of Health estimation methodologies for lithium-ion batteries in the context of circular economy. CIRP Journal of Manufacturing Science and Technology, 32, 517–528.

Bonsu, N. O. (2020). Towards a circular and low-carbon economy: Insights from the transitioning to electric vehicles and net zero economy. Journal of Cleaner Production, 256, 120659.

Deng, D. (2015). Li-ion batteries: basics, progress, and challenges. Energy Science & Engineering, 3(5), 385–418.

Deveci, M., Simic, V., & Torkayesh, A. E. (2021). Remanufacturing facility location for automotive Lithium-ion batteries: An integrated neutrosophic decision-making model, Journal of Cleaner Production, 317, 128438.

Elgowainy, A., Han, J., Ward, J., Joseck, F., Gohlke, D., Lindauer, A., & Wallington, T. J. (2018). Current and future United States light-duty vehicle pathways: Cradle-to-grave lifecycle greenhouse gas emissions and economic assessment, Environmental Science & Technology, 52(4), 2392–2399.

European Commission (2020) Regulation of the European Parliament and of the Council concerning batteries and waste batteries, repealing Directive 2006/66/EC and Ameding Regulation (EU) No 2019/1020. European Commission: Brussels.

Fallah, N., Fitzpatrick, C., Killian, S., & Johnson, M. (2021). End-of-life electric vehicle battery stock estimation in Ireland through integrated energy and circular economy modelling. Resources, Conservation and Recycling, 174, 105753.

Groenewald, J., Grandjean, T., & Marco.. (2017). Accelerated energy capacity measurement of lithium-ion cells to support future circular economy strategies for electric vehicles, Renewable and Sustainable Energy Reviews, 69 (March), 98–111.

Harper, G., Sommerville, R., Kendrick, E., Driscoll, L., Slater, P., Stolkin, R., Walton, A., Christensen, P., Heidrich, O., Lambert, S., Abbott, A., Ryder, K., Gaines, L., & Anderson, P. (2019). Recycling lithium-ion batteries from electric vehicles, Nature, 575(7781), 75–86

Helbig, C., Bradshaw, A. M., Wietschel, L., Thorenz, A., & Tuma, A. (2018). Supply risks associated with lithium-ion battery materials. Journal of Cleaner Production, 172, 274–286.

Hu, X., Yan, W., Zhang, X., Feng, Z., Wang, Y., Ying, B., & Zhang, H. (2022). LRP-based design of sustainable recycling network for electric vehicle batteries. Processes, 10(2), 273.

Jaffe, S. (2017). Vulnerable links in the lithium-ion battery supply chain. Joule, 1(2), 225–228.

Martínez, O. V., Van Den Boogaart, K. G., Lundström, M., Santasalo-Aarnio, A., Reuter, M., & Serna-Guerrero, R. (2019). Statistical entropy analysis as tool for circular economy: Proof of concept by optimizing a lithium-ion battery waste sieving system. Journal of Cleaner Production, 212, 1568–1579.

Mossali, E., Picone, N., Gentilini, L., Rodrìguez, O., Pérez, J.M., & Colledani, M. (2020). Lithium-ion batteries towards circular economy: A literature review of opportunities and issues of recycling treatments, Journal of Environmental Management, 264, 110500, 1–12.

Neumann, J., Petranikova, M., Meeus, M., Gamarra, J. D., Younesi, R., Winter, M., & Nowak, S. (2022). Recycling of lithium-ion batteries—current state of the art, circular economy, and next generation recycling. Advanced energy materials, 12(17), 2102917.

Olsson, L., Fallahi, S., Schnurr, M., Diener, D., & Van Loon, P. (2018). Circular business models for extended EV battery life. Batteries, 4(4), 57.

Park, Y.W., Sugie, R., & Mizuguchi, K. (2024). Circular Economy Strategy of Japanese Firms: A Comparative Study of Manufacturing and Other Industries. Communication of JIMA, 34(1), 15–22.

Reinhardt, R., Christodoulou, I., Gassó-Domingo, S., & García, B. A. (2019). Towards sustainable business models for electric vehicle battery second use: A critical review. Journal of environmental management, 245, 432–446.

Richa, K., Babbitt, C. W., & Gaustad, G. (2017). Eco-efficiency analysis of a lithium-ion battery waste hierarchy inspired by circular economy. Journal of Industrial Ecology, 21(3), 715–730.

Rönkkö, P., Majava, J., Hyvärinen, T., Oksanen, I., Tervonen, P., & Lassi, U. (2024). The circular economy of electric vehicle batteries: a Finnish case study. Environment Systems and Decisions, 44(1), 100–113.

Roy, J. J., Rarotra, S., Krikstolaityte, V., Zhuoran, K. W., Cindy, Y. D. I., Tan, X. Y., & Srinivasan, M. (2022). Green recycling methods to treat lithium-ion batteries E-waste: a circular approach to sustainability. Advanced Materials, 34(25), 2103346.

Saxena, S., Le Floch, C., MacDonald, J., & Moura, S. (2015). Quantifying EV battery end-of-life through analysis of travel needs with vehicle powertrain models. Journal of Power Sources, 282, 265–276.

Shakhnoza, N. K., & Park, Y. W. (2023). Circular Economy in Automobile Industry: Literature Analysis, Management Review: An International Journal,18(1), 83–113.

Velázquez-Martínez, O., Valio, J., Santasalo-Aarnio, A., Reuter, M., & Serna-Guerrero, R. (2019). A critical review of lithium-ion battery recycling processes from a circular economy perspective. Batteries, 5(4), 68.

Wegener, K., Chen, W. H., Dietrich, F., Dröder, K., & Kara, S. (2015). Robot assisted disassembly for the recycling of electric vehicle batteries. Procedia Cirp, 29, 716–721.

Yanamandra, K., Pinisetty, D., Daoud, A., Gupta, N. (2022). Recycling of Li-ion and lead acid batteries: a review, Journal of the Indian Institute of Science, 102, 281–295.

Chapter 8
CE Strategy in the Chemical Industry

Young Won Park

8.1 Introduction

The Circular Economy (CE) represents a transformative shift from traditional linear economic models, characterized by a "take-make-dispose" approach, to regenerative and restorative systems. This paradigm aims to optimize resource utilization, minimize waste generation, and maximize the lifecycle of products and materials. By integrating principles such as designing waste and pollution out of the system, extending product and material utility, and regenerating natural systems, CE seeks to decouple economic growth from environmental degradation.

The Japanese chemical industry exemplifies the strategic implementation of CE principles, underscoring its pivotal role within industrial ecosystems. As a foundational supplier to sectors like automotive, electronics, and consumer goods, the chemical industry significantly influences resource efficiency, sustainability, and innovation. In response to challenges such as rising material costs, resource scarcity, and supply chain vulnerabilities, Japan's chemical sector is advancing CE practices through innovative technologies, collaborative partnerships, and systemic changes.

The CE principles, as articulated by the Ellen MacArthur Foundation, advocate designing waste out of systems, keeping materials in use, and regenerating natural resources. These principles challenge industries to rethink conventional practices, innovate business models, and foster cross-sectoral collaboration. The chemical industry's contribution to CE encompasses several key areas, including the adoption of advanced recycling technologies, the development of bio-based materials, and the establishment of closed-loop systems.

For instance, chemical recycling methods such as depolymerization and pyrolysis are gaining traction, addressing limitations of traditional mechanical recycling by enabling the recovery of high-quality raw materials from complex waste streams. Bio-based materials offer renewable alternatives to fossil-based inputs, reducing carbon footprints and aligning with global sustainability goals. The integration of closed-loop systems ensures that end-of-life materials re-enter production cycles, fostering resource efficiency and waste minimization.

Y. W. Park and K. Tamaki, *Circular Economy Strategy for SDG Business Management*,
https://doi.org/10.1007/978-981-96-4194-9_8

Japan's commitment to CE is driven by its reliance on imported raw materials and the need for resilient economic models. The linear economy's inefficiencies are evident in substantial resource wastage, with significant amounts of plastics, metals, and organic waste ending up in landfills or incinerators. Global disruptions, such as the COVID-19 pandemic and geopolitical tensions, have exposed vulnerabilities in supply chains, emphasizing the importance of adopting CE principles to enhance sustainability and competitiveness.

The Japanese chemical industry faces unique challenges, including the rising costs of raw materials, semiconductor shortages, and the complexity of global trade dynamics. These pressures necessitate adopting CE strategies to mitigate risks and improve resource efficiency. Innovations in recycling, material efficiency, and renewable feedstocks offer opportunities for the industry to lead in sustainable development.

The 9R framework provides a comprehensive approach to achieving CE. Each strategy addresses specific stages of a product's lifecycle, aiming to minimize resource extraction and maximize utility. For example, the refusal of single-use plastics and hazardous chemicals reduces environmental impact at the design stage. Rethinking business models, such as adopting product-as-a-service systems, promotes systemic innovation. Advanced recycling technologies enable material recovery and reintegration into production cycles, ensuring sustainability.

The chemical industry's adoption of the 9R framework is exemplified through pioneering initiatives. Mitsui Chemicals, Mitsubishi Chemical, and Kaneka have demonstrated leadership in advancing CE principles. Mitsui Chemicals focuses on chemical recycling and bio-based materials, utilizing technologies like pyrolysis to recover raw materials. Mitsubishi Chemical invests in large-scale recycling facilities and explores renewable energy integration through artificial photosynthesis. Kaneka has developed biodegradable plastics like Green Planet®, promoting zero-waste practices and addressing marine pollution.

The transition to a CE offers significant economic, social, and environmental benefits for the chemical industry. Resource efficiency reduces dependency on virgin resources, while waste valorization lowers production and waste management costs. CE practices stimulate innovation in materials, technologies, and business models, driving competitiveness and fostering collaboration across value chains.

The Japanese chemical industry is well positioned to lead the global CE transition. By embedding CE principles into operations and supply chains, the industry can address pressing environmental challenges while unlocking growth opportunities. The synergy between engineering innovations and supply chain management is crucial for operationalizing the 9R framework, enabling industries to achieve systemic sustainability.

This chapter explores the advancements and challenges in Japan's chemical industry within the context of CE. It provides a detailed analysis of global and domestic trends, showcases case studies of leading companies implementing CE principles, and highlights the 9R framework's application in achieving circularity. Through innovation, collaboration, and commitment, the Japanese chemical industry can lead the way in addressing some of the most pressing environmental and economic challenges of our time, contributing to a sustainable and regenerative future.

8.2 The Circular Economy Strategy in the Japanese Chemical Industry

8.2.1 The Circular Economy Trends in the Japanese Chemical Industry

The chemical industry plays a pivotal role in the transition toward a circular economy, acting as both a driver and an enabler of sustainable practices across value chains. Its unique position within industrial ecosystems—providing raw materials for numerous sectors—makes it essential for achieving resource efficiency, reducing waste, and fostering innovation. This section explores the key trends influencing the adoption of circular economy principles in the chemical industry, focusing on the challenges and opportunities specific to Japan's manufacturing sector and the broader global context.

Circular Economy Challenges in the Manufacturing Sector

The Japanese manufacturing sector, including the chemical industry, faces pressing challenges that necessitate the adoption of circular economy practices. Economic disruptions such as the COVID-19 pandemic, geopolitical tensions, and material shortages have significantly impacted supply chains and production processes. These challenges underscore the need for industries to innovate and optimize resource use to ensure resilience and sustainability.

Resource scarcity and rising raw material costs have intensified the urgency of adopting circular practices. Japan, heavily reliant on imports for critical resources, is particularly vulnerable to global supply chain disruptions. This dependence has highlighted the need for robust strategies that minimize waste, maximize material recovery, and reduce dependency on non-renewable inputs.

The circular economy offers a pathway to address these challenges while unlocking economic and environmental benefits. By extending the lifecycle of products and materials, industries can reduce waste, lower production costs, and enhance sustainability. For example, the implementation of advanced recycling technologies enables the recovery of valuable raw materials from waste streams, reducing reliance on virgin resources.

Innovations and Collaborative Efforts in the Chemical Industry

In the context of the chemical industry, the transition from linear to circular systems involves rethinking traditional practices and adopting innovative approaches. Chemical companies in Japan are exploring a range of strategies to enhance resource efficiency and promote sustainability. These include the development of bio-based materials, investment in cutting-edge recycling technologies, and collaboration with stakeholders across the value chain.

One significant trend is the growing emphasis on chemical recycling. Unlike mechanical recycling, which typically involves physical processes to repurpose materials, chemical recycling breaks down waste into its molecular components, enabling the production of high-quality raw materials. This approach addresses the limitations of mechanical recycling, particularly for complex or contaminated waste streams. Techniques such as depolymerization, pyrolysis, and gasification are gaining traction, providing scalable solutions for managing plastic waste and other materials.

Another key development is the shift toward bio-based materials. By utilizing renewable feedstocks such as biomass, the chemical industry can reduce its reliance on fossil fuels and contribute to carbon neutrality. Bio-based polymers and chemicals are being developed as sustainable alternatives to traditional petrochemical products, offering opportunities to align industrial processes with environmental goals.

The integration of circular economy principles into business models also requires collaboration across sectors. Partnerships between chemical companies, consumer goods manufacturers, and waste management firms are essential for establishing closed-loop systems. These collaborations enable the creation of value chains where materials are recovered, recycled, and reintegrated into production processes, reducing waste and environmental impact.

Japan's chemical industry has demonstrated leadership in advancing circular economy practices through various initiatives. For instance, Mitsui Chemicals has launched projects focusing on chemical recycling and bio-based materials, such as its "BePLAYER®" and "RePLAYER®" brands. Similarly, Mitsubishi Chemical is investing in innovative technologies to convert waste plastics into raw materials, contributing to resource efficiency and sustainability.

The circular economy is not only a response to resource scarcity and environmental challenges but also an opportunity for the chemical industry to drive innovation and competitiveness. By embracing sustainable practices, companies can position themselves as leaders in the global transition toward a circular economy.

The Chemical Industry as a Catalyst for Sustainability

The Japanese chemical industry is actively addressing the challenges posed by linear economic systems through circular economy initiatives. The adoption of advanced recycling technologies and the development of bio-based materials are transforming the industry's approach to resource management. Collaboration across value chains is fostering innovation and enabling the creation of sustainable ecosystems. These efforts position the chemical industry as a catalyst for achieving a circular and sustainable future.

8.2.2 *Literature Review*

Circular Economy in the Chemical Industry

The chemical industry occupies a central role in the global transition toward a circular economy, being pivotal in resource recovery, waste minimization, and sustainable production systems. This review examines key scholarly contributions, highlighting the evolution, application, and challenges of circular economy (CE) principles within the sector.

The concept of the circular economy has matured over decades, with foundational ideas tracing back to systems thinking and industrial ecology. Winans et al. (2017) identified the CE framework as an approach that prioritizes material valuation within closed-loop systems, aiming to sustain economic growth while minimizing natural resource depletion and pollution. They emphasize the variability in CE application across industries and regions, underscoring the importance of tailored strategies for different sectors, including chemicals. Their thematic categorization of policies, value chains, and technological innovation provides a roadmap for applying CE principles to complex industrial systems.

Process engineering, as discussed by Reh (2013), plays a critical role in achieving CE objectives in the chemical sector. The discipline's focus on efficient resource transformation aligns with CE goals of reducing entropy and recovering valuable materials from diffuse waste streams. He underscores the 3R principles—Reduce, Reuse, and Recycle—as essential but complex drivers of circular systems. He also points to the statistical challenges in quantifying global reductions in raw material consumption, an issue particularly pertinent in the chemical industry's high-material throughput environment.

Expanding beyond the 3R framework, Kaur et al. (2018) introduced the concept of regenerative industrial systems. These systems focus on maximizing resource value through renewable energy, bio-benign products, and innovative business models. In the chemical industry, this involves advanced material design to enhance recyclability and biodegradability. Kaur et al. (2018) highlighted the importance of collaborative efforts among policymakers, businesses, and researchers to embed CE principles in industrial practices, which resonates with the chemical sector's reliance on interconnected value chains.

The European Union's CE action plan provides a benchmark for developing quality standards for secondary raw materials and ecodesign strategies that improve product durability and repairability. The emphasis on regulatory frameworks and economic incentives is particularly relevant for the chemical industry, where regulatory compliance and innovation must align to achieve sustainability.

Lifecycle assessment (LCA), as articulated by Genovese et al. (2017), emerges as a powerful tool in the transition to CE practices. The chemical industry, characterized by its complex supply chains, benefits from LCA's ability to evaluate environmental impacts across product lifecycles. The integration of process (bottom-up) and macro-economic (top-down) methodologies, through hybrid LCA, enables a more comprehensive understanding of resource and energy flows in chemical processes. This approach highlights opportunities for improving efficiency and reducing carbon hotspots, aligning with CE's goals.

Geng and Doberstein (2008) provided insights into China's implementation of CE principles, presenting lessons applicable to the global chemical industry. Their work illustrates the role of legislation, policy frameworks, and long-term planning in fostering CE adoption. By integrating CE goals into national development strategies, China has demonstrated the potential for "leapfrog development" that avoids traditional industrialization pitfalls.

The shift toward chemically recyclable polymers represents a specific innovation within the chemical sector. Hong and Chen (2017) explored the development of these materials, emphasizing their potential to create closed-loop systems that address the end-of-life challenges associated with traditional polymers. Chemically recyclable polymers enable depolymerization and repurposing without compromising material integrity, offering a sustainable alternative to conventional recycling methods that often degrade material quality.

Lieder and Rashid (2016) proposed a comprehensive CE framework encompassing environmental, resource, and economic dimensions. Their emphasis on stakeholder collaboration and the dual use of top-down and bottom-up strategies provides a practical roadmap for implementing CE in the chemical industry. Their findings highlight the need for integrated approaches that combine policy, technology, and market-driven solutions to achieve a regenerative economy.

Finally, Mathews and Tan (2011) examined eco-industrial initiatives as exemplars of CE in action. Their discussion of industrial symbiosis, wherein waste from one industry becomes a resource for another, resonates strongly with the chemical sector's potential for cross-industry collaboration. Their evolutionary perspective on CE underscores the dynamic nature of implementing circular principles, requiring iterative innovation and adaptation over time.

In summary, the chemical industry serves as a critical arena for advancing circular economy principles. The literature underscores the importance of integrating policy frameworks, technological innovation, and collaborative strategies to overcome the unique challenges faced by the sector. The chemical industry's capacity to transform waste into valuable inputs positions it as a key driver of sustainable development, aligning with the broader goals of a circular and regenerative economy.

The 9R Strategy for Circular Economy

This chapter adopts a modified 9R framework, consolidating "Recover" under "Recycle" to prioritize preserving material value over energy recovery. This approach reflects the growing acknowledgment that energy recovery through incineration contradicts the principles of circularity by permanently removing materials from the economic cycle (Park et al. 2024). The framework emphasizes strategies that retain and maximize the utility of materials and products within the system, aiming to extend their lifecycle and reduce resource consumption.

Engineering and supply chain management are instrumental in operationalizing the 9R framework, particularly within the chemical industry. Engineering innovations, such as design-for-disassembly and material optimization, support strategies like reuse, remanufacturing, and recycling. For instance, advanced technologies, including 3D printing and digital twins, enhance precision in production and reduce material waste. These practices align closely with circular economy principles, as outlined in the literature. Reh (2013) emphasized the role of process engineering in recovering valuable components from diffuse material flows, highlighting the importance of minimizing entropy, and optimizing resource recovery.

Supply chain management complements engineering efforts by ensuring efficient material and product flows within circular systems. Circular supply chains integrate reverse logistics to facilitate the collection, sorting, and processing of used products for refurbishment, remanufacturing, or recycling. Emerging technologies such as blockchain and IoT enhance transparency, enabling stakeholders to track material flows and measure progress toward circularity goals. Genovese et al. (2017) underscored the importance of lifecycle assessment (LCA) in identifying inefficiencies and hotspots within supply chains, offering a holistic approach to improving sustainability in production systems.

The synergy between engineering and supply chain management is vital for achieving circularity, particularly in complex sectors like chemicals. For instance, modular product designs simplify disassembly and repair, while efficient supply chain processes ensure materials are reintroduced into production cycles. However, implementing these practices entails challenges such as high initial costs, technological barriers, and fragmented global supply chains. Overcoming these obstacles requires collaborative efforts among policymakers, industry leaders, and researchers. Kaur et al. (2018) highlighted the role of multi-stakeholder participation and regulatory incentives in fostering CE adoption, particularly in industries reliant on complex value chains.

The 9R framework provides a comprehensive visualization of these strategies across engineering and supply chain phases. It includes Refuse, Rethink, Reduce, Reuse, Repair, Refurbish, Remanufacture, Repurpose, and Recycle, each aimed at minimizing resource extraction, reducing waste, and maximizing product lifespan. Refuse eliminates unnecessary materials at the design stage, such as avoiding single-use plastics or hazardous chemicals, aligning with Kaur et al.'s (2018) emphasis on bio-benign materials. Rethink encourages reimagining business models, including sharing economies and product-as-a-service systems, which resonate with the systemic innovations discussed by Winans et al. (2017).

Reduce emphasizes resource efficiency by minimizing material inputs and energy use, as seen in lightweight packaging and energy-efficient production processes. Reuse extends product life through second-hand markets or minimal processing, supporting the development of circular supply chains discussed by Genovese et al. (2018). Repair focuses on prolonging product utility by addressing functionality issues, thereby reducing waste generation. Refurbish and Remanufacture rebuild products to extend their lifecycle, which is particularly relevant for high-value sectors like chemicals and electronics. Hong and Chen (2017) highlighted the potential of chemically recyclable polymers in this context, showcasing innovations that enhance material recovery without quality degradation.

Repurpose involves adapting products or components for entirely new applications, fostering creativity and innovation, as illustrated in the chemical industry's use of by-products for secondary applications. Recycle focuses on material recovery for new production, positioned as a last resort within the framework. This prioritization reflects the literature's emphasis on strategies that retain material value, such as the hybrid LCA methodology proposed by Genovese et al. (2017), which integrates top-down and bottom-up approaches to optimize resource use.

In summary, the 9R framework offers a structured approach to achieving circularity by addressing various stages of a product's lifecycle. It aligns with insights from the chemical industry literature, emphasizing the critical roles of engineering innovation and supply chain management. Together, these disciplines drive the operationalization of circular economy principles, advancing sustainability in one of the most resource-intensive industrial sectors.

8.3 Case Study

The shift to a circular economy is not only a global imperative but also a transformative opportunity for industries. The chemical sector, a cornerstone of modern manufacturing, has embraced this transformation by adopting innovative approaches to resource utilization, waste reduction, and sustainability. This section explores three exemplary case studies—Mitsui Chemicals, Mitsubishi Chemical, and Kaneka—each demonstrating unique strategies for achieving circular economy objectives. These cases highlight diverse pathways for addressing environmental challenges while driving industrial growth.

8.3.1 Mitsui Chemicals: Chemical Recycling and Collaboration for Resource Circulation

Mitsui Chemicals has positioned itself as a leader in advancing circular economy principles through chemical recycling. With an emphasis on reducing plastic waste and enhancing resource efficiency, the company launched innovative projects such as BePLAYER® and RePLAYER®. These initiatives aim to replace fossil fuel-based inputs with bio-based alternatives and recycle end-of-life plastics into new materials.

One notable achievement is Mitsui Chemicals' partnership with Kao Corporation and CFP Co. This collaboration focuses on converting hard-to-recycle plastic waste into usable raw materials through chemical recycling. Unlike traditional recycling methods, chemical recycling decomposes plastics to their molecular components, producing high-quality materials suitable for manufacturing. Utilizing CFP's technology, the project transforms waste plastics into oil, which is then processed in Mitsui Chemicals' crackers to create new plastics. This approach addresses the limitations of mechanical recycling, such as material degradation and odor retention, and demonstrates the scalability of chemical recycling.

Mitsui Chemicals employs a mass balance approach to allocate the recycled content in its products. This methodology ensures traceability and compliance with sustainability certifications, thereby promoting broader acceptance of recycled materials in the market. In 2024, the company successfully integrated chemically recycled materials into Kao's product packaging, including detergent refill pouches and cosmetic bottles. These efforts exemplify the potential of closed-loop systems in minimizing waste and maximizing resource recovery.

However, chemical recycling faces challenges, particularly related to cost and infrastructure. Mitsui Chemicals is investing heavily in technology and capacity expansion to overcome these barriers. The company's commitment to innovation and collaboration underscores its role as a catalyst for sustainable development.

In terms of the 9R framework, Mitsui Chemicals mainly shows 3R strategies. The pressing issue of plastic waste has driven Mitsui Chemicals, along with partners such as Kao Corporation and CFP Co., Ltd., to innovate sustainable solutions. Guided by the principles of the 3R (Reduce, Reuse, Recycle) framework, Mitsui Chemicals also demonstrates leadership in expanding toward the 9R model (Refuse, Rethink, Reduce, Reuse, Repair, Refurbish, Remanufacture, Repurpose, Recycle). By fostering systemic changes, the company integrates technological advancements and stakeholder collaborations to minimize waste and enhance resource circularity.

Japan generates over 8.2 million tons of plastic waste annually, of which 13% is incinerated or landfilled. While the remaining waste is recycled, over half undergoes thermal recycling, converting waste into heat energy rather than reclaiming materials for reuse. Recognizing the limitations of this linear approach, Mitsui Chemicals advances chemical recycling as a robust complement to mechanical recycling (Table 8.1).

8.3.2 Mitsubishi Chemical: Transitioning from Linear to Circular Systems

Mitsubishi Chemical is at the forefront of transforming the chemical industry's linear production model into a circular one. The company has established a Circular Economy Promotion Division to drive sustainability initiatives, including the recycling of plastics and addressing climate change.

Table 8.1 R Strategies of Mitsui Chemicals

Refuse and Rethink	At the outset, Mitsui Chemicals commits to redesigning its materials and systems to discourage unnecessary waste generation. Through its "BePLAYER®" and "RePLAYER®" initiatives, the company shifts the paradigm by promoting bio-based feedstocks and advanced recycling systems. For example, its projects with CFP involve transforming complex plastic waste into oil, subsequently utilized as feedstock in their chemical production processes
Reduce	By employing mass balance approaches, Mitsui Chemicals minimizes reliance on virgin resources. These techniques allow for the precise allocation of bio-based and recycled content within chemical products, significantly reducing the carbon footprint. Mass balance tracking ensures transparency and accountability, aligning with global sustainability standards
Reuse and Repair	Mitsui Chemicals collaborates with Kao Corporation to establish systems for direct material reuse. Kao employs recycled plastic in its packaging, pioneering horizontal recycling where old containers are processed into new ones. This process also incorporates advanced cleaning and processing technologies to retain material quality, ensuring durability and usability over multiple cycles
Recycle	Chemical recycling lies at the core of Mitsui Chemicals' strategy. Unlike traditional methods, this process decomposes plastic waste into molecular components, enabling the creation of high-quality raw materials. Technologies such as pyrolysis and depolymerization address contamination issues, allowing for the recycling of mixed or degraded plastics previously unsuitable for conventional recycling Through these efforts, Mitsui Chemicals not only addresses immediate waste management challenges but also establishes a scalable and replicable model for circularity. The integration of 9R practices has laid the groundwork for a regenerative economy where resources are continuously cycled, reducing environmental impacts

One of Mitsubishi Chemical's flagship projects involves the construction of a state-of-the-art plastic-to-oil conversion facility at its Ibaraki plant. With an annual processing capacity of 20,000 tons, this facility employs advanced pyrolysis technology to convert waste plastics into feedstock for chemical production. The resultant materials are reintegrated into Mitsubishi Chemical's existing infrastructure, such as naphtha crackers and refining units, to produce new plastics and chemicals. This closed-loop approach minimizes reliance on virgin resources and reduces environmental impact.

The company's efforts extend beyond recycling. Mitsubishi Chemical is also a pioneer in artificial photosynthesis, a cutting-edge technology that uses carbon dioxide and sunlight to produce chemical feedstocks. This innovation exemplifies the potential for harnessing renewable energy to mitigate greenhouse gas emissions while advancing chemical manufacturing.

Collaboration is central to Mitsubishi Chemical's circular economy strategy. Partnerships with industry leaders, academic institutions, and startups have facilitated the development of new technologies and business models. For instance, the company's alliance with Honda Motor Corporation explores the recycling of acrylic resin from end-of-life vehicles, further exemplifying its commitment to resource efficiency. Mitsubishi Chemical's approach demonstrates the importance of integrating sustainability into corporate strategy. By aligning its operations with environmental objectives, the company not only addresses global challenges but also enhances its competitive advantage in the evolving market landscape.

In terms of the 9R framework, let us analyze the strategies of Mitsubishi Chemical. Mitsubishi Chemical leads the transition from a linear economy to a circular economy by embedding the 3R and 9R frameworks into its operational and strategic goals. By emphasizing waste reduction, innovative recycling, and resource recovery, the company positions itself as a key enabler of sustainable development. The adoption of the 9R framework reinforces Mitsubishi Chemical's leadership in sustainable practices. Its strategies balance innovation, collaboration, and environmental stewardship, demonstrating how holistic approaches can drive systemic changes across industries (Table 8.2).

Table 8.2 R Strategies of Mitsubishi Chemical

Refuse and Rethink	Mitsubishi Chemical prioritizes the elimination of non-essential plastic use, fostering awareness and rethinking material selection. Collaborating with ENEOS Corporation, it transforms waste plastics into raw materials for petrochemical production. This partnership aligns with the refuse principle by addressing excessive dependency on virgin materials
Reduce	The company's integration of advanced chemical processes significantly reduces raw material consumption. Mitsubishi Chemical's "mass balance" approach, similar to Mitsui Chemicals', quantifies the use of recycled materials, ensuring that resource conservation translates into tangible outcomes
Repair and Refurbish	The refurbishment of existing materials and equipment forms a significant part of Mitsubishi Chemical's strategy. By adopting innovative processes such as supercritical water depolymerization, the company revitalizes degraded plastics, transforming them into valuable inputs for high-quality products
Remanufacture and Repurpose	Mitsubishi Chemical expands its capabilities to include remanufacturing techniques. Its acrylic resin recycling initiatives highlight this commitment. Using microwave technologies in partnership with MicroWave Chemical, Mitsubishi Chemical efficiently converts waste acrylic products into feedstock. Collaborations with automotive manufacturers like Honda further illustrate their ability to repurpose materials from discarded vehicles
Recycle	Recycling stands central to Mitsubishi Chemical's circular approach. The company's efforts include oilification technologies capable of processing up to 20,000 tons of plastic annually. This not only diverts waste from landfills but also replaces fossil-based feedstocks with recycled alternatives in petrochemical and plastic production

8.3.3 *Kaneka: Biodegradable Plastics and Zero-Waste Initiatives*

Kaneka has emerged as a pioneer in developing biodegradable plastics and promoting zero-waste practices. The company's flagship product, Green Planet®, is a 100% plant-based biodegradable polymer designed to address plastic pollution and marine debris.

Green Planet® offers an environmentally friendly alternative to conventional plastics, with applications ranging from disposable cutlery to agricultural films. Its superior biodegradability under various environmental conditions, including marine settings, has garnered certifications such as "OK Biodegradable MARINE." Kaneka's collaboration with global retailers like Seven-Eleven and FamilyMart has accelerated the adoption of Green Planet® in everyday products, such as straws, shopping bags, and food packaging.

In addition to product innovation, Kaneka has implemented comprehensive waste reduction programs. The company's 3R (Reduce, Reuse, Recycle) initiatives aim to minimize industrial waste and enhance resource recovery. By stabilizing production processes, improving material yields, and segregating waste streams for recycling, Kaneka has achieved 16 consecutive years of zero-emission status. This achievement underscores its commitment to sustainable manufacturing.

Kaneka's efforts extend to education and community engagement. The company conducts e-learning programs for employees on circular economy principles and collaborates with municipalities on waste management projects. One notable example is the use of waste cooking oil to produce Green Planet®, which is then used to manufacture compostable garbage bags. This initiative exemplifies the potential of circular systems in addressing local and global environmental challenges.

Looking ahead, Kaneka plans to expand its production capacity for Green Planet® to meet growing demand. The company's investment in research and development, coupled with its commitment to sustainability, positions it as a leader in the transition to a circular economy.

In terms of the 9R framework, let us analyze the strategies of Kaneka. Kaneka exemplifies the successful application of 3R and 9R principles in addressing plastic pollution. With its flagship product, Green Planet®, Kaneka provides biodegradable plastic solutions that integrate seamlessly into circular systems, transforming waste management practices globally. Kaneka's adherence to the 9R model positions it as a trailblazer in bioplastic innovation. By aligning with circular economy principles, the company transforms challenges into opportunities, leading the way in sustainable material solutions (Table 8.3).

Table 8.3 R Strategies of Kaneka

Refuse and Rethink	Kaneka's development of Green Planet® emerged from a commitment to rethinking material functionality. By introducing a 100% plant-based plastic, the company reduces dependence on petroleum-derived inputs while enhancing environmental compatibility. Kaneka's refusal to rely on traditional materials exemplifies a proactive approach to sustainability
Reduce	The company's emphasis on bioplastics significantly lowers greenhouse gas emissions compared to conventional plastics. By utilizing renewable feedstocks and optimizing production methods, Kaneka achieves notable reductions in resource consumption and carbon footprints
Repair, Refurbish and Reuse	While repair may not traditionally apply to single-use items, Kaneka's innovations enable broader reuse. For instance, the integration of biodegradable plastics into compostable products ensures that resources can be naturally replenished after use, closing the material loop
Remanufacture and Repurpose	Kaneka's partnerships with local governments and industries illustrate its ability to remanufacture materials. Collaborations such as the "Green Planet®" composting initiative transform biodegradable plastics into nutrient-rich soil amendments, repurposing waste into agricultural inputs
Recycle	Although biodegradable plastics like Green Planet® often bypass traditional recycling, Kaneka enhances circularity by designing products compatible with existing waste management systems. Efforts to integrate these materials into composting processes bridge the gap between biological and technical cycles, contributing to a holistic waste management ecosystem

8.3.4 Comparison of 3 Cases

These case studies highlight the transformative potential of the circular economy in the chemical industry. Mitsui Chemicals, Mitsubishi Chemical, and Kaneka each demonstrate innovative approaches to resource management, waste reduction, and sustainable development. Their efforts underscore the importance of collaboration, technology, and strategic vision in achieving circular economy objectives. By embracing circular practices, these companies not only address pressing environmental challenges but also unlock new opportunities for growth and competitiveness. As the world transitions toward a more sustainable future, the chemical industry's role as an enabler of circular solutions will continue to evolve and expand.

The 9R framework expands beyond the traditional 3R model by introducing additional dimensions that emphasize preventive measures over end-of-life solutions. This comparative analysis evaluates Mitsui Chemicals, Mitsubishi Chemical, and Kaneka through the lens of these nine principles.

Refusal focuses on avoiding unnecessary material usage. Kaneka stands out by developing Green Planet®, a fully plant-based biodegradable plastic that eliminates the need for conventional fossil-based plastics. Mitsui Chemicals reduces reliance on virgin materials through its "RePLAYER®" initiative, which transforms waste plastics into reusable materials. Mitsubishi Chemical emphasizes the adoption of sustainable alternatives like bio-based and recycled materials, particularly those certified by ISCC.

Reduction aims to minimize material and energy consumption during production and use. Mitsui Chemicals employs chemical recycling to decrease dependency on virgin resources and lower greenhouse gas emissions. Mitsubishi Chemical emphasizes process improvements, optimizing energy use and minimizing waste during production. Kaneka reduces industrial waste through optimized manufacturing processes and recycling, aligning its practices with waste minimization objectives.

Reuse involves designing products and systems for repeated use. Mitsui Chemicals collaborates with Kao Corporation to collect, process, and reuse plastics in consumer product containers, creating a closed-loop system. Mitsubishi Chemical incorporates used plastics into production processes to manufacture new products. Kaneka encourages the reuse of its durable Green Planet® materials in packaging and agricultural applications, extending their lifecycle.

Repair focuses on maintaining and restoring products to prolong usability. Mitsui Chemicals emphasizes material recovery over direct repair efforts. Mitsubishi Chemical supports systems that align with sustainable product designs, though specific repair-related initiatives are limited. Kaneka designs its biodegradable products with recycling in mind, indirectly reducing the need for repair.

Refurbishing involves upgrading or restoring products to enhance functionality. Mitsui Chemicals introduces recycled materials into production processes, enabling refurbished applications in various industries. Mitsubishi Chemical uses chemically recycled materials to maintain high-quality standards, suitable for applications like automotive parts. Kaneka focuses on leveraging material innovations for new purposes rather than direct refurbishment.

Remanufacturing involves rebuilding products to their original specifications. Mitsui Chemicals utilizes molecular recycling to create materials comparable to virgin products for diverse applications. Mitsubishi Chemical integrates chemically recycled inputs into new production cycles through large-scale industrial partnerships. Kaneka contributes by replacing traditional materials with its innovative biodegradable options.

Repurposing focuses on finding new uses for products or materials outside their original design. Mitsui Chemicals converts waste plastics into raw materials for various chemical products. Mitsubishi Chemical transforms used plastics into energy sources and industrial applications. Kaneka demonstrates versatility in repurposing biodegradable materials for agriculture, packaging, and compostable products.

Recycling reclaims materials from end-of-life products for new production. Mitsui Chemicals adopts chemical recycling as a cornerstone of its sustainability efforts, breaking down plastics into molecular components for reuse. Mitsubishi Chemical employs advanced recycling techniques, including pyrolysis and depolymerization, to process plastics on a large scale. Kaneka achieves high recycling rates through a combination of traditional and innovative methods. As discussed, each company contributes uniquely to advancing sustainability within the chemical industry through the principles of the 9R framework.

8.4 Conclusion

The transition to a circular economy (CE) is a vital opportunity for the chemical industry to address pressing global challenges related to sustainability, resource efficiency, and environmental impact. By shifting from a linear economic model to a restorative and regenerative system, the chemical industry can play a transformative role in creating a more sustainable future. This transition involves rethinking traditional practices, integrating innovative technologies, and fostering collaboration across value chains to maximize resource utility and minimize waste.

The chemical industry occupies a pivotal position in this transformation, serving as both a driver and an enabler of CE practices. By adopting the 9R framework, the industry can address each stage of a product's lifecycle, emphasizing prevention and the retention of material value over end-of-life solutions. These principles challenge companies to redesign processes, products, and systems to align with CE objectives, from reducing reliance on virgin resources to creating closed-loop systems.

The Japanese chemical industry has demonstrated significant progress in operationalizing CE principles through innovative initiatives. Mitsui Chemicals has embraced chemical recycling technologies to recover high-quality raw materials from plastic waste, reducing dependency on virgin inputs and promoting material circularity. Mitsubishi Chemical has advanced large-scale recycling efforts, integrating chemically recycled materials into production processes while exploring groundbreaking technologies such as artificial photosynthesis to achieve carbon neutrality. Kaneka has pioneered the development of biodegradable plastics, exemplified by its Green Planet® product, which addresses plastic pollution and offers a sustainable alternative to fossil-based materials.

These efforts highlight the critical role of innovation in driving CE adoption. Advanced technologies such as chemical recycling, bio-based material production, and renewable energy integration are essential for achieving CE goals. For instance, Mitsui Chemicals' use of mass balance approaches ensures traceability and transparency in recycled material allocation, while Kaneka's biodegradable plastics showcase how material design can contribute to environmental sustainability. These innovations not only address immediate environmental challenges but also create opportunities for market competitiveness and economic growth.

Collaboration across industries and sectors is another cornerstone of the CE transition. The chemical industry's ability to partner with downstream stakeholders, including manufacturers, waste management firms, and policymakers, is crucial for establishing circular ecosystems. Collaborative projects, such as Mitsubishi Chemical's partnerships with automotive companies to recycle acrylic resin, demonstrate the potential for systemic change when value chains are interconnected.

However, the journey toward a circular economy is not without challenges. High upfront costs, technological barriers, and fragmented supply chains pose significant obstacles to widespread CE adoption. Addressing these challenges requires coordinated efforts among stakeholders, including governments, industry leaders, researchers, and consumers. Policymakers must create regulatory frameworks and incentives that support CE practices, while companies need to invest in research, development, and infrastructure to scale innovative solutions.

Consumer engagement is also a critical factor in driving CE adoption. By promoting sustainable consumption and raising awareness about the benefits of circular products, industries can foster a cultural shift toward sustainability. Transparency in reporting and measurable outcomes can further build trust and accountability, encouraging broader participation in CE initiatives.

The transition to a circular economy represents both a responsibility and an opportunity for the chemical industry. By leveraging the principles of the 9R framework, embracing innovation, and fostering collaboration, the industry can lead the way in addressing global sustainability challenges. The Japanese chemical industry's efforts provide a blueprint for others, illustrating how strategic actions can create economic, social, and environmental value.

As the world grapples with resource scarcity, climate change, and environmental degradation, the importance of circular practices cannot be overstated. The chemical industry's ability to transform waste into valuable inputs, reduce reliance on non-renewable resources, and create sustainable systems underscores its potential to drive a regenerative economy. By aligning business strategies with CE principles, the industry can not only mitigate risks but also unlock new opportunities for growth, innovation, and competitiveness. The path forward requires resilience, commitment, and collaboration, ensuring that the transition to a circular economy becomes a cornerstone of global sustainability efforts.

References

Geng, Y., & Doberstein, B. (2008). Developing the circular economy in China: Challenges and opportunities for achieving 'leapfrog development'. International Journal of Sustainable Development & World Ecology, 15(3), 231–239. https://doi.org/10.3843/SusDev.15.3:6.

Genovese, A., Acquaye, A. A., Figueroa, A., & Koh, S. C. L. (2017). Sustainable supply chain management and the transition towards a circular economy: Evidence and some applications. Omega, 66(Part B), 344–357. https://doi.org/10.1016/j.omega.2015.05.015.

Hong, M., & Chen, E. Y. X. (2017). Chemically recyclable polymers: A circular economy approach to sustainability. Green Chemistry, 19(16), 3692-3706.

Kaur, G., Uisan, K., Ong, K. L., & Lin, C. S. K. (2018). Recent trends in green and sustainable chemistry & waste valorization: Rethinking plastics in a circular economy. Current Opinion in Green and Sustainable Chemistry, 9, 30–39. https://doi.org/10.1016/j.cogsc.2017.11.003.

Lieder, M., & Rashid, A. (2016). Towards circular economy implementation: A comprehensive review in context of manufacturing industry. Journal of Cleaner Production, 115, 36–51. https://doi.org/10.1016/j.jclepro.2015.12.042.

Mathews, J. A., & Tan, H. (2011). Progress toward a circular economy in China: The drivers (and inhibitors) of eco-industrial initiative. Journal of Industrial Ecology, 15(3), 435-457. https://doi.org/10.1111/j.1530-9290.2011.00332.x.

Park, Y.W., Sugie, R., & Mizuguchi, K. (2024). Circular Economy Strategy of Japanese Firms: A Comparative Study of Manufacturing and Other Industries. Communication of JIMA, 34(1), 15–22.

Reh, L. (2013). Process engineering in circular economies. Particuology, 11(2), 119–133. https://doi.org/10.1016/j.partic.2012.11.001.

Winans, K., Kendall, A., & Deng, H. (2017). The history and current applications of the circular economy concept. Renewable and Sustainable Energy Reviews, 68(Part 1), 825–833. https://doi.org/10.1016/j.rser.2016.09.123.

Chapter 9
Advancing CE Strategies for a Sustainable Future

Young Won Park and Kin'ya Tamaki

9.1 Introduction

This chapter explores the transformative potential of the Circular Economy (CE) in addressing global environmental, economic, and social challenges. Positioned at the intersection of Digital Transformation (DX), Sustainability Transformation (SX), and Green Transformation (GX), CE offers a framework for decoupling economic growth from resource consumption while fostering innovation and resilience. Building on previous chapters and integrating insights from Japan's current and future strategies, this chapter examines emerging trends, challenges, and opportunities in CE implementation worldwide.

The convergence of DX, SX, and GX creates unprecedented opportunities for scaling CE practices. Advanced technologies such as Artificial Intelligence (AI), the Internet of Things (IoT), and blockchain enable real-time tracking of materials, optimize resource efficiency, and enhance transparency across global supply chains. These tools facilitate the adoption of innovative models, including product-as-a-service (PaaS), reverse logistics, and closed-loop systems, driving systemic change.

The preceding chapters provide detailed examples of CE principles in action across various sectors. The automotive industry demonstrates leadership in remanufacturing and shared mobility, while the chemical sector pioneers advanced recycling and bio-based materials. Similarly, consumer-focused industries such as cosmetics and food leverage CE principles to reduce waste, innovate packaging, and engage stakeholders. However, persistent challenges, including regulatory gaps, infrastructure limitations, and consumer awareness, require concerted multi-stakeholder efforts.

This chapter integrates specific examples from Japan's Circular Economy Vision 2020 and related initiatives, emphasizing the importance of technological innovation, policy alignment, and collaborative approaches. By drawing comparisons with global strategies, including those of the EU, USA, China, and South Korea, this chapter underscores the critical role of international collaboration in advancing CE practices.

Y. W. Park and K. Tamaki, *Circular Economy Strategy for SDG Business Management*,
https://doi.org/10.1007/978-981-96-4194-9_9

Looking forward, this chapter advocates for research and innovation to address emerging global challenges such as climate change, geopolitical uncertainties, and resource scarcity. Through technology integration, policy innovation, and stakeholder engagement, CE can serve as a cornerstone for sustainable development, ensuring economic growth and environmental preservation for future generations.

9.2 Current and Future Circular Economy Strategies of the Japanese Government

9.2.1 Current Circular Economy Strategies of the Japanese Government

The Japanese government has made significant strides in advancing Circular Economy (CE) initiatives, reflecting a commitment to transforming traditional resource management practices into sustainable economic models. The Circular Economy Vision 2020 introduced a strategic framework emphasizing the integration of economic growth and environmental sustainability. This vision shifted the focus from merely reducing waste to creating value through innovative practices, positioning CE as a critical component of Japan's economic strategy.

Over recent years, policies and legislation have strengthened this framework. The introduction of the Plastic Resource Circulation Act in 2022 marked a turning point in Japan's approach to managing plastic waste. By establishing design standards for recyclable products and promoting chemical and material recycling technologies, the act has fostered collaboration between corporations, municipalities, and technology developers. Additionally, initiatives such as the Japan Partnership for Circular Economy (J4CE), launched in 2021, have facilitated dialogues between government, industry, and academia, enabling the identification of challenges and collaborative solutions to scale CE practices.

The government's focus on CE aligns closely with international efforts. Japan actively participates in global platforms, including UNEA treaty negotiations on plastic pollution and the development of international CE standards through ISO/TC323. These efforts underscore Japan's role as a global leader in fostering sustainable resource management and reducing environmental impact (Table 9.1).

9.2.2 Future Circular Economy Strategies of the Japanese Government

Looking ahead, Japan aims to establish a growth-oriented, resource-autonomous economy. This strategy addresses the vulnerabilities exposed by global supply chain disruptions and geopolitical uncertainties. By diversifying resource dependencies

Table 9.1 Current circular economy strategies of the Japanese Government

Circular Economy Vision 2020	This framework integrates economic and environmental perspectives, promoting innovative models that generate economic value while reducing waste and resource dependence
Sustainable Finance Guidance	Released in 2021, this guidance fosters transparent dialogues between corporations and investors about CE strategies, driving sustainable financial practices
J4CE (Japan Circular Economy Partnership)	Established in 2021, this platform facilitates dialogue among government, industry, and academia to identify challenges and solutions for CE adoption across supply chains
Plastic Resource Circulation Act (2022)	This legislation enhances plastic waste management through design standards for recycling and innovative recycling technologies. It has catalyzed collaboration between corporations and municipalities to establish effective resource recovery systems
Global Engagement	Japan plays an active role in global initiatives like the UNEA treaty negotiations on plastic pollution and contributes to international CE standards (ISO/TC323)

and enhancing domestic capabilities, Japan seeks to mitigate risks and strengthen economic resilience. The development of advanced recycling technologies and bio-based manufacturing processes is central to this vision, enabling the production of sustainable alternatives to imported resources.

Another critical aspect of Japan's future CE strategy is the integration of CE principles into the broader goal of achieving carbon neutrality by 2050. By aligning resource management with decarbonization objectives, Japan intends to reduce supply chain emissions and promote the use of sustainable materials. This alignment positions CE as a foundational element in achieving long-term environmental and economic goals.

Challenges remain, including the need to enhance consumer awareness and acceptance of CE practices. Infrastructure limitations in waste collection and recycling also pose barriers to scaling CE initiatives. High initial costs and technological complexities require sustained government support and industry innovation. Despite these challenges, the potential for CE to drive economic resilience and sustainability presents a compelling opportunity for Japan.

The government envisions a future where CE principles are seamlessly integrated into global and domestic economic systems. This includes fostering innovation in material reuse, resource sharing, and product longevity, while ensuring that CE practices contribute to economic security and environmental preservation. Japan's leadership in exporting CE technologies and systems further enhances its influence in shaping a global transition toward circularity.

Through collaborative efforts among policymakers, industries, and citizens, Japan continues to advance its CE agenda, striving to build a sustainable and competitive economy. This commitment reflects a forward-thinking approach to addressing environmental challenges and ensuring economic resilience in an increasingly interconnected and resource-constrained world (Table 9.2).

Table 9.2 Future circular economy strategies of the Japanese Government

Technological Innovation	Development of advanced recycling technologies (e.g., chemical recycling, bioplastics) and bio-manufacturing processes to reduce reliance on imported resources
Resource Autonomy and Economic Security	Policies aim to mitigate supply chain risks by diversifying resource dependencies and fostering domestic alternatives, particularly for critical materials like rare metals and semiconductors
Expanding the Circular Economy Framework	The government identifies four strategic categories: -Resource Reuse and Recycling ($1 \times n$): Enhance low-cost and high-efficiency resource circulation -Resource Creation ($0 \rightarrow 1$): Develop bio-based materials and innovative resource generation methods -Resource Sharing ($1/n$): Expand sharing economy applications beyond mobility and hospitality -Resource Longevity ($1 + n$): Promote restoration, remanufacturing, and secondary markets for durable goods
Carbon Neutrality Integration	Align CE strategies with Japan's 2050 carbon neutrality goal, emphasizing supply chain decarbonization and sustainable materials management
Global Collaboration	Strengthen Japan's leadership in CE by exporting Japanese CE technologies and systems, fostering international cooperation, and aligning with global sustainability goals

9.3 Global Trends of Circular Economy: Key Regional Strategies

The Circular Economy (CE) has become a global imperative as countries and regions strive to balance economic growth with environmental sustainability. Leading nations are advancing CE through diverse strategies that include regulatory frameworks, technological innovation, and public–private collaboration. This section explores the approaches of the European Union (EU), the United States (USA), China, and South Korea, highlighting their unique contributions and examples.

Global efforts in CE highlight the importance of region-specific strategies while underscoring the need for international collaboration. Whether through the EU's regulatory leadership, the USA's market-driven innovation, China's industrial symbiosis, or South Korea's technological prowess, each approach contributes uniquely to the global CE movement. By learning from these models and fostering cross-border partnerships, nations can accelerate the transition to a sustainable and resilient economy.

9.3.1 *European Union: Regulatory Leadership and Comprehensive Frameworks*

The European Union has established itself as a global frontrunner in CE, embedding circular principles into its broader sustainability initiatives. The Circular Economy Action Plan (CEAP) is central to its strategy, serving as a key component of the European Green Deal, which aims for climate neutrality by 2050. This comprehensive approach focuses on waste reduction, sustainable product design, and material reuse (European Commission 2020).

Ecodesign regulations ensure products meet strict durability, repairability, and recyclability standards, reducing environmental impacts from production to end-of-life. Initiatives such as the Single-Use Plastics Directive have tackled marine pollution by banning problematic plastics and setting ambitious recycling targets. The Digital Product Passport (DPP) provides traceability and accountability in product lifecycles, a significant step in creating closed loop systems.

Collaboration is another hallmark of the EU's approach. The Horizon Europe program funds innovation in bio-based materials and recycling technologies, while initiatives like Catena-X in the automotive sector leverage blockchain to enhance supply chain transparency and promote material recovery. Examples include the Netherlands' commitment to becoming fully circular by 2050 and France's focus on repairability ratings for consumer goods, ensuring citizens are empowered to make sustainable choices.

9.3.2 *United States: Market-Driven Innovation and Emerging Policies*

The United States pursues CE through a combination of private-sector innovation and evolving public policies. The National Recycling Strategy emphasizes improving the quality and efficiency of recycling systems, reducing contamination, and supporting secondary material markets. Meanwhile, state-level initiatives, such as California's Extended Producer Responsibility (EPR) laws, hold manufacturers accountable for product end-of-life management.

Corporate leadership has been instrumental in advancing CE in the United States. Apple's Daisy robot, which dismantles electronic devices to recover valuable materials, exemplifies innovation in resource recovery. Similarly, Patagonia's Worn Wear program promotes product longevity through repair and reuse, aligning with circular principles.

Public–private partnerships have emerged as powerful tools for scaling CE initiatives. The Closed Loop Partners fund supports ventures focused on material recovery, waste reduction, and innovative business models. Cities like New York are integrating circularity into urban planning, with composting programs and public education campaigns driving citizen engagement.

While CE in the United States is still largely market-driven, increasing collaboration between businesses, municipalities, and federal agencies signals a shift toward a more cohesive national strategy.

9.3.3 China: Industrial Innovation and Policy-Driven Circularity

China's rapid industrial growth has necessitated a robust CE framework to address resource inefficiencies and environmental degradation. CE principles are embedded in national strategies, with the Circular Economy Promotion Law serving as a foundational policy. The 14th Five-Year Plan further emphasizes CE, setting ambitious targets for recycling, resource conservation, and waste reduction across industries.

Industrial symbiosis is a hallmark of China's approach. Cities like Suzhou and Tianjin host eco-industrial parks where waste from one industry serves as a resource for another. These systems optimize resource use while reducing emissions and waste.

China has made significant strides in technological innovation, particularly in battery and plastic recycling. Companies like CATL lead in electric vehicle battery recycling, recovering critical materials such as lithium and cobalt. In the plastics sector, chemical recycling methods such as pyrolysis and depolymerization are transforming waste management. Digital tools, including AI-driven sorting systems, enhance recycling efficiency and reduce contamination.

Globally, China's Belt and Road Initiative incorporates CE practices, focusing on sustainable infrastructure and waste management systems in partner countries. Shenzhen's urban circular systems exemplify China's commitment to integrating technology, policy, and public participation to achieve sustainability goals.

9.3.4 South Korea: Technology-Driven Circularity and Public Engagement

South Korea blends advanced technology, policy innovation, and consumer involvement to advance its CE agenda. The Resource Circulation Act and the Green New Deal provide a policy foundation that aligns economic recovery with environmental sustainability.

Technological innovation underpins South Korea's CE efforts. AI and IoT optimize waste management, with IoT-enabled systems tracking material flows and AI improving sorting accuracy. Blockchain pilots ensure traceability and compliance in recycling, particularly in electronics and packaging industries.

South Korea's EPR system extends to a wide range of products, encouraging companies like Samsung and LG Electronics to develop take-back and recycling programs. Urban mining initiatives recover rare metals from electronic waste, reducing dependency on imports and aligning with resource efficiency goals.

Public participation is a cornerstone of South Korea's strategy. Campaigns like the Zero Waste Movement promote sustainable behaviors, while cities like Seoul are implementing ambitious food waste recycling programs. Collaboration between government, industry, and academia strengthens these initiatives, fostering innovation and ensuring scalability.

9.3.5 *Comparing Japan's Circular Economy Strategy with Global Trends*

Japan's approach to the Circular Economy (CE) demonstrates a unique blend of technological innovation, robust policy frameworks, and cultural values like mottainai (a sense of not wasting). By comparing Japan's CE strategies with those of the European Union (EU), the United States (USA), China, and South Korea, we can identify similarities, differences, and opportunities for collaboration.

Technological Innovation and Industry Leadership

Japan is a global leader in advanced recycling technologies and material recovery, particularly in plastics and batteries. Companies like Mitsubishi Chemical and Panasonic are pioneers in chemical recycling and battery recovery systems, aligning with efforts seen in South Korea and China. However, Japan's focus on IoT-enabled material tracking and AI-driven recycling aligns more closely with South Korea's technology-driven strategies.

Unlike the USA, where private-sector innovation drives much of the CE progress, Japan benefits from close government-industry collaboration. Similar programs such as the EU's Digital Product Passport (DPP) initiative, which embeds unique product identifiers for lifecycle tracking, mirror EU efforts under the European Green Deal.

Policy and Governance Frameworks

Japan's Circular Economy Vision 2020 provides a comprehensive framework, akin to the EU's Circular Economy Action Plan. Both emphasize reducing waste, increasing resource efficiency, and fostering innovation. However, while the EU has a strong regional integration component, Japan focuses on bilateral and regional partnerships, such as collaborating with ASEAN countries to harmonize waste trade and recycling standards.

Incentives like Japan's Advanced Resource Recycling Act align with South Korea's Resource Circulation Act and China's Circular Economy Promotion Law, reflecting a shared focus on legislative support for CE. Unlike the USA, which lacks a cohesive federal CE policy, Japan's centralized approach provides clearer guidance to industries.

Cultural and Behavioral Influences

Japan's mottainai ethos encourages responsible consumption and waste reduction, paralleling South Korea's public engagement initiatives, such as the Zero Waste Movement. Both countries emphasize consumer education and behavior change as critical components of CE.

The EU's repairability ratings and second-hand marketplaces align with Japan's consumer-focused programs like refillable packaging initiatives by Muji and platforms like Mercari. The USA also has similar private-sector-led second-hand marketplaces, but they lack the cultural depth seen in Japan and South Korea.

Industrial Symbiosis and Urban Circular Systems

Japan's industrial symbiosis efforts, such as the development of eco-industrial parks in Kawasaki, share similarities with China's eco-parks in Suzhou and Tianjin. Both countries excel in creating closed-loop systems within industrial clusters. However, Japan places greater emphasis on leveraging advanced technologies like blockchain for supply chain transparency, a strategy increasingly adopted in the EU and South Korea.

Japan's urban circular systems, such as the Kobe Circular City Initiative, echo South Korea's Seoul initiatives and China's Shenzhen models. These urban systems focus on integrating waste reduction, recycling, and sustainable infrastructure, showcasing a shared commitment to circular urbanization.

Challenges and Opportunities

While Japan excels in technological innovation and public–private partnerships, it faces challenges in scaling CE practices across industries and engaging global markets. The EU's harmonized policies and standardization efforts provide a model for Japan to strengthen international collaboration. Meanwhile, the USA's private-sector-driven innovation offers insights into fostering entrepreneurial approaches within a CE framework.

China's advancements in industrial symbiosis and resource recovery infrastructure highlight opportunities for Japan to expand its own initiatives. Collaboration with South Korea on AI and IoT applications in recycling could further enhance both countries' leadership in CE technologies.

By examining these comparisons, it's clear that Japan's CE strategies are robust but can benefit from deeper alignment with international standards and enhance collaboration with global leaders. Leveraging its technological expertise, cultural values, and policy frameworks, Japan is well positioned to play a pivotal role in advancing the global Circular Economy agenda.

9.4 Future Strategies for the Circular Economy: Advancing Through Technology and Policy Integration

The transition to a Circular Economy (CE) is essential for addressing global challenges such as resource scarcity, environmental degradation, and climate change. Grounded in the 9R framework—Refuse, Rethink, Reduce, Reuse, Repair, Refurbish, Remanufacture, Repurpose, and Recycle—future CE strategies demand a holistic approach that integrates technological innovation, robust policy frameworks, cross-sector collaboration, and consumer engagement (Park et al. 2024). The following sections outline comprehensive strategies to realize the vision of a sustainable and regenerative economy (METI 2023; Japanese Cabinet Office 2023; PWC 2024). Then, we elaborate on strategies for implementing the 9R principles at scale while incorporating examples from Japan and beyond.

9.4.1 Technological Innovation: Enabling Circular Systems

Technology is at the heart of CE, enabling efficient resource use, extending product lifecycles, and advancing material recovery. In particular, technology plays a pivotal role in actualizing the 9R framework by enabling efficient resource use, extending product lifecycles, and advancing material recovery.

Data-Driven Decision-Making and Digital Platforms

Advanced technologies like IoT, AI, and blockchain are transforming resource management. In Japan, Hitachi leverages IoT to monitor elevators and escalators, ensuring predictive maintenance and reducing downtime. This approach extends product lifespans and minimizes material waste. Mitsubishi Chemical uses AI-driven algorithms to optimize production processes, reducing material input and waste. On a larger scale, the EU's Digital Product Passport (DPP) initiative tracks material flows by embedding unique identifiers into products, enhancing transparency and accountability. Similarly, Europe's Catena-X blockchain platform enables end-to-end traceability in automotive supply chains, fostering circularity.

In terms of the 9R framework, technologies such as IoT, AI, and blockchain enhance the application of Rethink and Recycle by tracking materials and optimizing resource flows. For example, Hitachi's IoT-enabled monitoring of elevators aligns with Reduce by minimizing downtime and material wastage. Mitsubishi Chemical applies AI to optimize production, reducing material input and supporting Reduce and Recycle principles.

Modular Design and Product-As-A-Service Models

Modular design simplifies disassembly, repair, and recycling. Toyota's hybrid vehicles feature components designed for easy disassembly and material recovery. In electronics, Dell produces modular laptops that allow users to replace individual components, reducing electronic waste. The Product-as-a-Service (PaaS) model shifts ownership from consumers to manufacturers, incentivizing durability and reuse. Panasonic's air conditioning systems are offered as a service, where customers lease the units, and the company retains responsibility for maintenance and recycling.

In terms of the 9R framework, modular design aligns with Repair, Refurbish, and Remanufacture, enabling the easy replacement of worn-out components. Toyota's hybrid vehicles, designed for straightforward disassembly and recycling, exemplify this approach. Product-as-a-Service (PaaS) models support Reuse by shifting ownership from consumers to manufacturers. Panasonic's air conditioning systems, leased rather than sold, ensure materials remain in a controlled loop, fostering Remanufacture and Repurpose.

Advanced Recycling Technologies

Innovative recycling technologies are critical for processing complex waste streams. In Japan, Mitsui Chemicals employs depolymerization to break down plastics into raw materials. Sumitomo Chemical has invested in pyrolysis technology, capable of processing mixed and contaminated plastic waste to produce high-quality feedstocks.

Honda's battery recycling systems recover valuable materials like lithium and cobalt from electric vehicle batteries, creating closed-loop supply chains. Additionally, Japan's municipal waste facilities are piloting AI-driven sorting systems, increasing efficiency and material recovery rates.

In terms of the 9R framework, innovative recycling technologies address complex waste streams, advancing the Recycle and Repurpose principles. Mitsui Chemicals' depolymerization processes and Sumitomo Chemical's pyrolysis plants are transforming the plastics sector in Japan, ensuring high-quality outputs for reuse. Honda's battery recycling initiatives recover critical metals like lithium, aligning with Remanufacture to close the loop in the automotive sector.

9.4.2 Policy and Governance: Establishing a Circular Framework

Strong policy frameworks and governance mechanisms institutionalize CE practices and foster innovation. Strong governance is also crucial for institutionalizing the 9R framework.

Harmonized Policies and Global Standards

Aligning national and international policies simplifies trade and collaboration. Japan's Circular Economy Vision 2020 incorporates global standards like the ISO 59000 series, providing a blueprint for CE implementation. This harmonization is evident in Japan's collaboration with ASEAN countries to establish shared recycling and waste management standards. The European Union's Circular Economy Action Plan complements these efforts by setting benchmarks for sustainable practices, creating a cohesive global framework for CE. In terms of the 9R framework, policies integrating Refuse, Reduce, and Recycle principles are crucial for global alignment.

Incentivizing Circular Business Models

Governments can promote CE through financial incentives. In terms of the 9R framework, government incentives drive businesses toward Reuse and Repair. For instance, Japan's Advanced Resource Recycling Act offers subsidies for resource-efficient practices, encouraging companies like Sony to establish take-back programs for electronics. Extended Producer Responsibility (EPR) laws, such as those applied to packaging and electronics, hold manufacturers accountable for Recycle and Reuse, incentivizing ecodesign.

Public–Private Partnerships (PPPs)

Collaboration between governments, industries, and academia enhances CE implementation. The Japan Partnership for Circular Economy (J4CE) fosters innovation through shared resources and expertise. For instance, Kaneka collaborates with municipalities to develop biodegradable plastics compatible with local waste management systems.

The Kobe Circular City initiative showcases successful PPPs, where stakeholders work together to create urban systems that minimize waste and optimize recycling.

In terms of the 9R framework, collaborative platforms like the Japan Partnership for Circular Economy (J4CE) facilitate innovation in Repurpose and Recycle, as shown in Kaneka's partnership with municipalities to develop biodegradable plastics and integrate Reduce into existing waste management systems. The Kobe Circular City initiative also fosters urban circular systems through public–private collaboration, addressing Rethink and Repair.

9.4.3 Innovation and Collaboration: Building a Sustainable Ecosystem

Creating a circular ecosystem requires investment in R&D, fostering partnerships, and engaging consumers. A sustainable ecosystem also requires investment in R&D to embrace the 9R framework.

Research and Development (R&D)

Investments in R&D drive advancements in CE technologies. In terms of the 9R framework, R&D drives innovation across the 9R spectrum. Kaneka's Green Planet® biodegradable plastics address Reduce and Repurpose by providing alternatives to petrochemicals. Toyota's research into hydrogen fuel cells supports Rethink and Refurbish, aligning with decarbonization goals. Panasonic's focus on battery recycling contributes to Recycle and Remanufacture, closing the loop in energy systems.

Cross-Sector Partnerships

Inter-industry collaboration establishes closed-loop systems. Collaborations between industries amplify the impact of Reuse and Remanufacture. Mitsubishi Chemical and Kao Corporation partnered to develop chemical recycling methods, advancing Recycle and Repurpose. Toyota and Panasonic's battery recycling systems demonstrate the potential of cross-sector synergies to reduce waste and enhance efficiency.

Consumer Engagement and Behavioral Change

Consumer participation is critical for realizing Refuse, Repair, and Reuse. Platforms like Mercari promote the resale of goods, reducing waste and extending lifecycles. Muji's refillable packaging initiatives align with Reduce and Reuse, fostering responsible consumption. Government-led education campaigns further incentivize consumers to embrace CE principles, ensuring widespread adoption.

9.4.4 Addressing Challenges: Overcoming Barriers to CE Implementation

Despite its potential, CE faces barriers such as high costs, infrastructural limitations, and regulatory complexity. Addressing these challenges is essential to fully implement the 9R framework.

Financing and Infrastructure Development

Innovative financing mechanisms, such as Mizuho Bank's green loans, support businesses transitioning to CE practices. Public–private partnerships fund critical infrastructure projects, including Japan's advanced waste-to-energy plants that integrate recycling and material recovery systems.

In terms of the 9R framework, green loans, such as those offered by Mizuho Bank, support businesses transitioning to Reuse, Remanufacture, and Recycle. Public–private partnerships fund waste-to-energy plants incorporating advanced sorting systems, ensuring efficient material recovery aligned with Recycle and Repurpose.

Regulatory Harmonization

Navigating diverse regulatory landscapes is challenging for multinational companies. Japan's leadership in ISO initiatives is helping develop universal CE standards, ensuring consistency in metrics and practices. The Ministry of Economy, Trade, and Industry (METI) is also streamlining domestic regulations to support CE adoption. In terms of the 9R framework, harmonized regulations also simplify compliance across borders, facilitating Recycle and Repurpose at scale.

Inclusivity and Equity

Ensuring equitable access to CE benefits is crucial. Japan's Society 5.0 integrates technology with social objectives, creating job opportunities in recycling industries and extending CE services to underserved regions. Initiatives like community-based waste management systems in rural Japan ensure inclusivity in CE practices. In terms of the 9R framework, integrating Rethink and Repair into community-based waste systems ensures equitable access to CE benefits.

9.4.5 Envisioning a Resilient Future

The transition to a CE offers a transformative opportunity to address global challenges while fostering economic growth. Companies like Fujifilm, with its multi-function printer leasing model, demonstrate how businesses can embed CE principles into operations, reducing waste and improving efficiency. Consumers, empowered by accessible services and educational campaigns, are key drivers of CE adoption. Governments must continue to provide regulatory and financial frameworks to enable this transformation. By leveraging advanced technologies, fostering collaboration, and implementing forward-thinking policies, CE can become the foundation of sustainable and resilient economies. Through these strategies and examples, the Circular Economy is poised to reshape industries, align economic activities with environmental goals, and ensure prosperity for current and future generations.

The 9R framework provides a comprehensive roadmap for transitioning to a Circular Economy that addresses environmental, economic, and social challenges. Through technological innovation, policy alignment, and multi-stakeholder collaboration, industries can embrace sustainable practices that balance growth with environmental responsibility. By embedding principles like Refuse, Repair, and Recycle into global strategies, CE can foster resilience and ensure prosperity for future generations.

9.5 Conclusion

The Circular Economy (CE) represents a transformative approach to achieving sustainable development, addressing global challenges such as resource scarcity, environmental degradation, and climate change. As explored throughout this discussion, CE provides a framework that transcends traditional economic models by integrating environmental, economic, and social imperatives. Its potential lies in decoupling growth from resource consumption, fostering innovation, and building resilience in industries and societies.

The integration of Digital Transformation (DX), Sustainability Transformation (SX), and Green Transformation (GX) into CE strategies offers unprecedented opportunities to enhance circularity at scale. Technologies such as AI, IoT, and blockchain have already demonstrated their ability to optimize resource flows, increase transparency, and enable closed-loop systems. Examples from Japan, such as Mitsubishi Chemical's AI-driven production optimization and Hitachi's IoT-enabled monitoring of elevators, highlight the role of advanced technologies in fostering traceability and resource efficiency across supply chains.

Globally, CE has been embraced with varying approaches, reflecting the unique contexts of regions like the EU, USA, China, and South Korea. The EU has established itself as a leader in regulatory frameworks and comprehensive action plans, while the USA emphasizes market-driven innovation and public–private partnerships. China's industrial symbiosis and large-scale recycling infrastructure exemplify policy-driven circularity, whereas South Korea's technology-centric strategies prioritize traceability and consumer engagement. Japan, with its innovative recycling technologies, collaborative governance models, and cultural ethos of mottainai, exemplifies a balanced approach that integrates technological, policy, and cultural dimensions.

Despite the progress, CE adoption faces persistent barriers. High costs of infrastructure and technology, fragmented regulatory frameworks, and consumer skepticism remain significant challenges. Addressing these requires cohesive strategies. Governments must establish robust policy frameworks, as seen in Japan's Advanced Resource Recycling Act and the EU's Circular Economy Action Plan. Industries should continue to innovate, investing in modular design, advanced recycling, and bio-based materials. Public–private partnerships and cross-sector collaborations are essential to bridge gaps in infrastructure, scale innovations, and promote inclusive circular systems.

Consumer engagement is another critical factor for CE success. Initiatives such as Japan's refillable packaging by Muji and second-hand marketplaces like Mercari illustrate the importance of behavioral shifts in driving circular practices. Education campaigns, incentives for sustainable choices, and the integration of digital tools to facilitate reuse, repair, and recycling are key to fostering consumer participation.

Looking ahead, the CE's role in addressing emerging global challenges cannot be overstated. As the world grapples with climate change, geopolitical tensions, and resource insecurity, CE offers a pathway to resilience. Aligning circular practices with carbon neutrality goals, as envisioned in Japan's 2050 targets, demonstrates the synergy between environmental and economic objectives. Research into scalable solutions for bio-based materials, renewable energy integration, and localized circular business models will further strengthen CE implementation.

In conclusion, CE stands as a vital framework for creating a sustainable and regenerative future. Its success depends on collective action—governments, industries, academia, and consumers must align their efforts to build resilient systems. By leveraging technological advancements, fostering collaboration, and embedding sustainability into every aspect of economic activity, CE can transform industries, preserve the environment, and ensure long-term prosperity for generations to come.

References

European Commission. (2020). A new Circular Economy Action Plan for a cleaner and more competitive Europe. Brussels: European Union. https://eur-lex.europa.eu/resource.html?uri=cellar:9903b325-6388-11ea-b735-01aa75ed71a1.0017.02/DOC_1&format=PDF.

Japanese Cabinet Office. (2023). Strategic Innovation Promotion Program (SIP) Building a Circular Economy System: Strategy and R&D Plan for Social Implementation (draft). Tokyo: Japanese Cabinet Office. https://www8.cao.go.jp/cstp/stmain/pdf/230201_besshi_7.pdf.

METI. (2023). Growth-oriented resource-autonomous economic strategy (draft). Tokyo: METI (Ministry of Economy, Trade, and Industry). https://www.meti.go.jp/shingikai/energy_environment/shigen_jiritsu/pdf/007_03_00.pdf.

PWC. (2024). Technological Utilization for Realizing a Circular Economy: Strategies for Industry Transformation. PWC Global Report. https://www.pwc.com/jp/ja/knowledge/thoughtleadership/2023/assets/pdf/technology-utilization-for-realizing-a-circular-economy.pdf.

Park, Y.W., Sugie, R., & Mizuguchi, K. (2024). Circular Economy Strategy of Japanese Firms: A Comparative Study of Manufacturing and Other Industries. Communication of JIMA, 34(1), 15–22.

The manufacturer's authorised representative in the EU is Springer Nature Customer Service Centre GmbH, Europaplatz 3, 69115 Heidelberg, Germany. If you have any concerns regarding our products, please contact ProductSafety@springernature.com

Printed and bound by CPI Group (UK) Ltd, Croydon, CR0 4YY
01/10/2026
02225934-0019